THE HISTORY OF BEVERLEY
From the Earliest Times to the Year 2003

by

Pamela Hopkins

BLACKTHORN PRESS

Blackthorn Press, Blackthorn House
Middleton Rd, Pickering YO18 8AL
United Kingdom

www.blackthornpress.com

ISBN 0 9540535 9 1

ILLUSTRATION CREDITS

The publisher and author are grateful to the following for help
with providing illustrations:

Beverley Library and Art Gallery, Humber Archaeology
Partnership, National Heritage, Oxford University Press

Printed and Bound by The Cromwell Press
Trowbridge, Wiltshire

CONTENTS

12. 1900 – 2003. CHANGES IN THE LANDSCAPE

COLOUR PLATES

Plate 1. Beverley Minster from the south west. This was the church of the Canons of the Collegiate Church of St John the Evangelist and was built round the tomb of St John of Beverley who had died in 721. The east end and the transepts (1220 – 1260) are in the Early English style, the nave (1309 – 1349) in the Decorated style and the west end (1380 – 1400) in the Perpendicular style. The porch and east window were added in the early 15th century. *Photo: Michael Askin.*

Plate 2. St Mary's church from the south west. This was the church of the merchants and the guilds. It began as a chapel of ease to the Minster in 1150 but grew and expanded as the town developed. It was completed in 1524.

Plate 3. North Bar – the northern entrance into the town. Built in 1409, it is one of the earliest remaining brick buildings in England.

Plate 4. A 15th century crown-post building in Flemingate with Beverley Minster in the background. Until the 17th century most buildings in Beverley were of timber construction.

Plate 5. Norwood House in Norwood. Built 1760 it is perhaps the best Georgian house in Beverley.

Plate 6. The Court Room in the Guildhall. The elected governors of the town, the keepers, bought this medieval house in 1501. In 1762 it was re-designed by William Middleton, a local builder. Giuseppe Cortese, the plasterer, constructed the Rococo ceiling with the seated figure of Justice, open-eyed, in the centre. Cortese also was responsible for the royal arms of George III above the mayor's seat. Edmund Foster of Hull carved the Rococo surround of the mayor's seat. The Chippendale style chairs were made by William Thompson of Beverley, 1762.

Plate 7. Saturday Market – the northern market in Beverley – with St Mary's church in the background from a postcard dated 1908. Note the absence of cars.

Plate 8. The Regeneration of the Beck. New brick houses constructed in 2002.

ILLUSTRATIONS IN THE TEXT

Front End Paper. The Westwood looking towards the town in 2003.

Back End Paper. David Hick's map of Beverley dated 1811. *(Beverley Art Gallery)* made in the early 18th century when it hung near the entrance to the choir. Today it hangs in the south transept of Beverley Minster. 20

and authorising the Recorder and 12 governors to act as Justices
of the Peace. 161

A NOTE ON WEIGHTS, MEASURES AND MONEY

The weights, measures and monetary values used in this book are the ones contemporaries used. These may be summarised as:

Money:

4 farthings	=	1d (penny)
12d (pence)	=	1s (shilling)
1s	=	5p
20s (shillings)	=	£1 (pound)
21s (shillings)	=	1 guinea

Weight:

16oz (ounces)	=	1lb (pound)
1lb	=	0.45 kilograms
14lb (pounds)	=	1 stone
1 stone	=	6.35 kilograms
2 stones	=	1qr (quarter)
1qr	=	12.70 kilograms
4qr (quarters)	=	1cwt (hundredweight)
1cwt	=	50.80 kilograms
20cwt	=	1 ton
1 ton	=	1.02 tonnes

Volume:

2 pints	=	1 quart
1 quart	=	1.14 litres
4 quarts	=	1 gallon
1 gallon	=	4.55 litres
2 gallons	=	1 peck
1 peck	=	9.09 litres
4 pecks	=	1 bushel
1 bushel	=	36.40 litres
8 bushels	=	1qr (quarter)
1 quarter	=	2.91 hectolitres

Distance:

12in (inches)	=	1ft (foot)
1ft	=	0.305 metres
3ft (feet)	=	1yd (yard)
1yd	=	0.91 metres
22yds (yards)	=	1 chain
1 chain	=	20.12 metres
10 chains	=	1 furlong
1 furlong	=	201.17 metres
8 furlongs	=	1 mile
1 mile	=	1.61 kilometres

Area:

30¼ sq yds	=	1 perch
1 perch	=	25.29 sq metres

40 perches = 1 rood = 1210 sq yds = 1011.56 sq metres
4 roods = 1 acre = 4840 sq yds = 0.405 hectares

Prepared by Stephen Harrison

INTRODUCTION

The gathering of information for this book has taken about twenty-five years. It is the result of conversations with many people, both those with an academic approach and those with no formal historical training but who have grown up with a love of the town. When for five years I ran Local History classes it was a two way learning process – I learnt as much as I gave. Students often gave me photos of Beverley or photocopies of documents which I had not come across previously. Conversations not only gave information but also spark off ideas which then need investigating. The result was hours of reading about a fascinating subject. My research also took the form of walking around the town and the Westwood, looking at and observing the direction of the streets, the lie of the land, the shape of the buildings, the design of windows above shop fronts and details of carvings in churches - in fact to get a feel of the history of the town.

In the town of Beverley the same area of land has been changed and altered over the centuries. People come, build their houses, set up industries and make developments suitable for their time. Then the next generation comes along and alteration takes place as needs and fashions change. I have chosen the chronological approach to portray the history of Beverley as I feel that this best shows the changes and developments which took place in each century and can often explain the reasons for those changes. In our own century the speed of change has quickened and residents of the town often feel that they are no longer in control of how the town will develop.

There has been so much recent research into Beverley's past and new techniques in archaeology have added much to our knowledge. I have tended to use modern sources in the search for historical accuracy rather than Victorian favourites. The backbone for this book has been the Victoria County History of Beverley. Obviously, this one volume cannot contain all the history of this ancient town and I hope that the bibliography will help to point directions in which a particular interest can be followed.

In putting the history down on paper I am particularly grateful to a number of people: my brother, Michael Gurney, who lives in France and therefore could comment on the contents as an outsider, Drs David and Susan Neave who went through the text testing for historical accuracy and Jane Lancaster who scrupulously checked the script. If there are any errors or omissions, they are entirely my own. Without their help and encouragement I could not have completed this book. Thanks also go to the staff at Beverley Library and to Sally Hayes at the Art Gallery.

Lastly, my thanks also go to Alan Avery of the Blackthorn Press who has given me the opportunity to write this history for the people of 21st century Beverley.

Pamela Hopkins
August 2003

CHAPTER 1

FROM NOMADS TO ROMANS

From whichever direction the East Yorkshire town of Beverley is approached, the twin towers of the Minster and the single tower of St Mary's dominate the skyline. On a summer's evening the sun will cast a golden light on the rich coloured stone of these buildings, widely believed to be two of the finest Gothic churches in the country. For hundreds of years these two churches have acted as beacons drawing the traveller and the pilgrim on to the ancient market town of Beverley.

The story of the town began, however, long before these churches were built. It began long before Beverley became a rich commercial centre, long before the freemen of the town were granted permission to graze their cattle on the common land to the west of the town, before medieval kings and pilgrims came to visit one of the most venerated shrines in the north of England. The story of the town began in 721AD with the death of Bishop John of York in a monastery he had founded on the place where Beverley Minster now stands.

Yet, for thousands of years before the life and death of Bishop John, later St John of Beverley, people lived in this area.

500,000 – 10,000BC. The Palaeolithic Period – The Ice Age

Beverley lies within the arc of the Yorkshire chalk land. Thousands of years ago the North Sea extended over that part of East Yorkshire known as Holderness up to the cliff line of the Yorkshire Wolds. The coast line ran through the present-day towns and villages of Carnaby, Haisthorpe, Burton Agnes,

1

Map 1
Beverley: location map

Nafferton, Lockington, Beverley and southwards to Hessle situated on the edge of the Humber.

During the Ice Age the whole of northern Europe was covered with a thick mantle of ice. Enormous glaciers slowly edged southwards from the Polar region scouring and scraping as they advanced and carrying great boulders and other debris in their path. As the ice melted the debris was deposited often far from its place of origin. In Holderness this debris, once deposited, formed a new land. A walk across Holderness today reveals deposits from Scandinavia, sandstones from the Pennines in north-west England, basalts from the Lake District, quartz from Northumberland and the central lowlands of Scotland and chalk and flint from the Yorkshire Wolds.

Most of the deposits in Holderness are boulder clay, sand and gravel settled on a bedrock of chalk. The boulder clay is impermeable, forcing rivers and streams to remain underground, and above ground trapped water formed inland lakes and meres. Over thousands of years the water receded, the lakes dried up and the only inland lake which remains today is Hornsea Mere. Deciduous woodlands grew on the boulder clay, trees and leaves grew, died and decomposed forming marshy peat areas known today as 'carrs'.

The undulating slopes and dry valleys of the Westwood Pasture, together with the Hurn, form 600 acres of land to the west of the town of Beverley. This area features in the history of the area from early times to the present day and as much of it has never been ploughed is a rich source of pre-historic remains.

The underlying rock is hard chalk (of the Cretaceous system), approximately 1,000 feet thick. Today chalk is exposed in Newbegin pits, but elsewhere the surface is covered by boulder clay. The chalk is permeable but the boulder clay is not and after heavy rain water stands for long periods in the hollows of the surface. Nowadays, the only spring to be seen breaking through the boulder clay is at Willow Row Bridge. This spring, dry in summer, flows freely after rains and during the winter. In recent years, particularly heavy rains have caused other springs to force their way to the surface.

10,000 – 4,000BC. The Mesolithic Period – Hunter Gatherers

At the end of the Ice Age land which had been compressed by the weight of ice bounced back, a process which is still continuing. The melting of the ice caused sea levels to rise and about 6,600BC the lower land linking present day Britain with Europe flooded so that Britain became an island. With the melting of the ice, rivers flowed swiftly but over time the amount of water decreased and rivers became silted up into narrow channels.

The people who lived during the Mesolithic period were nomadic hunter gatherers. They moved from place to place following the trail of the wild ox, the red deer, the boar, the red fox and the wolf which inhabited dense forests of hazel, oak, lime and elm on the higher ground and alder and willow on lower, damper ground.

Bands of hunter gatherers using simple tools and weapons of wood, horn and shaped stone, would travel up what is now known as the river Hull to the rich fishing and fowling grounds of Holderness. They travelled along an ancient route to the west of the river over land made firmer by deposits of sand and gravel, an area which was to become the northern boundary of the town of Beverley, to find the dry hunting grounds of the Yorkshire Wolds.

4,000 – 2,200BC. The Neolithic Period – The New Stone Age

Gradually a primitive form of farming developed and people began to settle. During the Neolithic Period woodland was cleared for a settlement and opened up to expose land for growing cereals. Higher ground in the area now known as East Yorkshire was heavily populated during this period and trees were cleared from much of the 'Westwood'. The remains of a long barrow, a burial place for a number of people, dating to this period has been found near the highest point of the Westwood.

2,200 – 700 BC. The Bronze Age

Over hundreds of years more and more people settled in this area which offered rich farming lands. About 2,000 BC large numbers of immigrants, often referred to as the Beaker people because of their distinctive beaker-shaped pottery, came from Europe bringing with them skills in manufacturing bronze implements. Burial customs changed. Bronze Age people favoured individual rather than communal graves. These single graves, which often contained grave goods, were covered with a mound of chalk, or grass which was cut from around the graves revealing the chalk beneath. They must have been a distinctive feature in the landscape. On the Westwood the outline of at least three round burial mounds (30-40 yards in diameter) can be seen close to Black Mill.

700BC – 71AD. The Iron Age

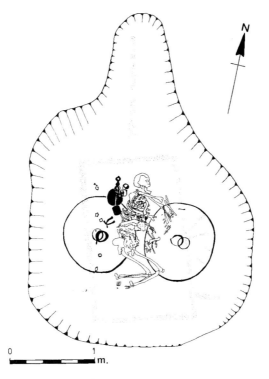

An Iron Age Cart Burial

About 700BC new migrants began to arrive from the over-populated area of northern France. Known as the Parisi people, they appear to have been a peaceful tribe seeking new lands and places of settlement. They manufactured tools and weapons of iron.

An Iron Age ditch (8 – 10 feet deep) stretches across the Westwood alongside Newbald Road to the plateau where Black Mill now stands. In places the ditch meanders, perhaps as a result of an obstruction such as a group of trees or a particularly large tree which stood in its path when the ditch was dug. The ditch probably defined a boundary, or if topped with a palisade, would have enclosed cattle.

A distinctive feature of the Parisi people is the burial of their dead in individual graves under a barrow surrounded by a square ditch; these graves are often grouped together into a cemetery. The largest such cemetery is near Market Weighton, at Arras which has given its name to this method of burial. There are seventeen Parisi burial sites in East Yorkshire and others in the Paris Basin in France. A further feature of the Arras Culture is the burial of a two-wheeled cart and several artefacts beneath the body of a man or woman, presumably of high status. In 1875 the Reverend Canon Greenwell, vicar of Beverley Minster, investigated an Iron Age cemetery between Black Mill and Archbishop's Pits on the Beverley Westwood. Here he found a cart burial the remains of which are now in the British Museum.

71 – 410AD. The Romans

With the arrival of the Romans we move out of pre-history into the period when written records assist in a search of the past. Four Roman legions, comprising about 20,000 men of the Roman Imperial Army, plus auxiliary units, invaded southern Britain in 43AD with the aim of subduing this northern island. At first Roman occupation stretched as far north as the Humber. In 71AD Petillius Cersalis, governor of Britain, came north through Lincolnshire and crossed the Humber at Petuaria (now known as Brough) in order to quell the Brigantes tribe who had rebelled against Roman rule. A route was made from Petuaria to present-day Market Weighton, (seven miles to the west of where Beverley now is), where it divided, one section continuing north to the fort at Derventia (now known as Malton), the other going north-west to Ebor (now known as York). For the next 350 years a Roman legion was stationed at this important military garrison and commercial settlement and soldiers were dispatched to suppress uprisings north of Hadrian's Wall.

A Typical Roman Tiled House

There is relatively little evidence of Roman occupation amongst the Parisi people of East Yorkshire. Aerial photography of the Westwood reveals two rectangular fields, typical of Roman agriculture, adjoining the Iron Age enclosure. Roman coins and pottery of the third and fourth centuries have been found on the ancient route along the northern boundary of the later medieval town of Beverley. Archaeologists have discovered evidence of a substantial amount of Roman tile making along the banks of the Beck. As tiles are difficult to transport it can be assumed that there were a number of houses built here or nearby, either by Romans or Romanised Britains, during the Roman period.

In 410AD the Roman garrison in Britain was recalled to Italy to protect Rome against invasion and the Britons were told to look to their own defences. During the 400 years of occupation the country had been administered and controlled by the Romans but after their departure warring groups developed and mercenaries from Europe were summoned to aid various leaders. These newcomers soon turned against their employers and claimed areas of the country as their own.

Angles from northern Germany settled in the area of Holderness. As the waters continued to recede, more low lying land became available for habitation. The higher places, such as the Westwood, were abandoned and the woods left to regenerate. Settlements were on the lower land where islands of boulder clay stood high above the marshland. Few Celtic place names remain in Holderness and from this we can infer that the Parisi either fled from the area or were killed by the new occupants.

During the fifth and sixth centuries invaders came from Denmark, and Saxony and colonized much of England. Small groups welded into distinct kingdoms. The area north of the Humber came to be known as Northumbria, the land stretching from the Humber to the Tees being known as Deira and land from the Tees to Scotland known as Bernicia. In 616AD Edwin was proclaimed king of Bernicia as well as Deira and thus became the first ruler of the kingdom of Northumbria.

One particular area of boulder clay, set on the spring line at the foot of the dip slope of the chalk wolds, surrounded by a large lake to the north and marsh land to the south and east, lay between the higher ground of the Westwood and the low land alongside the river Hull. Here was an area of dry ground which was large enough to support a small settlement. This was where Bishop John of York chose to found his monastery.

Beverley Westwood and the Hurn

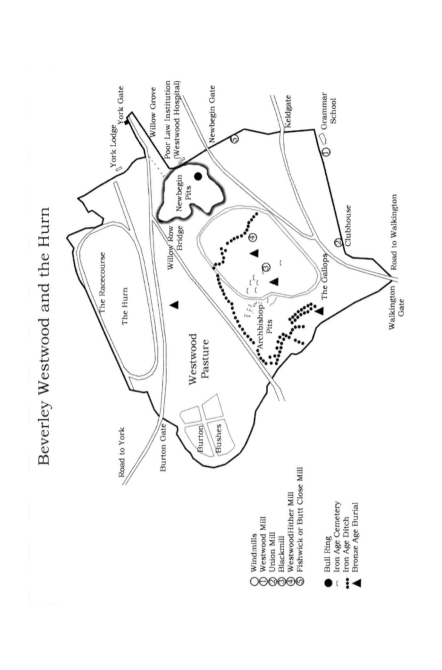

Windmills
① Westwood Mill
② Union Mill
③ Blackmill
④ Westwood/Hither Mill
⑤ Fishwick or Butt Close Mill

● Bull Ring
⟨ Iron Age Cemetery
⋮⋮ Iron Age Ditch
◀ Bronze Age Burial

CHAPTER 2

THE ANGLO-SAXON SETTLEMENT

Knowledge of early Christianity in Britain comes from the writings of St Bede. At the age of seven Bede was placed in a monastery at Jarrow in Northumbria and here he was to stay until his death in 735. He wrote over 100 books the most famous of which is *The Ecclesiastical History of the English People*. It is from this book that we receive the only contemporary information we have of the life of John, first Bishop of Hexham, then of York and much later to become known as St John of Beverley.

The Early Christian Northumbria

Christianity first came to England during the time of the Roman occupation. After the departure of the Romans, pagan invaders from Scandinavia drove Christianity to the far north, to the south west and to Wales where communities kept the faith alive in remote monastic communities. In 563 St Columba left Ireland with twelve companions and landed on the west coast of Britain on the island of Iona where he founded a Celtic monastery. From here he and his followers went out to the people in the surrounding countryside to convert them to the Celtic form of Christianity.

Soon after the death of St Columba, in 597, St Augustine, with several followers, landed in Kent with the intention of converting the English to the Roman form of Christianity. Four years later he was joined by an Italian monk, Paulinus. Ethelbert, king of Kent, received them kindly and when his daughter, Ethelberga, who had been converted to Christianity, travelled north to marry Edwin, King of Northumbria, Paulinus was permitted to accompany her.

In Northumbria Paulinus preached the Christian gospel to Edwin and his people. After miraculously escaping an assassination attempt the king gave thanks to his own gods and idols. Paulinus then told the king that his avoidance of death had been only because of Paulinus's prayers to the Christian God. Edwin agreed to be instructed in the Christian faith and his infant daughter and eleven members of his household were baptised. Edwin, reluctant to renounce his own gods, summoned his councillors to his great hall to discuss whether Christianity should be adopted as the official religion in Northumbria. After each councillor had spoken Bede tells us that the king:

> publicly accepted the gospel which Paulinus preached, renounced idolatry, and confessed his faith in Christ.'

The pagan high priest, Coifi, asked the king to provide him with arms and riding a stallion set out to destroy the idols at his temple at a place called Goodmanham (two miles east of Market Weighton).

On Easter Day in 627 King Edwin, with all his nobles and a number of the common people, was baptised at York in a hastily built wooden church dedicated to St Peter the Apostle. Soon after a greater and more magnificent stone church was built – later to become York Minster.

In 633 King Edwin was assassinated and pagans overran Northumbria slaughtering members of the church and the people. Northumbria reverted to paganism and was once again divided into two kingdoms and Ethelberga and Paulinus were forced to flee to Kent. Two years later Oswald, King Edwin's nephew, drove out the heathens and re-united the two Northumbrian kingdoms of Bernici and Deira. Christianity was restored.

One of the main differences between the Celtic and the Roman form of Christianity was the date for the celebration of Easter. This made for difficulties in the royal household where King Oswiu was a Celtic Christian and would cease his fasting on

St John

one day, while Queen Eanfled was a Roman Christian and would cease her fasting on another. A Synod was held at the monastery at Whitby, under the direction of Abbess Hilda, in 664 to resolve this question. Various viewpoints were put forward but eventually King Oswiu decided that the Roman form of Christianity should be adopted and concluded by saying that as:

St Peter is the guardian of the gates of heaven, I shall not contradict him ….otherwise when I come to the gates of heaven there may be no one to open them, because he who holds the keys has turned away.

Although for some time many continued to follow the old traditions, from then onwards the accepted form of the English Church was the Roman practice.

The Life of Bishop John

It was into this scenario that John, later St John of Beverley, was born. There is no record of his date of birth but as Bede refers to him as dying at 'a great age' in 721, it is probable that he was born in the first half of the 7th century – maybe 640. Although not mentioned by Bede, tradition has always maintained that John's birthplace was Harpham, nine miles north of the place where he was later to found a monastery. Bede tells us that John studied at Streanaeshalch (an abbey at Whitby) under Abbess Hilda.

In 687 John was consecrated bishop of Hexham. Bede writes that Bishop John travelled to the monastery at Jarrow in 691 and ordained him a deacon and in 702 ordained him a priest. Bede recalls two miracles which were attributed to Bishop John while he was Bishop of Hexham.

Bishop John liked, whenever possible, and especially during Lent, to go with a few companions to an isolated house set amongst scattered trees at a place one and a half miles from Hexham, across the River Tyne, to read and pray. One year, during his stay, the bishop gave accommodation to a youth who was dumb and had no hair on his head.

On the second Sunday in Lent, he ordered the poor man to come in to him and then he told him to put out his tongue and show it him. Thereupon he took him by the chin and made the sign of the holy cross on his tongue; after this he told him to put his tongue in again and say something. 'Say some word,' he said'. The boy said at once what the bishop told him to say the bonds of his tongue being unloosed. The bishop then added the names of the letters: 'Say A', and he said it. 'Say B', and he said that too. When he had repeated the names of the letters after the bishop, the latter added syllables and words for the youth to repeat after him. When he had repeated them all, one after the other, the bishop taught him to say longer sentences, which he did.

As a result of this miracle Bishop John was later to become the patron saint of the deaf and those with speech impediments. The bishop then ordered the physician to cure his scaly head. This was done

'And so', writes Bede, 'the youth gained a clear complexion, ready speech, and beautiful curly hair, whereas he had once been ugly, destitute, and dumb'.

A second miracle is the story told to Bede by Heribald, one of Bishop John's followers. Heribald once, against the bishop's wishes, galloped his horse in a contest with other young men. The horse stumbled and Herebald fell cracking his head on a stone. All night the bishop prayed over him and by morning Herebald had fully recovered his health.

In 705 Wilfrid, a somewhat turbulent priest, after a long exile was restored to the bishopric at Hexham. John, after the death of the saintly Bosa, become Bishop of York (the archbishopric was not formed until 735). The date of the foundation of a monastery at Inderawuda (meaning in the wood of the men of Deira) – later Beverley – twenty-seven miles east of York is uncertain but it is likely to have been while John was Bishop of York.

In the 16th century John Leland (keeper of Henry VIII's libraries), using an unknown source, wrote about the life of St John of Beverley. This source said that Bishop John founded a church in Beverley dedicated to St John the Evangelist which he subsequently converted into a monastery. He added a new presbytery, or choir, and to the south of the church he constructed an oratory dedicated to St Martin in which he later installed nuns. In the main church he placed seven priests and an equal number of clerks. According to this unproven source the monastery was established in 692 when Bishop John was still bishop of Hexham.

The Monastery at Inderawuda

Archaeology and tradition substantiate the claim that Bishop John's monastery at Inderawuda was on the site where Beverley Minster now stands.

Archaeological evidence suggests that the area was already inhabited in the 7th century. During Excavations in 1979 – 82 (undertaken by the Humberside Archaeological Unit – now Humber Archaeology Partnership), on land to the south of the Minster, pollen cores taken at a number of sites show that by the onset of the Iron Age (700 BC) the environment here was mixed oak forest. 1,000 years later parts of the forest had been cleared to allow for the cultivation of cereals. By the beginning of the 8th century the area was still mostly covered with woodland in which oak trees were common together with water loving trees such as alder and willow but there is evidence that at this time surrounding woodland was cleared to create new fields – inferring that the size of the community was growing. The remains of a number of major buildings of this period have been found; it is likely that the remains of the church lie beneath the present Minster.

There were also traces of an enclosure and ramparts to keep wild animals and unwanted visitors out. Excavation to the south of where the Saxon monastery is believed to have been established, revealed a large enclosure surrounded by a precinct ditch (2.5m. wide and 0.8m deep) and rampart. The combined width of the bank and ditch was 4.5m. If topped with a palisade the bank would be 4.5m high

It is impossible to be sure what that first church looked like. It was probably built of timber because the nearest source of freestone, as opposed to chalk, was oolitic limestone from the area where the villages of North and South Cave and Newbald now stand. It may have resembled other churches of this period which usually consisted of a nave and chancel with an apse, a rounded east end, and often contained side chambers, attached to the north or south walls, each entered by its own door from the nave, in which important burials would be placed.

The only visible survival of the Saxon church is the round-backed stone chair which today stands beside the High Altar in Beverley Minster. This may well have been the abbot's chair placed in the apse of the church. There is a similar chair in Hexham Abbey.

Late 7th Century Saxon Stone Chair

Leland, using his unknown source, states that two nobles who lived near the monastery were most generous in their gifts. Puch, who lived at the manor of South Burton (Bishop Burton), placed his daughter, Yolfrida, as a nun in the monastery. After she had died in May 742 he endowed the monastery with the manor of Walkington. Addi, the other nobleman, gave the manor of North Burton (Cherry Burton) to the monastery.

Bede tells the story of two miracles relating to these men.

The first abbot of the monastery at Inderawuda was one of Bishop John's deacons, Berhthun. Berhthun recounted to Bede the story of how the bishop had been invited by Puch, to dedicate his church at South Burton. After the dedication John was persuaded to dine in Puch's house. Bishop John, having been told that Puch's wife had been severely ill for nearly forty days, instructed one of the monks accompanying him to give her some of the holy water which he had blessed for the dedication of the church, and to apply some of the water as a lotion to the place where the worst pain lay. As soon as this was done, the lady was cured, rose from her sickbed and, bringing the cup to the Bishop and his followers, served them with drinks until the close of the meal.

On a similar occasion, Bishop John dedicated the church of the nobleman named Addi. One of Addi's serving lads was very ill and his coffin lay beside him awaiting his death. The Bishop went to see the boy, prayed over him, gave him his blessing and wished him a quick recovery. Later when all were seated at supper the boy sent a message saying that he was thirsty. Addi sent him some wine which had been blessed by Bishop John. As soon as the boy had drunk he got up, threw off his lethargy and weakness and dressed. He then joined Addi and the Bishop at supper.

A third miracle told by Berhthun and recorded by Bede is the story of an event which took place when he and the Bishop visited a convent of nuns at Wetadun (by tradition believed to be Watton). One of the nuns was seriously ill with an arm so swollen that it could hardly be encircled by both hands and she was likely to die from the pain. The Bishop visited the girl, stood over her, gave her his blessing and went out. Later Abbot Berhthun entered the room where the young girl lay and after he had given her a drink she told him that she had begun to feel better as soon as the Bishop had blessed her and gone away. The pain had entirely left her arm.

Death of Bishop John

Bede tells us that when Bishop John's advanced years prevented him from administering his bishopric, (probably in the year 714) he consecrated his priest Wilfrid to the See of York and retired to his monastery at Inderawuda to end his days in a manner pleasing to God. In this monastery, on 7th May 721, Bishop John died and was buried in St Peter's chapel.

In Beverley Minster today there is a stone slab which marks the burial place of Bishop John, later St John of Beverley, who died almost 1300 years ago.

After the death of Bishop John, Alcuin (735 – 804), librarian of the cathedral church of York, and who was later to become adviser to the Emperor Charlemagne, wrote a verse history of Northumbria. He included the life of Bishop John, as told by Bede, to demonstrate John's honesty and virtue which proved his worthiness to be venerated as a saint.

The miracles which took place during his life showed Bishop John's powers as an intercessor with God. Soon miracles occurred to those visiting his place of death. For 800 years the tomb of Bishop John was to draw pilgrims in ever increasing numbers.

CHAPTER 3

NEW ARRIVALS : THE VIKINGS AND THE NORMANS

A Viking Raid on the East Coast

The invasion of the Northmen, a name given by the English to all the inhabitants of Denmark and the Scandinavian peninsula, began in 787. The first evidence of the invaders over-wintering in Britain is 851. To begin with invasions were on a small scale but in 865 this was to change when a large army of Danish invaders entered England, crossed the Humber and captured York. After negotiations between the invaders and the Saxon rulers in 880 the kingdoms of Northumbria, East Anglia and central England became known as Dane Law and became subject to Danish jurisdiction. With their capital at York the Vikings followed their own customs and traditions and continued trading throughout northern Europe. The Danes brought new words into the English vocabulary. Many of East Yorkshire place-names with suffixes such as 'by', 'thorpe' and 'wick' are of Scandinavian origin.

Danish settlement in Beverley is demonstrated by the use of the Norwegian word for street - 'garta'- being used in many street names (Lairgate, Hengate, and Highgate) although many streets received their names long after the Viking kingdom had gone.

The Danish invaders were pagans and had little initial respect for the Christian communities they found. Gradually they came to tolerate Christianity and the Minster at York returned to being a centre of Christian teaching and learning.

Archaeology shows us that by the mid 9th century the Saxon monastery at Beverley had been abandoned, perhaps as a result of Danish attacks, although there is no evidence of destruction. A purse-hoard of twenty-three Saxon coins and stycas dating to 851 was buried close to the precinct ramparts suggesting that perhaps the site was abandoned when the Viking army first over-wintered in England.

By the early 10th century a community of some renown, centred round the cult of Bishop John, had been established on the site of the monastery at Inderawuda. Archaeology shows that at this time the area of the monastery was cleared, old timber used for buildings, debris was thrown into the precinct ditch and a new layout of buildings and enclosures was made. Evidence of the use of glazed windows and a building roofed with lead indicates that a new church was built of stone.

King Athelstan Visits the Tomb of Bishop John

In 925 Athelstan, whose aim was to unite the whole of England, Scotland and Wales under one lordship, was crowned king of the West Saxons and the Mercians. After the death of the Danish king, Athelstan marched into Yorkshire and established himself as lord. Northumbria submitted to his rule, the Kings of the Scots and of Strathclyde acknowledged him as their ruler and the Welsh princes agreed to pay tribute. In 937 a rebellion of minor kings rose against him which caused Athelstan to raise an army and march north to confront the rebellion at Brunanburh. The location of Brunanburh is unknown but it is likely to have been in Northumbria.

**Late 17th Century panel of King
Athelstan and St John in Beverley Minster**

William Ketell, a canon of Beverley Minster, writing in the early 12th century, tells us that, on his way north to the battle, Athelstan and a few of his followers diverted from their path to visit the tomb of John of Beverley. Here the king prayed throughout the night, so that the pavement was drenched with his tears, and in the morning left his dagger on the altar promising that if he was successful in battle he would return and grant rights and privileges to the church which held the remains of the saint. During the night before the battle (Ketell relates) the king awoke to find John of Beverley standing by his bed. The saint told him that because of the king's devotion in visiting his tomb, he had entreated God on his behalf and God had heard his voice.

> Therefore, I shall be an enemy to your enemies and I shall strike those who strike you, and the grace of God will protect you.

The battle took place; Athelstan was victorious and became the first overlord of Britain. With such a protector as Bishop John it is no wonder that future kings felt the need to visit the tomb of this powerful saint and seek his support.

William, a 12th century monk at the abbey of Malmesbury, in his chronicles says that Athelstan:

King Athelstan

> cast all his predecessors into the shade by his piety, as well as the glory of all their triumphs by the splendour of his own. I forbear relating how many new and magnificent monasteries he founded; but I will not conceal that there was scarcely an old one in England which he did not embellish either with buildings, or ornaments, or books, or possessions.

Athelstan was certainly generous in his gifts to the church in Beverley and to the town. Ketell tells us that he confirmed certain rights to the church:

- the right of sanctuary – a right which may have already existed since Saxon times and which was to last for 600 years.

- The right of thraves (each plough in the East Riding was to contribute the equivalent of 96 sheaves of corn to the canons of Beverley Minster).

- the right of the canons to hold certain lands in the East Riding

- The right for the town of Beverley to be exempt from paying land-tax to the king.

- The right for the church, at that time the only religious community in the East Riding, to be a 'minster' with a College of Prebendaries (or canons) i.e. a collegiate church run by secular canons; (Ripon, York, and Southwell were also collegiate churches and thus called minster but as each of these churches is now the seat of a bishop they are also called cathedrals). The clergy of a minster were expected to provide religious support to surrounding areas which might not have their own priests.

Historians today believe that William Ketell's account of the visit of King Athelstan and the rights he granted to the church were merely an affirmation of already existing rights and privileges belonging to the minster at Beverley.

After his death in 939 Athelstan was buried in the abbey church at Malmesbury where his effigy can still be seen. For many centuries people considered Athlestan to be the founder of the religious settlement at Beverley and his image is represented in many carvings in the present church.

The name Bevreli or Beverlac (meaning beaver-lake or beaver-clearing) first appears in the 10th century for 'John of Bevreli' was included in the calendars of northern saints. The community became renowned as the place where the relics of that 'holy man', described by Bede, remained.

Since the arrival of the Danes monasteries had been destroyed, the clergy had become lax, ignorant and superstitious and much of Yorkshire had reverted to paganism. In 958 Oskytel became archbishop of York. A lover of monasticism, he tried to encourage the growth of religious communities throughout Yorkshire, particularly at York, Beverley and Southwell and to support these communities he restored land which had been plundered by the Danes. His successor, Wulfstan II (1003 – 1023), felt that priests should be missionaries converting the heathen.

The Last Three Saxon Archbishops of York

The last three Saxon archbishops of the northern province found the archdiocese of York too big to administer and promoted the churches at Ripon, Southwell and Beverley into almost cathedral status.

Archbishop Aelfric (1023 – 51) was of West Saxon origin. He had been a monk and then dean of Winchester before being appointed to York. He continued Wulfstan's work of reforming the church in the north and in particular he increased the endowment of the houses of secular canons, at York, Beverley and Southwell. He laid down strict rules for conduct: canons were to avoid the company of women, were to sleep in common dormitories, sing offices together in church and eat in the refectory. In Beverley he began the rebuilding of a dormitory and refectory for the canons, and he secured further estates for the Minster. In 1037 Bishop John was canonised and on 25th October his relics were translated to a magnificent new shrine of gold and silver with precious stones which was placed in the church. St John's saints days became the 7th May (the date of his death) and 25th October (the day of his translation).

Archbishop Cynesige (1051-60), a monk who had served in Edward the Confessor's chapel, was in 1051 appointed archbishop of York. He, like his predecessor, was a benefactor to houses of secular canons, especially at Beverley where he continued work on the dormitory and refectory and added a stone tower to the church.

Archbishop Ealdred (1060-69), first a monk at Worcester and then, from 1046, its bishop, was considered to be the most powerful prelate in England. He provided the secular canons at Beverley with new lands and completed the building of the dormitory and refectory at Beverley, Southwell and York. At Beverley he redecorated the church throughout, built a new presbytery at the eastern part of the chancel, provided a new pulpit above which hung a crucifix of bronze, silver and gold and enforced order and decency among the clergy, especially in their dress.

King Edward the Confessor (1042-1066) established Archbishop Ealdred as 'sole lord of the manor of Beverley' and granted the right of two annual fairs to the town.

A Trading Community Develops Near the Minster

Beverley, by the beginning of the 11th century, was a thriving community. Craft activities took place to the south of the Minster; these included textile production, leather working and the manufacture of objects out of antler. Considerable trading took place, as is indicated by archaeological finds of pottery vessels from Stamford and Northamptonshire, coins from Lincoln and York and lava querns from the Rhineland.

Archaeological finds of iron slags demonstrate the process of metal working. Much lead spillage in the surrounding ditch indicates lead working, perhaps for roofing and glazing the church. Pottery and glass vessels were in use. Industrial and domestic farm buildings were outside the precinct on the south side (Hall Garth field). Other archaeological finds in the area of the Minster relating to this period are copper and lead alloys, jewellery and dress fittings, worked bone pins and toggles, glass beads, antler combs, jet and worked bone amulets and pendants. Bones of mammals (sheep, pig roe deer, red deer), birds (goose and domestic fowls) and fishes (herring, pike, eel, sturgeon, carp, mackerel, salmon, smelt and turbot) have been found which give us an indication of the diet of members of this busy community.

Accounts of miracles which took place resulting from the intercession of St John, give us a picture of the area. William Ketell tells us of a man he knew who, when young, had been a deaf mute. The man had come to the tomb of the saint and having been cured of his infirmities remained not far from the monastery 'next to the lake flowing outside the cemetery' – a lake in which, perhaps, beavers played. A prisoner who escaped to Beverley from the castle at Cottingham, is described as crossing the 'rampart of the lake which encircled the town'. Archaeological excavations confirm these accounts for investigations carried out in 1983 reveal that the area round Eastgate, to the north of the

Minster, was, in the 8th century, a pool or depression and that over a period of 350 years infilling took place.

1066 – The Arrival of the Normans

On 5th January, 1066, Edward the Confessor, died childless. After Edward's death Harold Godwinson, who had been nominated heir presumptive by the dying king, was crowned king of England. In September Harald Hardrada, King of Norway, another claimant to the throne, and Tosti, brother to King Harold, sailed with a fleet of 330 ships to the Orkneys and from there south along Scotland and along the English coast until he came to land where 'it is called Cleveland'. A Norwegian saga gives us a flavour of the devastation of this army; one wonders how the settlement at Beverley, nine miles north of the Humber, was affected:

> He went ashore, harried and subjugated the land without resistance. Then he laid into Scarborough and fought against the townsfolk. He went up on the rock there is there and had a large bonfire built and set fire to it. When the fire was blazing they took large forks and threw it down into the town. Each house then caught fire from the next. The whole town went up in flames. The Norwegians killed many men and took all the booty they laid hands on. The English had no choice, if they were to live, but to submit to King Harald. He subjugated the whole country wherever he went. Then King Harald with all his army continued southwards down the coast and came in at Holderness. A concentration met him there and King Harald won another battle. Then he went to the Humber, up along the river and landed at Riccall.

A battle took place at Fulford with much slaughter, followed soon after by a battle at Stamford Bridge in which Harald Hardrada and Tosti were both killed and King Harold of England was victorious. However, news reached the king of the invasion of William of Normandy in the south of England and Harold and his army hastened south to repel them. At Hastings King Harold was killed and William claimed the throne of England. On

Christmas Day 1066 he was crowned king of England by Ealdred, archbishop of York.

Archbishop Ealdred was quick to make known to the Norman rulers the power of the saint whose remains lay at Beverley. In 1067 he ordered a monk, Folcard, from the monastery at S Omer, near Calais in France, to write responsories (an anthem sung in response to a priest) for St John, telling the story of his life and listing the miracles which had occurred at his tomb. Miracles such as:

- A blind boy, brought from Hexham, who recovered his sight at the tomb.

- A Scot, called Gillo, who was deformed, who, having passed the eve of St John's day by himself at the shrine, was cured.

- A citizen of York had a favourite son who became dumb. He recovered when he was taken to Beverley Minster.

In this biography Folcard writes that through the merits of the saint:

cripples were cured, demons were banished, the blind made to see, the deaf were made to hear, the mute were made to speak, the lame were made to walk; all kinds of ailments were put to flight.

As the news of miracles spread no wonder that pilgrims came to Beverley!

Harrying of the North

In 1068 Earl Morcar led a rebellion against the new king. As a result two motte-and-bailey timber castles were hastily built in York to guard the river Ouse. However, the northerners were not easily to be subdued by their new conquerors and on 11th September 1069, when a Danish fleet sailed into the Humber the whole of the north rose against the Norman rulers, killing the

king's appointed governor and the soldiers in the garrison in York. In 1069 William came north to suppress the northerners who had rebelled against his authority. He carried out what has later been called the 'Harrying of the North' in which the city of York was demolished and throughout Yorkshire and Northumbria, towns, villages, farms, cattle, houses were destroyed and the land made into a wasteland; a state from which it would take several generations to recover. The Anglo Saxon Chronicle says that 'William utterly raised and layed waste the entire shire of Yorkshire'.

The town of Beverley was, however, spared the king's vengeance. According to William Ketell this was due to the support of Beverley's saint.

William Ketell records the story of how a few of the king's soldiers left his camp and came to Beverley in order to plunder and rob the town. The soldiers proceeded to the enclosure of the churchyard where a large number of terrified people had gathered:

Their leader, Thurston, attacked a wretch who was trying to reach the safety of the sanctuary. He drew his sword and gave chase through the middle of the stunned people on his horse. The man escaped all the way inside the doors of the church. Suddenly there was a gathering of trembling people shouting unanimously imploring the help of St John. The soldier fell down paralysed from the horse he was riding and his misshapen face having been twisted behind his back, and his hands and feet bent back, just like an ugly monster, he drew the eyes of all the astonished people who were there. They broke out in praises and glorified the power of John.

The soldiers returned to the king who then summoned

Wise men from the church at Beverley who told him about the sanctity of the saint and the honours to the church which had been given by previous kings.

Consequently, King William reinforced with royal assent whatever had been given to the church.

With generous hands he adorned the church with votive offerings and enlarged the church with lands so that he might achieve forgiveness of his sins.

1085 Domesday Book

In the winter of 1085 King William ordered men to survey the land in order to assess the amount of tax due to the king. The consequences of this survey were likened to Domesday itself – the Last Judgement.

The King's commissioners visited every estate in the land in order to establish place names, the names of who had held the land before 1066 and who owned it in 1085, the amount of taxable plough land with the number of ploughs before and since 1066, the number of villagers, cottagers, slaves and free men, the number of mills and fishponds, the amount of meadow, pasture and woodland and the difference in tax potential between 1066 and 1086. Within 18 months the survey was complete.

In Bevreli', it was found; 'St John' carucate (the amount of taxable ploughland) was always free from the king's geld (i.e. a tax paid on land holding). The canons have there on the demesne (manorial lands reserved for the lord of the manor's personal benefit and on which tenants gave free service) 1 plough, and 18 villeins and 15 bordars having 6 ploughs, and 3 mills of 13s (annual value), and a fishery of 7,000 eels. Pasturable wood (land) 3 leagues in length and one and a half in breadth.

Whereas in other areas of the north of England, as a result of the 'Harrying of the North', the value of the land had dropped between the death of King Edward and the compilation of the Domesday Book, in Beverley it remained almost the same.

The Domesday Book did not tax land belonging to the canons at the Minster. Therefore there are no figures for population on this land. However, the fact that Beverley had three mills at this time for grinding corn indicates that it had the capability of supplying flour for a population of several thousand people. The mills would have been water mills or horse mills, windmills were not known until 12th century, and would have probably been situated near the Beck.

After the death of Ealdred in 1069, Thomas of Bayeaux, a Norman, was appointed archbishop of York. He created his nephew, Thomas the Younger, (a royal chaplain) as Provost of Beverley Minster. While Beverley had remained unscathed by the 'Harrying of the North', the lands of the canons had not and thus revenues from the collection of thraves had fallen considerably. The job of the provost was to oversee the organisation of assets to the canons and thus to the Minster. His first task was to resolve disputes among the canons. One effect of his appointment was to ensure the continuation of communal life in the completed dormitory and refectory for the following century by withholding 'corrodies' (allowances for food and clothing) unless the canons were present in Beverley. The provost did not have a stall in the choir or place in the chapter and had no voting rights within the Minster. He was merely the nominee of the archbishop and it was the canons who permitted him admittance in the church.

Over a period of 450 years forty-one provosts were appointed to the Collegiate Church of St John at Beverley. Twenty-three of these, who included five chancellors of England, one royal treasurer, two keepers of the privy seal and two keepers of the royal wardrobe and others were highly placed royal servants. Thirteen provosts became bishops, five of them archbishops. They were considered to be among the wealthiest men in Yorkshire. Their lands in Holderness, from which their thraves came, far exceeded in size the lands which supplied thraves to the canons of Beverley Minster.

By the end of the 11th century Beverley, supported by king and archbishop, had developed into a strong trading community. The Collegiate Church of St John the Evangelist, one of the wealthiest monastic establishments in Yorkshire, had long been attracting large numbers of pilgrims to the shrine of its saint. Over the next 300 years Beverley was destined to become one of the most prosperous and highly populated towns in the realm.

The town of Beverley now stood poised to climb the mountain of success.

CHAPTER 4

1100 – 1200. EVER UPWARDS AND ONWARDS

The 12th century opened with a new king on the throne. During the reign of Henry I (1100 – 1135) there was peace in the country which gave the opportunity for commerce to flourish. However, when his nephew, Stephen (1135 -1154), was king a different claimant to the thrown caused uprisings and discord for much of his reign. On Stephen's death the grandson of Henry I became king, Henry II (1154 – 1189). Much of his time was spent in France contesting ownership of his vast properties but in England he established the rule of law and peace reigned. He was followed by his son, Richard I (1180 – 1199) who imposed heavy taxes in order to finance his journeys to the crusades. He was abroad for most of his reign.

The commercial wealth in Europe of the 12th century made monastic expansion possible. In 1098 the first Cistercian monastery was founded at Cluny. It was soon followed by the re-founding or building of other monasteries throughout western Europe following, for example, the order of St Benedict or in England Gilbert of Sempringham, the only English Order.

During the 12th century Beverley developed from a settlement of several thousand people, centred round the church in which lay the bones of St John, to an extensive town. Marshland to the east and the south, and the archbishop's wood to the west meant that the town developed with the elongated street pattern which we see today stretching from the site of the northern boundary, the North Bar, to the Minster and down to the Beck.

Market Day in a Medieval Town

Soon after his accession to the throne, Henry I (1100- 1135) granted a charter to the people of Beverley confirming the town's rights to have markets and fairs. He agreed that the church and land of St John was to be exempt from paying the king's tax and from supplying soldiers for the king's army.

The people of Beverley did not easily accept the authority of their Norman rulers and disliked interference from the Norman archbishops of York. Archbishop Gerard (1101 – 1108), a Norman, was a reformer who was at variance with his canons at York as he tried to enforce the rule of celibacy amongst priests together with other reforms. His unpopularity included accusations of leading a licentious life, covetousness and practising magical arts. During the celebration of the mass at Beverley a servant of his, who was deaf and dumb, began to sing; whereupon the archbishop began to praise the power of St John of Beverley. A member of the local nobility stood up and said that in Beverley they were well accustomed to St John's miracles but it would be well if the archbishop took this event to heart and stopped interfering in the affairs of Beverley.

Episcopal Support and Royal Rebellions

In 1114 Thurstan, a Norman who had been educated in Caen, was appointed archbishop of York by King Henry, for whom he acted as chaplain. The new archbishop followed a disciplined, ascetic life; he wore a hair shirt, flagellated himself, ate and drank sparingly and was constantly at prayer. It was he who assisted in the foundation of Fountains Abbey and Byland Abbey in north Yorkshire.

As archbishop of York he became Lord of the Manor of Beverley and did much to aid the development of the town. In 1121 he obtained permission from the king to prolong the June fair held in the town, on the feast of St John the Baptist, from two to five days.

The following year the archbishop gave to the men of Beverley a charter in which he made the town a borough, administered by its twelve keepers. The charter granted the townsfolk of Beverley the right to have their own 'hanshus' – a hall in which they could make laws for the improvement of the town. The charter stipulated that the people of Beverley were to have the same liberties as those of York and pay no tolls throughout Yorkshire. This was an important concession to merchants and traders as they moved around the countryside. In return for an annual payment of £12 to the Archbishop, the people of Beverley were to have all tolls of those entering the town on market days on which fairs were held. However, the Archbishop was to keep the tolls taken on the three main fair days – events to which the greatest number of people came. Confirmation of this charter by Henry I meant that it could not be disputed. The king confirmed that merchants from Beverley need pay no tolls throughout the kingdom – another important concession.

Archbishop Thurstan was more than a religious leader. King Henry died in 1135 and his nephew, Stephen became king. However, Henry's daughter, Matilda, supported by the king of Scotland, claimed the throne of England for her son. In 1138 the Scots, taking advantage of the troubles in England, invaded Northumbria. Thurstan, the king's representative in the north, raised an army, estimated to be 20,000 strong, and prepared to resist Scottish intrusion into the heart of Yorkshire. Thurstan, now old and infirm and unable to make long journeys, was disuaded from leading the army into battle. A battle took place near Northallerton which came to be known as the Battle of the Standard. The banners of St John of Beverley, St Wilfrid of Ripon, St Cuthbert of Durham and St Peter the apostle were gathered up and taken to the field of battle where they were placed in a cart with the consecrated host above. All day the battle raged round the cart and when the Scots withdrew with over 1,000 dead, victory to the English was attributed to the intercession of the saints whose banners were in the midst of battle. On many occasions the banner of St John of Beverley was to accompany medieval kings in their struggle against the Scots.

When, in an effort to suppress the power of the church, Stephen imprisoned the Bishop of Lincoln and demanded that he relinquish his fortified palaces, the clergy became alarmed. The canons at Beverley paid the king £366 13s 4d in order to ensure royal protection. In 1141, at the Battle of Lincoln, the king was captured and taken to Bristol where he was imprisoned. Afterwards he was released; Matilda's rebellion failed and by 1148 peace was restored.

In 1147, after the death of Thurstan, William Fitzherbert, treasurer of the York chapter and one of the king's chaplains, was elected by the York chapter as archbishop. Many churchmen opposed this appointment and appealed to Rome, complaining that William was no more than a royal pawn and accusing him of selling ecclesiastical appointments. Stephen, meanwhile, imprisoned the archdeacon of York, together with other archdeacons, received William at Lincoln and accepted him as the new archbishop of York. The archbishop of Canterbury refused to consecrate him so William went to Rome and, despite disagreement, was consecrated archbishop by Pope Innocent II. However, on the death of the pope in 1147 the new pope, Eugenius III, ordered a new election at York. William was suspended and then deposed while the pope consecrated Henry Mucdoc, first abbot at Fountains Abbey, as the new Archbishop of York. The king and the canons at York objected to this appointment. The canons of York Minster barred his entry into the church and the citizens shut him out of the city. When he sought refuge at Beverley Minster Stephen fined the canons for receiving him. From Beverley, where he stayed for three years, he made known his feelings about the clergy and citizens at York. Eventually peace was made and he was enthroned at York on 26th January 1151.

Like Thurstan, Murdoc was a stern, religious ascetic who believed in the monastic way of life and who wore the traditional hair shirt and endured flagellations. In reparation of their sins he persuaded Eustace Fitzjohn in 1148 to refound the Saxon monastery at Watton and William le Gros, Lord of Holderness, in 1151 to found the Cistercian monastery at Meaux, six miles east of Beverley. Both these monasteries were to become large, wealthy institutions. The monks of Meaux and the canons of Beverley, on lands separated by the river Hull, would have watched the growth and development of their churches viewed across the flat land of the East Riding.

Henry II, son of Matilda, succeeded Stephen as king of England and in December 1154 was crowned without opposition. A charter to the town of York, in 1163, comments that Beverley weavers were among those permitted to make dyed cloth. By 1174 the status of the town had so increased, no doubt boosted by the oft proven power of Beverley's saint, that Henry permitted a nine-day fair to be held from Ascension Day to the Friday before Whitsun in addition to other fairs.

On Henry's death his son, Richard I became king. In December 1192, when returning to England from the crusades he was imprisoned by Leopold of Austria; his Charter re-establishing the rights of the men of Beverley was sealed and attested at Worms in Germany during negotiations about the £100,000 ransom which was to be paid for his freedom.

The Boundaries of the Town

To the north the boundary of Beverley extended to where the

Beverley Beck and the Minster

stream, coming from the wood to the west of the town (the Westwood) flowed past the northern entrance (where North Bar now stands), and to the east the boundary followed the course of that stream (which today continues to flow but is now covered over), as it ran south, parallel to the developing northern market *(see map on page 50)*. The stream continued down the street now called Walkergate, across Toll Gavel and then divided so that a tributary ran down what is now Eastgate, joining Flemingate and so to the river Hull, the other stream running west and then south of the Minster and so down to the river. The plan of the streets of Beverley followed the bends and twists of the streams flowing from the Wolds, through the town towards the River Hull. Several streams ran through the town but the Walkerbeck was the largest and after Archbishop Thurstan had encouraged the townsfolk 'to make a channel from the river of sufficient depth to carry barges', was widened and deepened to form the Beck - an important link for commercial traffic from Beverley with the river Hull and the Humber.

Beverley was never a walled town but to the west a ditch, first mentioned in 1169, ran along the boundary, past the end of Keldgate and Newbegin Bar and along the northern boundary as far as the North Bar. Bars, or gateways, were built mainly to serve as a method of collecting taxes from strangers entering and exiting the town rather than for defence - for, of course, Beverley had no need for defences; it had its saint to protect it.

Housing development was centred round the two markets, the Minster and the Beck. There was little development to the east of Walkergate apart from a track following the path of a now dried up stream to the small settlement at Grove Hill beside the river Hull. There were strips of cultivatable land between the central area of the town and the boundary. As the town grew houses were built and street names given.

The main street running through the town was the Alta Via (or High Street) which began at the northern entrance, continued along the western edge of the northern marketplace (Saturday Market), south along the streets now known as Toll Gavel and Butcher Row, and down the west side of the southern

Reconstruction of a Medieval Timber Framed Building

marketplace (Wednesday Market) to the Minster

Stone for churches was brought from quarries at North Cave and later from near Tadcaster, transported via rivers Ouse, Humber and Hull and so into the Beck; or ships might continue on the river Hull and deposit their loads at Grove hill.

The Market Places

The two markets occupied large open spaces. Three and a half centuries of infilling of the land immediately to the north-east of the Minster had meant that by the 12th century the canons had been able to establish a market on firm ground to the north of the church. This area, the northern part of which was known in medieval times as Fishmarket, stretched from the Minster to what we now call Butcher Row, and the street leading from it to the woods to the west of the town was called Fishmarketmoorgate (now Well Lane). Later, as another market developed in the northern, drier, part of the town the importance of the southern market decreased and so houses were built and new streets formed to make Eastgate and Highgate.

Archaeological excavations, undertaken in 1983-86 by the Humberside Archaeological Unit, in the area of number 33-35 Eastgate revealed hundreds of years of development. Originally the area consisted of a pond stretching between the present line of the street and the Walkerbeck. Between the 8th and 11th century efforts had been made to infill the area with organic material. By the beginning of the 12th century a street frontage had been developed and the area had been divided into three plots. Between 1102 and 1140 substantial houses replaced earlier buildings. By the middle of the 12th century the level of the plots had been raised, with fresh dumping of soil, and new post and wattle structures had been built in the north part of the site. The discovery of a large number of gullies and pits show that textile production was carried on in this area. Between the mid-to-late 12th century the entire site appears to have been occupied by a large dyeing complex with interlinked timber vats and drains on both halves of the site. For several centuries this area was devoted to the production of cloth making and leather working. The street served as a track linking the town with the west end of Flemingate and so on to Beckside and the river Hull.

Development also took place along Beckside, and throughout the post-Norman medieval period this was one of the most prosperous areas of the town. In 1160 a priest is mentioned at the church of St Nicholas. St Nicholas was the patron saint of sailors and the church, a chapel of ease to Beverley Minster, would have been built to serve the growing commercial community at Beckside. The medieval church was nearer to the Beck than is the 19th century church of that name which we see today.

The northern market, first recorded as 'the Market' (from 16th century referred to as Saturday Market) developed on land owned by the archbishop of York. It was a vast open space which stretched over the present area, up to where St Mary's Church and Hengate now are, and may even have encompassed land as far as the northern gate; the area of Ladygate was also part of that open space. In many large towns the Lord of the Manor would build a castle in which he and his bailiff would reside. In the case of Beverley the lord of the manor was based at York but by the 12th century the archbishop had his great hall in the centre of the northern market in Beverley from which to administer the area. This great stone hall belonging to the archbishop, named the Dings, (first mentioned in 1160) must have dominated the centre of the market place. By 1190 the archbishop's main residence in Beverley seems to have moved from his stone hall in the northern market to his timber hall to the south of the Minster in Hall Garth. It is probable that the twelve keepers of the town then met in the Dings and it was from here that a bell would be rung to indicate that trading might begin.

By the beginning of the 12th century Beverley merchants were exporting raw wool to the cloth towns of the Low Countries and merchants trading in Beverley gave their name to one of the principal streets, Flemingate.

Thurstan Grants Beverley Borough Status

As medieval towns developed, townsmen wanted to be self-governing. The Norman feudal system meant that taxes and dues were paid to the king. When the king allocated land to another, the recipient became lord of the manor of that area and in return would be expected, when required, to provide men for the king's army. Most dues and service (such as working on the lord's land) were paid to the lord of the manor. People living in towns preferred to own land and pay an annual fee to the lord of the town rather than give service.

Freemen could conduct a trade in their own right and would pledge to be true to the people of the borough in which they lived and obedient to the rulers. They were expected to take their turn in governing the town. To become a freeman a man needed to be the son of a freeman or have been apprenticed to a freeman, or bought a freedom. Freemen were entitled to claim any exemptions from tolls and a share in the profits of the town. They became the craftsmen and merchants who influenced the development of trade and industry and controlled the administration of the borough. They are also known as burgesses. A 'burgess' was someone who lived in a borough and held land in 'burgage tenure'.

Archbishop Thurstan's charter of 1122 granted Beverley borough status. Boroughs liked to hold their own courts of law so that all fines for offences went to the town rather than to the lord of the manor. A borough was a place where plots of land, or tofts, could be held on burgage tenure. In Beverley it is difficult to assess the original size of burgage plots for over the centuries plots have been amalgamated and altered. However, an idea of the pattern of land division can be seen in the series of plots on the east side of Saturday Market and between Eastgate and Highgate. In the main market areas plots were often narrow to allow a greater number of traders to have frontages to the street. Behind the house would be an area for keeping pigs or growing vegetables. Few domestic buildings in Beverley pre-date the 15th century but those timber buildings which still exist are in the less busy areas of the town where there was room to have houses fronting onto the street, such as St Mary's arcade in North Bar Within and the Sun Inn in Flemingate. The layout of the plot could be affected by the terrain or previous usage. At the junction of Walkergate and Toll Gavel, the running of the Walkerbeck caused a change in plot alignment. Between Saturday Market and Toll Gavel the plot length stretching to Lairgate increases from 20 feet in the north near in the area of Old Waste to over 85 feet near Landress Lane for here plots were laid over previously cultivated land. Individual burgage plots can still be identified in the town of Beverley; No. 2 Saturday Market (Prescott's jewellers) at the north end of Saturday market and no 13 Butcher Row (a hairdresser) both have narrow frontage directly onto the street. Shops such as No. 59 Saturday Market (Briggs and Powell) are long and narrow in design for here the area behind the original medieval building on this plot has been built over.

Those who rented burgage plots were expected to build a house, which could vary in design to provide accommodation for the freeman and his family and was a place from which he could conduct his business. Behind the house would be a small enclosure where livestock could be kept (geese, hens, ducks or pigs) or vegetables grown (such as beans, peas, leeks, and herbs - mint, rosemary or thyme). There might be a ditch – a useful place in which to dump rubbish – or bank around the plot. Access to the plot would be from the side or rear via a lane or alleyway running from the street alongside the plot. Fixed rents would be paid to the overlord, in the case of Beverley, the provost, the canons, the archbishop of York or the twelve keepers of the town. In 1130 Henry I granted the gift of free burgage which meant that plots could be freely transferred, bought and sold. This was an important privilege, confirmed by Archbishop Thurstan, for, together with grants of free toll and recognition of the borough's merchant guild, it encouraged economic and urban growth. A freeman was entitled to graze stock on the common land.

Houses were built of chalk, wood, turf or unbaked earth. With timber frames standing directly on the soil they were liable to rot and were frequently rebuilt. Some roofs would be thatched with branches of reeds grown on the riverbank while others would be tiled – by the end of the 12th century tilers were making bricks and tiles along Beckside. Building materials were mostly what was near at hand – trees, chalk, gravel, sand, and osiers which grew along the river bank. The majority of people lived in single or double storey timber houses with wattle and daub infill and thatched roofs but wealthy merchants or churchmen had larger houses with maybe brick infill and tiled roofs. The extremely wealthy would have houses made of stone. Inside, all houses would have one large room with a hole in the ceiling through which smoke from the peat fire in the centre of the room, used for cooking and heating, could escape. There being no glass, windows would be barred and shuttered. Floors were of earth, maybe covered with rushes. Furnishing included chairs, benches, tables and beds. Wealthier houses would have iron hearth equipment with gridirons and bronze cooking pots and pans. Unglazed pots were produced in kilns at Beverley but, no doubt, as merchants travelled out of Beverley and abroad they

Burgage Front. 13 Butcher Row

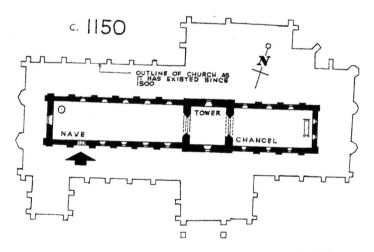

Plan of St Mary's showing its growth from around 1150

brought back pottery from other areas.

Weekly markets and seasonal fairs, which usually began with the celebration of a feast day of a popular saint, were important commercial events in the town. People would come in great numbers from the surrounding area, and even from abroad, to buy and sell goods.

At first temporary stalls would be set up in the market area, as they are today, on market day but as time went on permanent buildings would be erected.

The Collegiate Church of St John the Evangelist

12th Century Font in Beverley Minster

There is no documentary evidence of building work at the Minster during the 12th century. However, the presence of four large decorated arches, datable before 1160, placed high in the present nave roof space, indicate that part of the Norman church, including the nave, was rebuilt at this time. The font which stands

44

in the Minster today, carved of Frosterley marble from the river Weir, Durham, dates from the late 12th century; its size gives an indication of the size of the Norman church.

In the Norman minster at Beverley there were seven canons; later the number was increased to eight. Each canon was identified by the altar to which he was attached (a canon of the altar of St Martin's, of St Andrew, of St James, of St Mary, of St Michael, of St Peter and St Paul, of St Stephen, and of St Katherine). During the 12th century the canons seem mostly to have been resident in Beverley and were expected to live in the Bedern, whose buildings included a dormitory and a refectory; other buildings occupied a substantial block of land between Keldgate and Minster Moorgate fronting on to the present St John Street. As the wealth of the canons increased so they demanded private residences. A vicar appointed to an altar was responsible for the cure of souls and parochial duties, even if the canon was present. Each canon was represented in his choral duties by a clerk, who was not a priest, often referred to as 'berefellarii'.

In 1162 Thomas a Becket was appointed as provost of Beverley Minster but there is no evidence that he ever visited the town.

St Mary's Church provides chapels for the Guilds

In about 1120, probably under the instruction of Archbishop Thurstan, building work began on a church in the northern market. The church, dedicated to St Mary, was a chapel of ease to the altar of St Martin at the Minster. It consisted of a six bay nave, a square tower and a three bay chancel. Over the next 400 years, this church was to be extended and heightened into the beautiful church we have today.

A reason why the church, built on an east to west alignment, as was the tradition, is not parallel to the street may be that the road is older than the church. In medieval times parish churches were not only centres of religion but also provided useful repositories for documents and valuables and trading often took place within the church precincts.

From 12th century, different crafts were formed into trade guilds; these were religious fraternities which acted as protection societies for their members, making provision for the poor, sick and needy and promoting the interests of their craft. A guild of sufficient wealth would have an altar in the church dedicated to a particular saint and, if very wealthy, a priest to pray for the souls of its members.

Chapels required altars and altars required east walls. In 1180 the second stage of building began in St Mary's with the creation of the north transept and, after 1200 the south transept to accommodate the altars of the guilds. It was the wealth of the merchants and the guilds which was to result in such rich decorations in this splendid medieval church.

The Importance of Saints

In the second half of the 12th century, as the wealth of the country increased, the re-building and extension of churches became the norm and a way of financing such projects was by encouraging pilgrims. The 12th century was the age of pilgrimage and those unable to make the journey to the Holy Land, or the church of St Peter in Rome or the resting place of St James at Santiago de Compestella in Spain might well have to be content with doing penance at the shrines of the greatest saints in England.

For a holy person to be canonised there must have been reports of miracles occurring at the tomb in which he or she lay. Miracles would prove that the prayers and the soul of the diseased were accepted by God. Once canonized the tomb of the saint would become a focus for pilgrims.

The feast days of St John Beverley were observed in many churches in the north of England, in France, Italy and in Flanders. A church at St Jean de Breveli in Normandy today claims to have part of the jaw bone of St John of Beverley. It may have been taken there by a nephew of King Athelstan returning to his native land after spending several years at the court of this generous king.

During the 12th century the cult of St John of Beverley was widespread and William Ketell, a canon at Beverley Minster, in his *Miracula Sancti Johannis*, written during the first half of the 12th century, states that pilgrims to Beverley were mostly from Yorkshire but some came from as far away as Lincolnshire, Norfolk, Northumberland, Scotland, and Ireland.

Until this time Beverley had been the only religious centre in the area to have its own saint. During the second half of the 12th century many priestly figures who had died were canonized once miracles had occurred at their tombs. In 1166 Edward the Confessor had been canonised and pilgrims gathered at his tomb at Westminster, in 1170 Thomas a Becket, Archbishop of Canterbury, was murdered - three years later he was canonised and Canterbury became one of the most popular destinations of pilgrims. Nearer to home, in 1189, Gilbert of Sempringham, aged over 100, died and was buried in Lincoln Minster; he was canonised in 1202. In 1200 Bishop Hugh of Lincoln, who had begun the rebuilding of Lincoln Cathedral after the disastrous earthquake of 1186, died and was canonize in 1220. William Ketell tells the story of how, when severe drought had threatened the people of York with starvation, the canons of York Minster, having no saint of their own, came to Beverley, where the remains of St John, a former bishop of York, lay. They asked that the saint's shrine should be carried round the church on his feast day, followed by the 'clergy festively decorated with ornaments'. A truly colourful occasion; and effective. For the heavens opened and the canons were drenched. (This miracle demonstrated that not only did St John have power over the elements but also he could influence areas outside Beverley.) However, York was soon to have its own saint. In 1154 Archbishop William died, and soon after miracles were occurring at his tomb in York Minster – in 1180 indulgences of a year and 40 days relaxation of sins were promised to all who would devoutly visit his tomb; he was canonized in 1227. Saxon saints remained popular and throughout the middle ages the most popular destination for pilgrims in the north of England was the shrine of St Cuthbert at Durham, St Wilfrid at Ripon and St John at Beverley.

Fire Destroys Much of the Town

In 1188 a fire caused much damage to the town of Beverley and to its Minster - it would have spread with ease through the timber framed houses with their thatched roofs. Excavations in Hall Garth (the field to the south of the Minster) reveal that a large timbered hall, built with timbers felled after 1134, was gutted by fire at about this time. It was replaced by a new timber framed hall, which was to stand for the following 200 years, of sufficient grandeur to be the residence of an archbishop. Archaeology in Keldgate, opposite Keldgate Manor, has revealed that at this time there were two buildings fronting onto Keldgate which had pits at the rear containing leather off-cuts from shoemaking but in the late 12th century the buildings ceased to be used - perhaps as a result of the fire. The fire may also have damaged the great Norman tower of Beverley Minster.

One result of the fire was that the bones of St John were lost. Nine years later a search was made and the bones of the saint were rediscovered and reburied in a lead coffin. No doubt much publicity was given to the fact that this was no new saint, for miracles had been occurring at his tomb since his death in this place nearly 500 years before.

CHAPTER 5

1200-1300. THE STEADY CLIMB

Richard I died in 1199 and was succeeded by his younger brother, John (1199 – 1216). During his reign John was at variance with the pope's authority to appoint the archbishop of Canterbury and in rebellion with his barons who in 1214 forced him to sign the Magna Carta at Runneymede. By this charter some of the power of the king passed to the barons.

After his death John was succeeded by his nine year old son, Henry III (1216 – 1272). In his fifty-six year reign he managed to restore stability in the country in which commerce could flourish. It was during his reign that the term 'parliament' was used to describe gatherings of lay and ecclesiastical lords and the king's advisers. Henry III wanted to reproduce in England the greatest French art and architecture. He built Westminster Abbey to house the remains of Edward the Confessor and encouraged church building throughout the country.

By now hereditary monarchy was accepted and he was succeeded, without question, by his son Edward I (1272 – 1307). Aged thirty-three, Edward was already practised in government. He took great interest in all aspects of political life and attended to every detail. He worked with his barons rather than against them and gave parliament the right to pass laws. His dream was to unite all the British Isles under one rule.

In 1295 the first parliament was called which represented the three estates of the realm, the clergy, the nobility and the commonalty. The sheriff of each county was directed to send two knights to parliament, elected by his county, and two citizens and burgesses of each city or borough within his shire. For the next 500 years Beverley was to send two representatives to parliament.

49

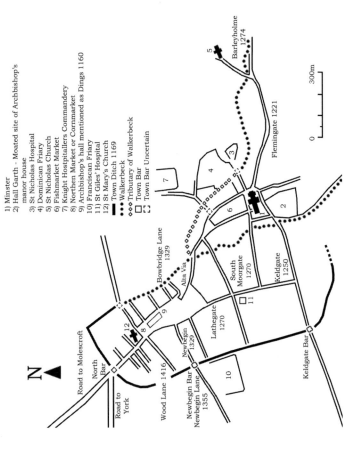

1) Minster
2) Hall Garth - Moated site of Archbishop's manor house
3) St Nicholas Hospital
4) Dominican Friary
5) St Nicholas Church
6) Fishmarket Market
7) Knight Hostpitallers Commandery
8) Northen Market or Cornmarket
9) Archbishop's hall mentioned as Dings 1160
10) Franciscan Friary
11) St Giles' Hospital
12) St Mary's Church
■ Town Ditch 1169
●●● Tributary of Walkerbeck
● Walkerbeck
□ Town Bar
⸬ Town Bar Uncertain

Road to Molescroft
North Bar
Road to York
Wood Lane 1416
Newbegin Bar
Newbegin Lane 1329
Newbegin Lane 1355
Bowbridge Lane 1329
Alta Via
Lathegate 1270
South Moorgate 1270
Keldgate 1250
Keldgate Bar
Flemingate 1221
Barleyholme 1274

0   300m

Map 3. Medieval Beverley giving dates when names first appear in the records.

Street Names

The rapid growth of the cloth industry and the expansion of regional trade were to continue during the 13th century. The names of the streets in Beverley tell us much about the development of the town. At first names seem mostly directional but later indicate occupation or are names of individual people. Over the centuries names have changed and altered, streets have been added and others disappeared. Below is a list of streets first documented in the 13th century:

- 1221 Flemingate the place where the merchants from Flanders had settled.

- 1250 St Mary Gate – street leading to St Mary's church. Now Ladygate.

- 1250 Bowbridge Lane – street leading from the northern market to the bridge over Walkerbeck. Since 1747 Dyer Lane.

- Newbegin – meaning 'new building' recorded in the 13th century as lying near Lairgate.

- 1270 Mynstermoregate – street leading from the Minster to the moor (Westwood). Sometimes referred to as Southmooregate or moorgate.

- Northmoregate – leading from the southern market to the moor – by 1320 Fishmarketmoorgate, now Well Lane.

- 1274 Barleyholme – south side of the Beck. Throughout the post Norman medieval period one of the wealthiest areas of the town. Early 19th century known as Beckside.

51

- Lathegate – street leading to the barn (perhaps it was in this street that the canons had their barns). Later Lairgate.

- 1282 Byscopdinge – where the archbishop had his hall in the northern market. Later Butterdings (an area in the centre of Saturday Market which now has a group of 18th century shops.)

Religious Institutions

St Francis

During the 12th century, crusades were sent to the Holy Land to fight the Saracens and regain the holy places for Christianity. The Knights Hospitallers (who took their name from their hospital in Jerusalem dedicated to St John the Baptist) was an international network of lay monks who had taken vows of chastity, obedience and poverty and whose aim was to care for the sick and the poor, both travellers and crusaders, to maintain a hospital in Jerusalem and to defend the route to the Holy Land. They wore a black dress on which was placed the Maltese cross. By 1144 their headquarters in England had been established at Clerkenwell, London.

The great wealth of the order was the result of gifts of land from kings and individuals. These lands were administered from commanderies or preceptories and at one time there were fifty-five such commanderies in England. Both they and the Knights Templer, a similar order, held considerable estates

A Nineteenth Century Representation of the Knights Hospitallers

in the East Riding. As well as administering the lands given to the Hospitallers, the commanderies also served as a training ground for future recruits to the order and offered hospitality to the traveller.

In 1201, Lady Sybil de Valines, widow of William, third Lord Percy, gave the Manor of Holy Trinity in Beverley – 2½ acres (in the area where the railway station now is) to the Order of Knights Hospitaller. The land was divided into the Inner and the Outer Trinities. The Inner Trinities was surrounded by a moat (moated perhaps not only for defence but also in order to drain the land), and contained a commandery and a chapel; entry was through a stone gateway. The Outer Trinity enclosed a large graveyard.

The two great orders of friars, the Franciscans and the Dominicans, originated in France in 1220 and 1221. They were an international brotherhood of individuals whose members were itinerant preachers, ministering to the needs, and dependent on the charity, of those who employed them or from whom they begged. By mid 13th century fewer monasteries were being founded but the orders of friars attracted those with a vocation and many grants of land were given to them by the wealthy. Most important medieval towns in England acquired Dominican and Franciscan friaries. The Order of Dominican, or Black Friars - so named because of the colour of their capes (also known as Friars Preacher) was established in England in 1221 and within fifty years had established forty-six houses. Shortly before 1240 Stephen Goldsmith, a cleric at the Minster, gave a 4½ acre site near the Minster to the Order of the Dominican Friars. Soon after, Thomas Holme gave a piece of ground 237 feet long and 120 feet broad for the erection of a house of the friars. Immediately a programme of building began. Excavations undertaken between 1960-1983 reveal that at first wooden buildings were erected which were later replaced, when funds became available, by stone. In 1263 Henry III gave fifteen oaks from the Forest of Galtres, north of York, to the friars. By the end of the century the friary consisted of a church with a nave and choir, a chapter house, a cloister, a dormitory and refectory and to the north a large timbered hall.

The Franciscan friars arrived in England in1224 and thirty-one years later had established forty-nine houses. In 1267 a Franciscan friary (Greyfriars also known as Friars Minor) was founded outside Newbegin Bar at an area known as High and Low Friars. It had several buildings and a fish pond. Thirty years later Greyfriars was moved to a new site outside Keldgate Bar. The land given for the second friary lay near St Helen's Chapel near Keldgate Bar.

Unlike the canons at the Minster the friars, known as the preaching friars, had no estates to manage and received their income from begging and from donations; the amount of building work which was carried out on the friary is a measure of their popularity. The friars' day was concerned with studying the scriptures, training novices and celebrating the mass. Their main commitment was to preaching both in the friary church and also in the open air in both Beverley and the surrounding area. Their sermons, unlike those of the canons, were lively, entertaining and illustrated with moral tales. By the end of the 13th century there were forty-four Dominican friars and thirty-six Franciscans in Beverley. They received a strong following from the townspeople and merchants, many of whom requested to be buried in their graveyard.

The friars became a source of irritation to the canons at the Minster who accused them of stealing members of their congregation. In 1269 Archbishop Giffard wrote to the Dominican Friary at Beverley about a licence he had issued to them and the Franciscans to hear confessions in their church. He had been informed that the Dominicans had admitted parishioners of St Martin's chapel in the Minster and from St Mary's church to confession and other sacraments which meant that tithes and other income had gone to the friary rather than to the parishes. Another incident occurred on Easter Sunday, 1309, when parishioners of the altar of St Martin had been given Holy Communion in the Dominican church. To make things worse one of the recipients had previously been excommunicated. The friar responsible, Friar John of Lockington, was ordered by his prior,

Walter of Grimsby, to ask for pardon on bended knee before the canons of Beverley.

In 1291 the archbishop organised a programme of preaching in support of the crusades to take place on Holy Cross Day (14th September). He instructed the Dominican friars at Beverley to preach at Preston or Hedon, at Ravenser and at Wyke (a port on the Humber). Franciscan friars were sent to South Cave, Driffield and Malton.

Hospitals were rest houses for cripples and pilgrims who became ill on their journey to visit holy places. St Giles, a late 8th century Greek, had lived as a hermit in the South of France. He had been wounded when a soldier and after his death became the patron saint of cripples. In Beverley, St Giles Hospital, with its church and courtyard is first recorded in the late 12th century and stood on the west side of Lairgate, to the north of Minster Moorgate and inside the town ditch. In 1277 Archbishop Walter Giffard, in exchange for a small estate, gave the hospital to the Prior of Warter Priory. In 1279 Archbishop Wickwane ordained that there should be four priest brethren at the hospital which was to care for six sick priests and have fifteen beds for other people.

Fall of the Tower of Beverley Minster

In October 1213 a priest at Beverley Minster, unable to sleep, rang the bell for matins an hour too soon. When the canons assembled in the chancel, a number of stones fell from the tower, causing the canons to leave their stalls, and, after a second fall of stones, they went to the west end of the nave in order to finish the service undisturbed. Hardly had they returned to their houses when the whole tower collapsed.

No record remains of the plan or size of the Norman church at Beverley, which perhaps may have had a nave and transepts of a similar size to those at Southwell Minster today, which date to 1108. However, it seems that Beverley Minster had been badly damaged by the collapse of the tower and probable that the choir was destroyed. By about 1220 a building programme - which was

Beverley Minster (1220 – 1260). North Transept

to take 200 years to complete - began, which resulted in a church of even greater splendour. Here was to be a change from the heavy, almost fortress-like, style of Norman architecture into a style that originated in France which has become known as the Early English, Decorated and Perpendicular Gothic styles with pillars soaring up to the heavens. Everything pointed upwards, pinnacles, windows, arches and vaults impressing on those who entered the building the need to forget the old pagan gods and their earthly life and look only towards the heavens where true glory was to be found.

Of course Beverley was not the only church to be rebuilt at this time. In 1215 Walter de Gray, the new archbishop of York, resolved to make York Minster the greatest church in the Kingdom; by 1220 the West front had been added to Ripon Minster, by 1234 a new Early English choir had been added to the Norman nave at Southwell Minster and the nave which we see today at Lincoln Cathedral was built 1200 – 1250.

The first phase of rebuilding Beverley Minster began, about 100 years after the building of St Mary's had begun, at the east end of the church. It included the choir and the double transepts which we see today - transepts with their east walls were needed for the altars belonging to the chapels of the eight canons. Stone from the previous church was re-used and in the windows at the east end of the Minster many inverted capitals from the Norman church can be seen; single lancet windows, dog tooth carvings and the stiff foliage of the acanthus leaf gave decoration while Purbeck marble, brought from Dorset, provided a contrast in colour. In 1252 Henry III gave 40 oaks from Sherwood Forest to the canons of the Minster for the roof of the new church.

The first phase of the re-building programme of Beverley Minster was completed by 1260 and it was to be another 50 years before there were sufficient funds for the second phase of building to begin. In 1290 Archbishop John le Romayn granted an indulgence of 40 days to anyone contributing to the repair of the building and in 1292 the canons ordered a new shrine to be made.

Beverley Minster. South Transept built 1220-1260

The Right of Sancturary

Sanctuary Cross on York Road

The 5th Century stone Saxon chair in the Minster, known as the Frith stool or chair of peace, is believed to be the chair on which one of the canons, or an officer of the church, would sit when delivering the Oath of Sanctuary. The right to claim sanctuary at Beverley is said to be one of the privileges granted by King Athelstan although this right may well have existed in earlier Saxon times. The importance of sanctuary was that a fugitive from the law could flee to a church where the sanctuary was exercised where he, or she, would come under the jurisdiction of Church Law, secure against arrest or violence. Penalties for violating sanctuary were high.

A mile from the perimeter of the town of Beverley were four sanctuary crosses. Three stumps of crosses remain (in each case the cross which once would have been on top of the stone base has vanished): on the road to Walkington, the road to Bishop Burton and the road to Hull – the fourth beyond Molescroft no longer exists. If a fugitive passed one of these and claimed sanctuary of the Collegiate Church of St John the Evangelist pursuers were no longer permitted to capture him, or her. If they did so they would have to pay a fine of £4. More stones were at the entry to the town; if stopped here the fine would be £16, if stopped inside the churchyard boundary the fine was £48, at the door of the church £96 and in the choir of the church £144 with the additional threat of excommunication. It was a rich and brave person indeed who could afford to pay such fines and was prepared to jeopardy his immortal soul.

The right of sanctuary existed in other churches – Ripon, York, Hexham and Durham - but Beverley was one of the major sanctuaries of the middle ages and was unusual in that the whole town and its environs, not just the Minster precinct, comprised the sanctuary. The Minster would probably, as at Durham, have had a doorknocker to which the fugitive could cling and by banging on the door summon help. Alured, a canon at Beverley during the 12th century, wrote that sanctuary was given by the canons or their ministers with much humanity. Sanctuary seekers were allowed to tarry for 30 days, were provided with food and a bed in the dormitory or in a house in the precincts. In Beverley the fugitive having stated his supposed crime, a church official, sitting in the Frith stool, would administer the oath:

> Sir, Take hede on your oath you shall be trew and faithful to my loard Archbishop of York Lord of this towne; to the Provost of the same, to the Chanons of this chirch and other ministers thereof. Also you shall bere gude het to the baille and twelve Govrnors of this town to all burges (Burgesses) and comyners of thes same. Also you shall bere no pointed wapon, dagger, knyfe ne none other wapen ayenst the king's pece. Also you shabe redy at all your power if ther be any debate or stryf or of sothan (sudden) case of fyre within the town to help scess it. Also ye shalbe redy at the obite of kyng Adelstan at the dirige and at the messe if such tyme as it is done at the warning of the bellman of the town and do your dewte in ryngng and for to offer at the mess on the morne so help you God and theis holy Evangelists.

The fugitive was then expected to kiss the Bible. Over a period of thirty days the canons would investigate the case and try to secure a pardon; if successful the fugitive would be allowed to go free. If a pardon was not achieved the fugitive would be escorted to the outer limits of the sanctuary to meet the Coroner and undergo the process of outlawry which was banishment from the country. The Coroner would then escort the sanctuary seeker, dressed in sackcloth, unshod, in his bare shirt as if he were about to be hanged, to the nearest port. In Beverley, however, there was another alternative for sanctuary men who were proved innocent for they were allowed to remain in the town if they swore allegiance to the Minster and the town authorities; they then became known as 'grithmen'. If anyone asked for sanctuary on three separate occasions he or she had to remain as a servant of the church for life.

Throughout the centuries there were several incidents in which it would appear that grithmen were not fully accepted by the townspeople; perhaps the fact that the majority of the sanctuary seekers were accused of homicide is a reason.

William Ketell (writing in the early 12th century) recounts the story of a young clerk from Lincoln who during the 'troubled reign of King Stephen' was imprisoned in a castle at Cottingham. As he lay bound with chains and watched over by the guards he prayed to St John of Beverley for deliverance. His captors threatened him with torture unless his parents paid the ransom money demanded.

One night, as the man was falling asleep in his cell, a man, 'dressed like a bishop' appeared before him and ordered him to stand up and leave. The young man pointed out that he could not do this for his arms were bound with iron rings and he was secured in a locked prison. The bishop told him not to be afraid. At that moment the clerk noticed that one of the rings on his legs had broken. With an old rag he bound the ring to his other leg. The bishop told him that he should not be afraid but should flee for refuge 'to his minster at Beverley'. He then led the young man out of the cell, through a hall, where the guards were sleeping, out of the door and across the huge defences of a broad moat. Having left the castle they passed through a wood, at times a cart going before them showing the route. The ground was marshy 'as is the condition of the region' and the inner skin of the soles of the feet of the clerk were pierced by sharp reeds and prickly shrubs.

'As twilight was closing in' the young man came near the minster and saw a house. He entered in order to warm himself for the 'cold oppressed him so much that he was barely able to walk'. Once he had been revived by the fire he went to the Minster as dawn was breaking. The doors of the church were already open and the custodians asked who he was and why he had fled there for refuge. He explained how St John had led him out of captivity and told him, to flee to his minster for refuge. As he spoke the ring fell from his second leg and all present offered thanks 'for such a happening'.

When

> the performance of this miracle was made known to all the people and clergy they broke out in praise of God and sang a hymn for the Lord who performs great wonders through his servant John, who is often made famous through miracles.

The clerk then offered the iron rings to the altar where they were suspended

> and many hoops of iron and shackles were hung up, that is to say on both sides of the tomb of John, the man of God.

The sacrist of the church was an old man, wise in ecclesiastical custom. He seeing that the soles of the feet of the clerk were greatly bruised and swollen, provided a medicinal compress and gave instructions that the young man be given sandals so that his feet should not be hurt by a shoe's upper. The clerk remained in the church for a long time until his mobility was restored. He told the story of his miraculous deliverance to all whom he met.

Extensions to St Mary's Church

During the second quarter of the century the nave and chancel of St Mary's were extended to their present length

The Crypt of St Mary's Church

and aisles were added to allow for processions. In 1269 the church acquired its own vicar. Towards the end of the century St Katherine's chapel was added, together with the crypt and Holy Trinity Chapel above. It appears that the original intention, judging from the depth of one of the pillars in the crypt, had been that the floor of Holy Trinity Chapel was to be at the same level as the floor of the church with the crypt beneath; this idea was abandoned, most probably because of water running at the lower level, for the level of the floor of the crypt was raised which necessitated steps to the chapel above. In the east wall of the chapel can be seen the piscina at the original intended level.

Over 200 masons' marks are visible in the crypt of St Mary's church. In medieval England masons would wander from place to place, carrying with them the tools of their trade, seeking work. A mason would arrive at the site where work was in progress and would knock at the door of the Master Mason's lodge. Before being admitted or being employed he would be asked specific questions about his previous work. If the questions were answered correctly, in a specified way (using signs and passwords) he would be recognised as a qualified mason. When employed the mason would be paid each day according to the number of stones he had cut or fitted into the building; on each stone he would scratch his personal mark. Masons' marks are to be found all over medieval buildings but most are less obvious than those in the crypt of St Mary's church, for this area was not intended to be visited but merely used for storing the bones of those skeletons dug up from the cemetery round the church where the building was being extended.

Disputes over Pannage, Toll and Turbary

A grievance between the townspeople and the archbishops was the lack of access to open land around the town. Deer hunting, which is thought to have been introduced by the Normans, was exceedingly popular in the middle ages. A large area of ground, preferably with a mixture of open grassland, woodland and coppice would be enclosed by a ditch surrounded by an earthen bank and topped by an oak palisade or pale. The archbishops of York owned extensive lands round Beverley at their manor at Bishop Burton (where part of the earth bank of the enclosed park still exists), to the west of the town (the Westwood) and to the south the archbishop's park (later to be named Beverley Parks). It was over this last area, which offered arable farming, grazing and peat or turf for use as fuel, that disputes arose. In the early 13th century the archbishop was intending to turn the area into an enclosed park. The townspeople complained to the king that the archbishop had dispossessed them of pasture, toll, turbary (the right to dig peat) and sandpit. In reply the archbishop, to the anger of the people, planted a hedge where before there had been a ditch so that access became harder. Once again the townspeople complained to King John who demanded a royal inquiry which resulted in confirming their claim and granting them the right to take possession of the land. The archbishop rejected the claim and excommunicated those people of Beverley who were involved. During the episcopacy of Sewall de Bovill (1255 – 1258) a compromise was reached in the king's court and the townspeople gave up the rights of common in the park and in Stone Carr, in Weel, and in return the archbishop granted them pasture and pannage (pasturage of pigs) in the Westwood, pannage in Hagg wood, and pasture in the meadow called Out ings which adjoined Figham.

However the dispute continued. Archbishops Giffard and Wickwane continued the aim of enclosing a park to the south of the town and tried to buy out the rights of others to the land. In 1267 burgesses, concerned about pasture rights which in the previous century had been granted by the archbishop but which now Giffard was trying to reassert control over, appointed a delegation to meet Archbishop Giffard. The result of the meeting was that the townspeople agreed to pay 1,000 marks to Archbishop Giffard for their trespass in his parks and in return they were allowed some pasture rights in two areas of the park although the archbishop still controlled the land.

A compromise had been reached but peace was not to last. In 1281 a group of townsmen appealed to the archbishop of Canterbury over the question of pasture. The king was asked to adjudicate and the case was to be tried in his own court. Whereupon, the archbishop of York imprisoned the townsmen involved so that they could not attend. In 1282 Archbishop Bovill's compromise was agreed but with the additional grant to the burgesses of the archbishop's hall in the northern market, the Dings. Having moved to his hall south of the Minster the archbishop no longer needed his hall in the market place. A separate agreement regulated pannage in Hagg wood.

Wealthy Merchants

Many rich merchants resided in the town, for Beverley had other important sources of wealth beside the church - the wool trade, the cloth trade, and the leather trade. By the end of the 13th century three of the four greatest exporters of wool through Hull were Beverley men and the cloth of Beverley had a national

Wool Merchants

reputation. Recent excavations on the sites of the Tesco building and the council offices in Champney Road, together with earlier excavations to the east of the town, reveal that cloth making took place throughout the town and was to remain an important industry until the 16th century. Presumably wool being exported from Meaux Abbey and Watton Priory would also come through Beverley and be put on ships going to the Humber.

The Support of Kings

Medieval kings patronized the town of Beverley and its saint. The freemen of Beverley continued to be free from paying tolls throughout England, except in London; King John accepted 500 marks from Beverley for granting this privilege. In 1266 Henry III, when summoning a royal army from the shire of York, declared that the town of Beverley need send only one man carrying the banner of St John

In 1286 Alexander III of Scotland died. As there was no obvious successor to the throne Edward I decided to push his own claim as overlord of Scotland and thereby achieve his ambition of uniting England and Scotland. In the spring of 1296 the first large scale military attack was launched against the Scots. The king removed the coronation stone from Scone, in Scotland, and placed it in Westminster Abbey where it was to stay for the following 700 years. The struggle against the Scots was to last until 1603 when James VI of Scotland became James I of England.

In 1296 Edward I stayed at the Dominican Friary for three days. During his stay, the king made a grant to the Chapter of the Minster for the establishment of a chantry chapel, in honour of St John, with a priest to celebrate mass and pray before the altar for the well-being of the king during his life and for his soul after his death.

In 1298 the king moved the major government offices (the Chancery, the Exchequer and the central law courts) to York where they stayed until 1305. While in York he several times came to Beverley to visit the shrine of St John. When in 1299 he left the area in order to travel further north to fight the Scots he took with him the banner of Beverley's saint.

At this time Wyke was a thriving port on the Humber. The town was considerably smaller than Beverley but was a strategic place from which to send ships and supplies in support of the king's campaigns against the Scots. It also controlled the ships leaving the river Hull and entering the Humber. In 1299 Edward I established Wyke as a Royal borough and the town was renamed King's Town upon Hull.

CHAPTER 6

1300 – 1400 REACHING THE PEAK

When Edward I died in 1307 he left a rich and prosperous country. His son, Edward II (1307-1327) lacked the statesmanlike qualities of his father and was more concerned with lavishing gifts on his friends than consulting with his councillors. Edward's favourite, Gaveston, so invoked the hatred of the nobles that after being imprisoned at Scarborough he was taken south and beheaded. Edward's attempts to subdue the Scots ended in complete failure in 1314 when much of the king's army was slaughtered at the Battle of Bannockburn. For years after that date the Scots were free to penetrate into northern England, stealing cattle and destroying villages. To make matters worse, between 1314 and 1325 atrocious weather caused starvation in England. There was a succession of wet summers in which torrential rain ruined harvests and the famine which followed caused the prior of Bridlington to speak of misery 'such as our age has never seen'; this famine was followed by a disease in sheep. In the early 40s there was further poor weather which destroyed harvests and weakened the population.

After the murder of Edward II in 1327, his son, Edward III, was to rule for the following fifty years. During his reign half the population of England was wiped out by the Black Death and many were to die in the Hundred Years War with France, including the king's eldest son the Black Prince. When Edward's grandson, Richard II (1377 - 1399) became king he imposed a poll-tax which ignited the Peasants' Revolt.

Yet, despite these terrible hardships the prosperity of the country increased. It was under the rule of Edward III that the system of parliamentary government developed and English, rather than French, became the common language. The kings of England continued to favour Beverley and its saint and the prosperity of the town increased so that by 1377 it was shown to be the tenth largest town in the country, after London. In the massive building programme in the two main churches in Beverley some of the highest limits of artistry were achieved.

Street Names

During the course of the 14th century the names of more streets are recorded.

- 1300 Fishmarketgate – road from north of Fishmarket (Wednesday Market) from 1633 known as Butcher's Shambles. From 19th century extended and known as Butcher Row.

- 1312 Friarygate – in 1330 recorded as being near the house of St Nicholas. Now Friars Lane

- 1320 Cornmarket – the northern market. During 13th century it was divided into different areas for selling different goods (ie. Butchers' Row – between the market place and Hengate, Glovers Row. From 1577 Saturday Market.

- 1324 Cross Bridge – The Walkerbeck flowed down over Walkergate and where it entered Toll Gavel there was a bridge situated near a cross. The stream is now covered over.

- 1327 Hengate – maybe hens were kept there. In the early days there was a bar at the end of the street which prevented unauthorised entry.

- 1329 Walkergate – street where the fullers 'walked' their cloth. Fullers bought cloth from the weavers.

They thickened the cloth by treading it ('walking' it) in running water in order to clean it and turn a loose weave into a matt weave. The cloth was then sold to the merchant tailors.

- 1329 Godchep Lane – good and cheap. Referred to in some documents as being off the High Street. 1790 it was called Landress Lane after a Roger Laundese who had an acre of land nearby.

- 1332 Humbergate, 1370 Chapel Lane, 1573 St Thomas Chapel Lane (after the chapel that was nearby), 1628 Queensgate – may have been the queans' or prostitutes' street.

- 1344 Toll Gavel – where tolls were collected from strangers entering the market ('Gavel' is Norse word meaning toll)

- 1347 Pottergate, 1407 Grovehill Road – road leading to the hamlet of Grovehill.

- 1355 Mention of a lane running from Newbegin to Westwood; 1743 Newbegin Lane; 1828 Westwood Road.

- 1360 Holme Kyrk Lane – could refer to Holme family who contributed towards the building of the medieval St Nicholas church, or refer to the damp ground over which it ran. Now Holme Church Lane but original line of the street altered.

- 1376 Trinity Lane – original line of the street now altered.

- 1381 North Bar Within (or within North Bar) and North Bar Without

- 1386 Vicar Lane – opposite St Mary's church

Beverley Minster – a New Shrine, a New Nave

In preparation for the second phase of rebuilding in 1306 the canons appointed John de Fitling as collector of alms for Beverley Minster. No doubt as John de Fitling visited other towns on his fund-raising activities he would extol the power of St John and the glory of the church which was being built around his tomb.

Edward I continued his support of Beverley's saint. In 1301, moved by his devotion to St John, he remitted half of a fine of 100 marks levied on the community; the remaining fifty marks were to go towards the cost of building a new shrine. In 1306, shortly before his death, he granted the canons of the Collegiate Church at Beverley £40 a year on condition that they distributed at each of the feast days of St John of Beverley one penny each to 3,000 poor people. He also gave money to the canons for two great wax candles for the High Altar before St John's shrine, two smaller ones before his standard and a chaplain daily celebrating mass.

In 1308 a new shrine, to contain the relics of St John of Beverley, was completed. In 1292 the canons had instructed Roger de Faringdon, a London silversmith that the shrine should be:

> Made from gold and silver, beautiful and adorned with plates and columns in architectural style with figures everywhere, and with canopies and pinnacles before and behind.

The carriage of the new shrine to its resting place near the High Altar must have been a momentous occasion. The Minster would have been filled with the canons, specially summoned to Beverley for the occasion, dressed in their sumptuous robes, accompanied by the vicars and other church officials. The merchants of Beverley would be there dressed in their finest livery. Townspeople and pilgrims, some of whom had travelled from afar, would be straining to catch a glimpse of the shrine as it passed - carried high on the shoulders of the eight Porters of the Shrine. Anticipation must have been high as the new shrine was carried into the church, through the door of the north transept, through the newly built choir and so to the High Altar, accompanied, no doubt, by the singing of the boys in the Minster choir.

In 1312 Queen Margaret, widow of Edward I, came to Beverley and heard mass in the Minster. She gave a round ornament of gold of moderate size which was at once fixed to St John's shrine.

The shrine of St John of Beverley was not the only shrine within the Minster. In the early 14th century a shrine, dedicated to St Berhthun (first abbot of the Saxon monastery at Inderawuda) was placed in the church. Another shrine was dedicated to a nun, St Yolfrida, who tradition said had been in charge of an oratory of St Martin, a chapel attached to the south west corner of the Minster. One of the most sought after burial places in the Minster was before the statue of the Virgin Mary above the red chest where offerings made before the statue on feast days amounted to almost as much as those at the shrine of St John. Pilgrims coming to the church would wander round and pray before the various images of the saints, the statues of the Virgin in the middle of the nave and another at the south door, the crucifix inside the north door, and the image of the Saviour at the west end of the church. There were at least sixteen altars belonging to the chapels of the canons and to the various chantries where prayers would be said and donations placed in the offertory box.

The Chapter Act Book of Beverley Minster records an occasion in 1318 when Lady Isabella of France, Queen and consort of Edward II, came to the church and was greeted as though she was a king. The clergy, dressed in silken copes, met her at the door; they then processed to the High Altar, where a collect was said over her as she knelt in prayer. She then distributed offerings: to the High Altar a cloth of gold; to the shrine of St John a precious jewel, to the small shrines thirteen shillings, to the tomb seven shillings. A carved woman's head in

Believed Carving of Lady Isabella of France. Beverley Minster

Musician in Beverley Minster

the south aisle, much restored, could be her likeness for by the time she arrived work had already begun on building the wall of the south aisle.

The Queen would have seen the Minster full of wooden scaffolding for by 1310 sufficient funds had been collected for work to begin on the nave. Masons would be measuring the cut stone and carrying each piece to its appointed place as they worked to build a new nave round the partly destroyed Norman church. By this time wide aisles were needed for processions to take place round the churches. In the Minster the South Aisle was built first up to the level of the windows with arches similar in design to those at the east end of the church. Next was the north aisle with arches in the new ogee style.

Architectural styles had changed since the completion of the east end of the church and the introduction of buttresses to take the weight of the roof made it possible to have larger window openings with decorative stonework and mullions. One of the glories of Beverley Minster is the feeling of architectural unity; Purbeck marble and dog tooth ornamentation had been used in the 13th century east end and transepts; they were also used in the clerestory of the 14th century nave, thus giving a sense of continuity throughout the building. Other 14th century carving in the nave and aisles followed the fashion of the day and is realistic in design rather than the stiff acanthus leaf of the 13th century. Work on the nave was to continue until 1349 when, after the Black Death, a shortage of masons caused all building work to cease.

Beverley's two major churches have the highest number of carvings of medieval musicians of any church in the country.

Provosts and Canons

The communal residence of the Minster clergy was the Bedern, which originally provided accommodation for the provost and vicars, the berefellarii or parsons and the canons. Later the provost built his own house. The provost's court and gaol were also part of the complex. The buildings are likely to have been in a line with a central gateway which led into an inner courtyard. Documentary evidence suggests that the Bedern and associated buildings occupied a large block of land between Keldgate and Minster Moorgate with the present day St John's street on the east side. In 1304 an inventory of the provost's possessions in the Bedern includes the great and small halls, great and small kitchens, larder, buttery, brew house, bake house and granary. In 1306 the butlers asked for absolution from excommunication for adding a chamber in the Bedern kitchen without first seeking permission.

Provosts were considered to be dignitaries rather than members of the church. However, by the 14th and 15th century several provosts had acquired a prebend (a portion of land allocated which provided a source of income) which entitled them to a seat in the Chapter House. The early 14th century provost, William Melton, was the representative of the king in Beverley and his authority was symbolised by the right of his servants to carry a

Tomb of Nicholas de Huggate

verge (a rod) when processing through the town. The provost employed a steward, a bailiff, a coroner and a receiver and had the right to hear cases in his own court and to have a gaol.

William Melton became provost of the Collegiate Church at Beverley in 1307. Ten years later he became archbishop of York. He replaced his archiepiscopal manor house south of the Minster (on Halls Garth) with a timber frame aisled hall, which had a tiled roof, beaten earth floors and five tiled hearths. In 1325 he added a moat to his land with a timber bridge at the northwest corner.

In 1318 Edward II appointed Nicholas de Huggate as provost of Beverley Minster. Nicholas de Huggate was a clerk in chancery, keeper of the wardrobe of Prince Edward, the Prince of Wales (later Edward III) and from 1324 receiver for Acquitaine and Gascony. Thus during his early years as provost he spent most of his time away from Beverley on royal service. He had preferments in many other churches. In 1332 Edward III granted him release of all debts 'in consideration of his manifold services to the King from boyhood'. Thereafter Huggate was frequently in residence in Beverley. He died in 1338 and his tomb chest now stands in the east side of the north transept. The costume of his effigy, which shows the coats of arms of many leading Yorkshire landowners, shows that this was a man of some importance.

The income from the prebends greatly increased the wealth of the canons at the Minster who, rather than live in the Bedern, built their own residencies. Several of these houses faced the Minster. In 1313 Canon John of Nassington, Prebend of the altar of St Martin (the wealthiest prebend), found his house, which lay to the north of the church between Highgate and Eastgate, too small and in disrepair (apart from the stables and a room above the gate) and so built a new hall with a double room and chapel, a kitchen, a brew-house and a bakery - timber from the old house was used. In his will he left to the Minster a red choir cope (as was customary) adorned with many figures in gold, silk and other colours worth £29 6s 8d, also eight chairs for the conductors of the choir and a beautiful grail. The prebendal houses of St Peter, St Katherine and St Mary lay in Highgate. In 1323 Queen Isabella stayed in the prebendal house of St Andrew in Flemingate, and declared that it was in a good state of repair and comfortably furnished. The prebends of St Stephen and of St James owned buildings in or near Lurk Lane. The houses of the chancellor, precentor, and sacrist were all in Minster Moorgate.

Extracts from the Chapter Act Book of St John the Evangelist at Beverley (1286 – 1347)

Chapter House of Beverley Minster

The canons of the Minster, or, if absent, their representatives, would meet in the Chapter House and discuss the affairs of the day. The meeting would begin with a reading of a chapter from the Rules of St Benedict, or from some other holy book. The topics discussed by the Chapter give us an idea of the problems of the day.

1306 3rd September
Some damnable sons of perdition, names unknown, have carried off the tithe sheaves from a piece of arable land called Gares in the

field of Etton, belonging to the fabric (i.e. the Minster) from time immemorial, and have damnably fallen into the sentence of excommunication.

The offender was duly proclaimed excommunicated in Etton church. The offender turned out to be the rector, John of Ardern, who promised to restore the tithes of corn which had been carried off by him in the belief that he was the owner – he obtained absolution.

1306 4th September

The Pope wrote to the Archbishop of York saying that the church was disturbed that its lands were wasted by civil war and that the Holy Land was held by the Babylonian enemy. He ordered that masses and prayers should be said for him. By November each priest celebrating masses on one day was ordered to say a mass for our Lord the Pope. The number of masses said at Beverley each week was 25.

1306 22nd November All Soul's Day

On 27th December 1304 Peter of Cranswick had been murdered.

Reconciliation of the Minster Yard after the pollution of bloodshed of Peter of Cranswick on 27th December 1304, no one having been buried there meanwhile. The tent in which Archbishop Greenfield blessed the water for sprinkling was fixed on the ash-trees at the churchyard gate towards the archbishop' manor.

1307 14th July

By the 14th century canons were often absent from Beverley and their duties in the Minster were performed by their vicars. A difficulty arose about their receiving thraves and other entitlements if absent. Soon after William Greenfield became archbishop of York, he wrote to the canons at Beverley ordering that the seven canons from the original foundation should reside in the Bedern for at least twelve weeks of the year. They were to have half of the offerings at the High Altar, and the whole of all other offerings and profits accruing to the chapter, or common fund. However, the Bedern corrody (allowance of food which was sometimes commuted to cash) was to be given to the prebendaries whether they were in residence or not; this differed from previous archbishops who stated that they only received corrody if they were present. Many of the canons appointed to an altar in Beverley Minster were royal officials and were mostly away on the king's business. The eighth canon was usually resident and received half the offerings at the High Altar and the Shrine of St John. The canon of St Martin's altar received tithes from St Mary's church and was expected to make payment to the vicar of St Mary's.

1308 7th July.

Letter from Archbishop Greenfield.

> A certain person has fled to Beverley for sanctuary, and you, we hear, attempt something about him to our prejudice. Stop it or expect further proceedings.'

The first mention of a schoolmaster is in the 12th century although it is possible that the church may have provided some schooling since the days of St John – for in medieval society it was the priests who could read and write. By the 15th century there were 33 pupils. Choristers were taught free but the school also included fee-paying pupils.

> The choir school to be kept in repair by the schoolmaster, but if re-building is needed, it is the duty of the Master of the Works.

1312 11th June

> On the feast of St Barnabas, oil flowed from the tomb of St John which was smeared on the eyes of some boys who had not

been able to see properly for three months. Immediately they began to see more clearly.'

1318 22nd July

Miracles wrought through the prayers of the Confessor John of Beverley should be known that God's glory in St John's church might be exalted by its being more frequented.

Let it be known therefore that Agnes of Sherburn in Elmet, had for six days endured madness. She was taken to the tomb of St John of Beverley and there was bound very harshly with very strong fetters and for another six days she continued in madness, tormented by continuous ragings; she disturbed the church and the neighbouring locality with continuous and horrible noise. Suddenly she was cured and she, who although her illness was so very strong that three men could hardly restrain her, having been made sane, was then made so weak that she could hardly walk or stand without human assistance.'

When her cure, as with all such occurrences before being declared miracles, was investigated by the officials of the church, she reported to the chapter that she seemed to see in her sleep

the aforesaid St John dressed in white pontifical clothes, walking next to her and saying 'Follow me because you have been restored to your former health'. Immediately, having been wakened, the fetters with which she had been bound having been broken, she knew that she was healthy and sane through the grace of God.

20th January 1322

John, son of William of North Ferriby, aged ten, became dumb; marked with a cross in the Priory of Ferriby, a vow to visit Beverley being made, his speech was restored. Next day be became blind. They brought him to St John's tomb and after a short stay he received his sight. We have examined him and he read a verse of the Psalm 'O praise the Lord with me'.

1322

It was ordered that

excommunication should take place with bells ringing and candles lit while the people are there in their thousands.

Building and Carving in the Decorated Style

By the second quarter of the 14th century Decorated Gothic architecture - so called because of the realistic decorations in stone of leaves, animals, Green Men and mythical beasts - was highly popular and the town must have been filled with skilled craftsmen who in St Mary's church built the Sacristy, St Michael's Chapel and the Priest's Room and in the Minster the Reredos and Percy tomb canopy and the nave in the Minster. All are decorated with rich carvings which today are recognised as being masterpieces of mid-14th century stonework.

The Pilgrim Rabbit, St Mary's Church

Carvings even extend to the clerestory of the Minster where they can only be seen in detail with binoculars. In St Mary's 14th century figures playing musical instruments are found in the ceiling of the Holy Trinity chapel and in the ceiling of St

Michael's chapel is a head which is believed to be in the likeness of Ivo de Roughton a master mason whose mark can be found in both the major churches in the town and who was involved in building work in other northern churches. In the Minster winged-figures on the label stops above the nave play a variety of medieval musical instruments; the faces above these musicians provide humorous comments on the quality of the sound produced. One of the angels is playing a shawm, a particularly loud instrument usually played in the open air; the figure above has his hands placed firmly over his ears. At ground level the walls of the north and south aisles have carvings which provide visitors to the church with a sermon in stone. Here the figures are misshapen, their bodies crooked (unlike those of the angels in the nave) or even beast-like as they play on instruments likely to lead to decadence and depravity. This is the fate of those who do not follow the teachings of the church. Some would say that they are an example of the masons having fun; unlikely, for as the canons were paying for the work they would want a moral message portrayed in order to keep the pilgrims on the path to righteousness.

In 1308 Henry Percy, First Lord Percy, received a licence from Edward II to crenellate his moated castle at Leconfield (2 miles north of Beverley) and for 200 years this powerful family seems to have made this place its favourite abode. Lord Percy died at the Battle of Bannockburn and his widow, Lady Eleanor (Fitz Alan), died in 1328. In 1340s their son commissioned the building of the reredos in the Minster with its concealed staircase. Attached to it is the tomb, generally believed to be that of his mother, with its richly decorated canopy – one of the sculptural glories of the Minster. One of the heraldic shields on the canopy bears the fleur-de-lis which was adopted as part of the king's heraldic arms after the battle of Crecy in 1346.

The Percy's became increasingly powerful and wealthy during the 14th century as with their vast estates and castles in Northumberland they took on the role of defending the North of England from invasion from Scotland.

The Percy Tomb, Beverley Minster

A Chapel at Molescroft

The land on either side of the road from Beverley to Leconfield was open fields leading to the hamlet of Molescroft. In 1323 a licence was granted by Edward II for Philip Ingleberd, rector of Keyingham, to build a chapel at Molescroft dedicated to St Mary. In 1325 Philip died and his heir Roger Ingleberd endowed land and rent in Molescroft, Beverley and Paull to endow a chantry chapel here dedicated to St Mary.

The Dominican Friary and Knights Hospitallers

By 1310 there were forty-two friars in the Dominican Friary and thirty-eight in the Franciscan. The Dominican friars added a south aisle to their church, built another cloister, a dormitory over the refectory and a guesthouse. They also enlarged the size of their burial grounds. Many Beverley merchants and local landowners left money to the friars with requests that they be buried in the friary cemetery:

> 1347 John Bron, tanner of Eastgate,
> 1349 Sir Henry Percy,
> 1378 Sir Marmaduke Constable,
> 1381 Lord William Latimer,
> 1388 Walter Chiltenham, vicar of Holy Trinity, Hull,
> 1391 Patrick Barton, rector of Catwick,
> 1394 Sir Brian Stapilton,
> 1397 Sir John de St Quintin.

By 1338 the Knights Hospitallers had thirty-eight commanderies in England with thirty-four knights, thirty-four chaplains and forty-eight sergeants in residence. The commandery at Beverley had one knight and two chaplains, three clerks, nine officials, servants and two pages. To be the

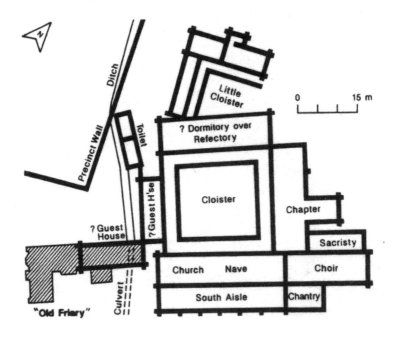

Plan of the Dominican Friary in the 14ᵗʰ Century

commander of a commandery a knight had to have completed three caravans (i.e. been to the Crusades three times) and to have been resident in the commandery for five years. In 1358 the Commander at Beverley was Robert Hales who in 1371 became the Grand Prior at Clerkenwell, London, head of the order in England and later became the King's chancellor. In 1389 he was implicated in the administration of a new form of taxation ordered by the king; Clerkenwell was stormed by the mob and burnt and Robert Hales and the archbishop of Canterbury were taken to Tower Hill and executed; their heads were then paraded through the streets of London. The chronicler Walsingham wrote of him: 'Prior Robert Hales, a magnanimous knight though the commons loved him not'.

Industries in 14th Century Beverley

The exporting of wool
and cloth from Beverley
continued to increase. In
1313 a group of Beverley
merchants sent £4,000 worth
of goods to Flanders in three
Flemish ships. By that time
the town of Beverley was
well known for its scarlet and
blue cloth. In 1330 Beverley
merchants maintained
European bases and some
were resident in Bruges. The
export of wool was to peak in
mid-century but had fallen
dramatically by the 15th
century.

Scene from the dyeing industry

The Holme family,
through several generations,
dealt in wool from abbeys
and priories such as Meaux, Sempringham, Malton and Thornton.
The wealth of the Holme family was such that religious houses
would borrow money from them - in 1326 the prior of
Sempringham owed Thomas de Holme of Beverley £300, and ten
year later the prior of Melton owed him £1,000. Thomas and his
son Richard raised hobelars (mounted troops who travelled on
horseback but fought on foot) and foot archers in Beverley for
Edward III. The Holme family, together with other wealthy
Beverley merchants such as the Copendales, Kelsternes,
Tyrrwhits, Frosts, Sigglesthorns and Alice Lumbard, made
substantial loans to the crown as Edward III continued his
hostilities with the Scots and the French. Sir Richard Holme, who
had married Joan, daughter of Sir William St Quintin of
Brandesburton, is listed as one of the 12 Keepers of the town in

1347 and 1354. He had property in Flemingate and Barleyholme and is credited with financing the building of the nave aisles, transepts, an extended chapel and the west tower of St Nicholas church. However, his will of 1366 makes no mention of St Nicholas church but asks that his body be buried in the church of the Dominican Friary. The name of Holme continues in the town documents throughout the 14th and 15th centuries.

Tanning was another industry important to the economy of Beverley and 30 tanners had been registered by 1366. Cows pastured on lands around Beverley and hides from other areas, brought by boat up the river Hull, meant that there was a continual supply of skins. The tanning industry also encouraged shoe making and the manufacture of other leather goods.

After the Romans left Britain in 410 there is little evidence of brick making for another 700 years. During the middle ages the earliest record of commercial brickyards in the country is at Beverley and Hull. In Beverley there is archaeological evidence of the use of brick in the late 12th century and during the later Middle Ages brick and tile making became an important industry. Beverley bricks were used in Beverley, York, Hull and Bridlington. Maybe the lack of stone in the East Riding and contact with the Low Countries, where brick was widely used, influenced the early making of brick in this area together with the availability of suitable clay along the Beck and the banks of the river Hull. Clay would be dug out in the autumn and left in heaps in order to be broken down by frosts during the winter months. The heaps would be turned from time to time and then, in late spring, would be dug over and moulded into bricks which would then be left for about a month to dry. They were then made into a clamp with turves, wood, refuse or coal and burnt, or put into simple kilns with an open top. The earliest evidence of the use of brick in Beverley is between the 14th century stone ribs of the vault of the nave of the Minster. The clay produced a brick of a dark red colour, which can be seen in North Bar (built 1409).

Clay was a closely guarded commodity and there were many disputes between the archbishops of York and the men of Hull about the use of clay along the riverbank. There were also disputes with the monks at Meaux Abbey. The Chronicle of Meaux, written by the late 15th century abbot, Thomas Burton tells of an argument which arose between the 'tilers' of Beverley and the Abbey of Meaux in 1385. The chronicle states that many houses in Beverley and elsewhere were covered with brick and that the brick makers, without gaining the permission of the abbot, secretly and frequently carried away in their boats soil from between the riverbanks at Wawne and Sutton (which were owned by the abbey) and the channel of the stream of the water of the river Hull, for the purpose of making bricks. In an effort to stop these activities members of the abbey removed the oars and 'other instruments' of the tile makers but still they did not desist. When members of the abbey took one of the tile maker's boats, which was laden with soil or clay, the Provost of Beverley, Robert de Manfield, tried to incite the archbishop and all the burgesses and inhabitants of Beverley by saying that the soil itself and the lordship of the water of Hull belonged to the archbishop of York and to his tenants of the provostry of Beverley, and that the burgesses and inhabitants of Beverley had always taken soil and clay in this manner. With threats and accusations they tried to get the abbey to repair the boat which they said had been damaged. A monk of the abbey was imprisoned in Beverley and even the Abbot himself threatened with violence. However, when brought before the court at Wawne the tile makers were forced to acknowledge that they were in the wrong.

Feasts and Holy Days

Throughout the year there would have been the excitement of visiting merchants and groups of pilgrims (maybe similar to those pilgrims recorded by Chaucer in his 'Canterbury Tales' – written in 1387). There was also the pomp and ceremony of the arrival of the king who with his nobles visited the shrine of Beverley's saint and prayed for support as he continued with his battles with the Scots.

The town must have been full of activity and the constant movement of people. Carts travelling from ships moored at

Beckside or Grovehill, carrying stone which had been quarried from pits near Tadcaster and brought in boats along the rivers, must frequently have been drawn through the crowded streets. The year's calendar was marked out by feast days of the saints. On feast days and fairs the town would have been filled with people from surrounding areas who came to celebrate the mass in the churches and see what was for sale in the markets. Merchants, pedlars, jugglers, householders, stewards of the Percys' castle at Leconfield, lay brothers from Meaux Abbey or from Watton Priory would all gather to see what was on sale in this wealthy town. Cloth, silks, ribbons, pots and pans, boots, shoes, wine, malt, butter and salt for the preparation of meat to be stored for winter, would, no doubt, all have been available.

The three main fairs took place on 25th October (the day on which St John was translated to the sainthood), 7th May (the day of his death) and 21st-25th June (the feast of St John the Baptist). The most important fair was the Cross Fair held in Highgate. This eleven day fair began on Ascension Day, after the Rogation Procession, and finished on Whitsunday. This procession, which tradition stated had been instituted by Archbishop Aelfric in the 11th century, was to continue until the mid-18th century.

On the Monday before Ascension Day (Rogation Monday) the shrine of St John of Beverley would be carried round the boundary of the town. This occasion gave the guilds an opportunity to demonstrate their importance and status. The shrine of the saint was taken from the Minster and carried in procession around the boundary of the town. Before the procession the eight Porters of the Shrine, an hereditary office which had the responsibility of guarding the shrine in times of danger, underwent a period of purification and restrictions. They were expected to drink no ale from the time that the shrine was carried from its resting place until its safe return when they would then take part in a celebratary feast in the refectory. The clergy would assemble at the High Altar to receive the shrine. The Porters of the Shrine would carry the gold and silver casket from its resting place, process around the church and out into the street. The procession would then make its way past the gateway of the

Bedern, where the provost or his representative would make an offering, continue up Highgate to Cross bridge and along Walkergate to St Mary's church. The procession would be watched by masters of recognised guilds, dressed in their finest livery (thus demonstrating their corporate identity), standing on wooden castles erected in prescribed areas in different parts of the town. The guild of weavers denied a place in the castle or procession to any master who was too poor to be clothed in the current livery. The castles were to be 'honestly covered' - the bow and arrow makers, who had a castle at the Bull Ring opposite the castle of the butchers, ensured this by ordering each brother to bring a suitable bedspread to be hung on the castle. In the afternoon the procession would continue, and members of the guilds would be expected to follow, to visit chapels at Hull Bridge, Thearne and Molescoft. On Ascension Day the shrine would be restored to its accustomed place and mass would be celebrated.

Another important day in the town's calendar was the performance of the Mystery Plays, first mentioned in the town records in 1377. The word 'mystery' comes from 'mastery' meaning that the plays were performed by those who were masters of their craft. On the feast of Corpus Christi, the Thursday after Trinity Sunday, members of the guilds were expected to act out scenes from the Bible, from the fall of Adam to the Ascension of Christ and the coronation of the Virgin Mary, at seven designated areas throughout the centre of the town. A stand would be erected at North Bar from where the Keepers could view the first play to be performed early in the morning. Throughout the day the cart on which the plays were acted would be trundled through the town, drawn by horses or men. It was often a triple-decker cart with a lower stage providing a dressing room and a place from which images concerned with hell, such as devils and weird spirits, could emerge through a trap door, a stage on which the play could take place, and above, at the back of the stage a raised platform on which God, often dressed as a pope, could appear. Having left North Bar the cart would stop at prescribed points to allow the performance of a play: at the

A Performance of a Mystery Play

bullring at the southern end of the northern market, at Cross
Bridge at the bottom of Walkergate, at the Fish Market, at the
bottom of Highgate and finally at the Beck.

On the day the mystery plays were performed the twelve
Keepers of the town, dressed in their colourful robes, walked at
the head of the craftsmen in the procession expressing the civic
pomp and importance of the town. This was not specifically a
guild occasion for some of the plays were presented by crafts
which did not have guild status – the vintners who played the
annunciation to the shepherds and the priests who performed the
coronation of the Virgin. A badly presented play was considered
an insult to the town and the offending guild would be fined by
the Keepers. In 1409 thirty-six plays are mentioned in the cycle at

Beverley but sadly, unlike York, none of Beverley's cycle of plays has survived.

Religious fraternities would have their own celebrations. St Helen, mother of the Roman emperor, Constantine, had gone to the Holy Land and discovered the places associated with the life and death of Jesus. On her feast day, 3rd May, members of the guild of St Helen, founded in Beverley in 1378, assembled and

> chose a fir youth, the fairest they can find who was clad as queen, like to St Ellene. An old man goes before the youth carrying a cross and another old man carrying a shovel, in token of the finding of the Cross.

Dressed in their best clothes, 'with much music' they went in procession to the church at the Franciscan friary to hear mass said at the altar of St Helen. Everyone gave a penny. After dinner they assembled

> In a room in the hall of the guild and there they eat bread and cheese and drank as much ale as is good for them.

In 1355 nine married couples, two married women and the vicar of St Mary's, founded the Guild of St Mary. On the saint's feast day guild members of both sexes gathered in the town and processed to the church 'with melody and rejoicing' led by two members dressed as angels carrying candleholders in the shape of bowls each with twenty-four tapers. Next would come a guild member 'nobly dressed and adorned' as the Virgin and two more dressed as Simeon and Joseph. The other members of the guild walked behind at a moderate pace, two by two, sisters first and then the brothers each holding a candle. Mass was celebrated in the church followed by their annual dinner 'in an honest place'. After dinner aldermen and stewards were elected who would be responsible for visiting poor and infirm members of the guild and supplying them with guild funds.

The Principal Streets are Repaved

The Keepers' collection of tolls from strangers as they entered the town was used mainly for the upkeep of the roads. In 1344 the keepers received 16,000 bricks from the tilers for the repair of the area known as the Dings in the northern marketplace. The Town Keepers Accounts Rolls refer to large quantities of white stone taken from the Westwood to consolidate certain streets. The levels of the roads and market squares in the centre of Beverley were then raised and the roads repaved with cobbles in an effort to provide a drier surface. Today we descend from the road of North Bar Within into the church of St Mary's which is built at the original level of the street. The undulations on the east side of the Westwood, known as Newbegin pits, are caused by chalk for hundreds of years having been dug from here, carried into town and used for upgrading roads and providing house foundations.

After the demolition of a medieval house in Highgate in 1958 archaeological excavations revealed that the street has eight layers. First was the dark grey clay loam of the Saxon period. Next was a thick layer of compressed peat and bog with a few chalk blocks and a quantity of twigs, wood shavings. The peat had been formed by large quantities of organic waste being dumped from nearby habitation over many centuries. Branches of hazel had been laid on the surface of the peat, always with their length across the street. Upon these were young trees, laid side by side, in some parts close enough to touch. On top of this was a layer of chalk and occasionally pieces of waste building stone; both the chalk and the building stones were in large regularly cut blocks so that each fitted with its neighbour. These were covered with brushwood, which was then covered with chalk - finally gravel was laid on top.

Beverley Pays Protection Money to the Scots

In 1306 Robert Bruce (1306 – 1329) was crowned king of Scotland. Edward II continued his father's campaign to be overlord of the the Scots. In 1310 he asked to borrow the banner of St John which was escorted north by one of the vicars choral. On 24th June 1314 a large army left York and marched north. A battle took place at Bannockburn in which the English army was humiliatingly defeated and destroyed as a fighting force. From then on the whole of the North of England was subject to raids from the Scots in which houses were burnt and cattle stolen. In 1319 there were many English casualites at a battle near Boroughbridge, in 1322 Edward II narrowly missed capture near Byland. In that year a raiding party reached Bootham Bar, in York, and for several days terrorised the neighbourhood. In 1322 the burgesses of Beverley petitioned Edward II for confirmation of earlier charters, which they, wrongly, claimed, allowed enclosure of the town with a wall. The King agreed to consult the archbishop and inspect the charters. However, no comment seems to have come and Beverley had to remain content with its existing ditches and gates for defence and to pay protection moncy to the Scots. Hull, however, was granted permission to build a brick wall round the town.

The Black Death

In the mid-1340s there was more bad weather which resulted in poor harvests and people weakened as a result of malnutrition. In 1349 came further devastation. The Black Death (so called because the first sign was lumps often turning to black boils in the groin, armpits or neck), which had been sweeping across Europe, arrived in England and no part of the country was safe. In June 1349 the archbishop ordered the consecration of the churchyard of St Thomas's chapel outside Keldgate bar as an additional burial ground. Although no reliable statistics exist, it is likely that in Beverley, as in other towns in England, almost half the population died. The size of the population of Beverley before the Black Death is unknown.

Beverley Tenth Largest Town

Soon after the eleven year old king, Richard II, was crowned king in 1377 a new form of taxation was imposed. This was the Poll Tax which was a direct tax on all males over the age of fourteen. The Poll Tax of 1377 is of particular interest because it provides the first reliable assessment of the population of Beverley. According to the returns, 2,663 people in Beverley were subject to tax. Taking into consideration the number of females and children who did not have to pay tax in the town it is likely that the full population was approximately 5,000. A comparison of these figures with those of other towns shows that at this stage Beverley was the 10th largest town in the country. It can be assumed that the population of Beverley before 1349 was considerably higher than in 1377.

One effect of the Black Death was a shortage of labour. Consequently, labourers could demand higher wages. In order to keep prices down and prevent labourers from leaving their masters for better paid work, in 1351 the Statute of Labourers fixed the maximum legal wage. However, by now labourers knew their worth and wages continued to rise.

A further effect was a loss of faith in bishops, monks and clergy of the church. The prayers of the priests had not averted the calamity which caused the death of half the population. In 1370s John Wyclif, a teacher at Oxford, claimed that the church was too wealthy and urged people to stop paying tithes. He organised the translation of the Bible from Latin to English so that it could be read and studied by the people. He pronounced that priests were not necessary for salvation and he questioned one of the most important Church teachings that during mass the bread and wine turned into the body and blood of Christ. His followers, known as Lollards, went into the countryside preaching and reading the Bible in English. Church authorities accused the Lollards of being heretics and a number of them were burnt at the stake.

Archbishop Neville 1374 – 1388. Rebellions and Uprisings

It was in this atmosphere that Alexander Neville, younger son of Ralph, the 4th Lord Neville of Raby, in 1374 was consecrated archbishop of York. His career has been described as displaying 'a dangerous combination of high ambition, exceptional litigiousness and an apparent lack of application to detailed business'. His time as archbishop was to witness two revolts in Beverley which questioned the very government of the town and the control of the Minster. The archbishop was said to be a fiery character who evoked fear among the people of Beverley.

Early in his reign Richard II, in honour of St John, exempted the burgesses of Beverley from contributing towards the cost of building ships and barges for use by the king. Instead, they were ordered to send soldiers to the king's army. The burgesses of Hull then tried to impose a tax on the burgesses of Beverley as payment towards their costs of building ships demanded by the king. They claimed that their great expense had reduced the town to poverty and they wanted assistance from more opulent towns such as York and Beverley. Beverley claimed that it was not a sea town and that the river was too narrow for large boats to navigate. Hull's relationship with the people of Beverley was already strained and cannot have been improved by the intervention of Archbishop Neville. The 19th century historian, JH Sheahan, describes the scene;

> the archbishop, with his servants, travelled to Hull to meet the mayor and claim the rights of the people of Beverley to use the river Hull. The mayor and a large train of followers in violation of the rights of hospitality rudely attacked him. The mayor snatched the archbishop's crosier and struck one of his attendants. There was then a general assault and bloodshed, the enraged magistrate laying about him manfully with the crosier, breaking the peace and the heads of his opponents.

The Westwood Granted to the People of Beverley

Concerns about the rights of pasture had continued from the previous century but mostly complaints from the archbishops were about the poaching of deer by individual townsmen in the archbishops' park. Archbishop Neville threatened that any offender caught poaching would be excommunicated.

In 1379 – 80 the people of Beverley were to receive one of their most precious resources – Beverley Westwood. This 600 acre wood, which for 400 years had belonged to the archbishops of York, had long been a cause of discontent between the archbishops of York and the people of Beverley. In 1381 Archbishop Neville granted it and its boundary ditches, plus 200 acres at Figham and 200 acres at Swinemoor (damp land from which peat could be dug) to the people of Beverley on condition that they paid him a fee of £5 a year (a good rent at the time). The archbishop reserved the right to keep one limekiln for his own use but undertook not to sell the lime produced. He also reserved the right of pannage for his tenants at Bishop Burton. Pannage was the practice of driving tame pigs into the woods in autumn to fatten on acorns before being slaughtered and salted down for winter food. The Westwood provided a source of income for the town; timber which could be sold for building houses or ships or used as firewood, chalk for foundations of houses and roads, and, as the area became cleared of trees, a place where the freemen of Beverley could graze their cattle and sheep. In 1386-7 the town received £1 4s 0d from the sale of wood and £3 10s 0d from the limekilns. Over the years the return was increased and the annual payment of £5 to the archbishop easily raised.

West fronts of the Minster and St Mary's church

In 1380 Archbishop Neville gave oaks from his park at Bishop Burton to the Minster as the canons prepared for the third, and final, stage of building. As masons were recruited the provost and canons applied to the court at Westminster for:

Beverley Minster, West Front

enlarged powers to preserve and prevent insubordination amongst work people by the adoption of summary methods punishments.

The nave was extended to its present length. The figures above the pillars to the west of the crossing in the Minster are no longer angels but waits carrying musical instruments and swords. A carving in the north aisle is of a nun sitting with a dog in her lap. Perhaps a reflection on a Church in which a nun paid more attention to her dog than her devotions.

During the middle ages Beverley gained a reputation for secular music through its waits and minstrels. The word 'wait' is a Nordic word meaning 'watcher' or 'guard'. In towns watchmen were often appointed to guard the city walls and gates during hours of darkness and to report any strangers or wrong-doers to the keepers. Often these watchmen formed themselves into bands of instrumentalists who would entertain the townsfolk and perform at civic functions. In Beverley the waits took an important part in the Rogationtide procession. In order to prevent vagabond musicians and buskers coming to the towns and taking the profits of the minstrels, Edward IV, in 1469, incorporated the royal minstrels as a guild and ordered that throughout the kingdom no minstrel was to perform unless he was a member of the guild.

By the end of the century the West Towers of the Minster had been built in the Perpendicular style with even larger and more spacious windows than previous styles had permitted. The glass in the great West Window was put in 1400.

The West Front of St Mary's was also completed with its perpendicular west window circular turrets, now replaced. Before the building of the east and west windows of St Mary's the interior of the church must have been quite dark for the highest point was the roof of Holy Trinity chapel. Clerestory's added to the nave and the chancel to raise the roof in line with the new windows must have brought in extra light.

Peasants' Revolt Spreads to Beverley

Throughout the 14th century kings needed new sources of taxation to fund the never ending expense of military campaigns against the Welsh, the Scots and the French. Parliament was summoned more and more in order to raise taxes. A further Poll Tax was levied in 1379 which was graduated, the amount of tax varied from £6 13s and 4d from a duke to one groat from the lowest paid. However, the government, still short of money, in 1381 imposed a further tax in which the poorest were to pay one shilling and the richest 20s (£1). There were accusations of ill-government and extravagance which resulted in demonstrations of unrest throughout the country. These culminated in the rising, known as the Peasants' Revolt, led by Wat Tyler in the summer of 1381 which was quickly followed by other uprisings in southern counties. Everywhere Manor-houses were fired and lawyers put to death. Converging on London the Kentish men, led by Wat Tyler, crossed the Thames at London Bridge, captured Simon of Sudbury, archbishop of Canterbury and the Chancellor, and Sir Robert Hales, the Treasurer (also at one time prior of the Knights Hospitallers commandery at Beverley), imprisoned them in the Tower were they were taken to Tower Hill and beheaded and their heads paraded through the streets of London. By this time disturbances in other parts of the country had already resulted in unrest in northern towns, especially York, Scarborough and Beverley. However, with no alternative to Royal government and with the death of Tyler at the hands of the Mayor of London, the rebellion petered out and many rebels were hanged.

Canons' Rebellion

Archbishop Neville was a man not unacquainted with dissension for he seems to have spent much of his time in quarrels first with the dean and chapter of York, then the church at Ripon and finally the canons of Beverley Minster.

The archbishops of York had been granted the ninth prebend of St Leonard at the Minster. As he was not a canon the archbishop was not entitled to a place in the chapter. Neville thought otherwise and in February 1381 announced his intention of making a formal visitation of the canons and clergy the following month. On 26th March he arrived to be met only by the precenter, the clerk of the Bedern and two chantry priests. Three days later the vicars appeared but refused to accept the archbishop's authority without the permission of their masters, the canons. Later two canons turned up, Richard de Thearne and Nicholas de Louth (who was also vicar of St Mary's, Cottingham, where his brass memorial tablet can be seen today). They both had other preferments in the province of York and so were somewhat dependent on the archbishop for continued support. In April the vicars left Beverley and were promptly excommunicated by the archbishop who then imported vicars choral from York in order that the services might continue.

The absent canons were all highly placed royal clerks, secure in rich preferments outside the grasp of Archbishop Neville. Walter de Skirlaugh (later to become Bishop of Durham and who was in 1404 to pay for the building of a church in the village of his birth, Skirlaugh) was overseas on king's business. Henry de Snaith and William de Birshell remained aloof from the archbishop. The two remaining canons were Richard de Ravensor (a distinguished Master in Chancery and former provost of Beverley Minster who led the rebellion against the archbishop) and John de Wellingborough, the king's clerk.

The archbishop had been within his rights in demanding a visitation; the main objection was that it was too sudden and that demanding a place in the chapter was going against the accepted custom. The practice of the non-residence of the canons was long-standing.

There was no resolution to this dispute until the downfall of Neville. In Beverley, once the dispute with the canons had evaporated there was unsettlement between the rulers of the town and the craftsmen.

The Craftsmen's Rebellion

In 1359 the town had received its Great Charter. This laid out the rules for the government of the town by the twelve Keepers.

- Outgoing Keepers were responsible for nominating eighteen men who had not been Keepers in the previous three years from whom the burgesses were to choose the next twelve Keepers. (This system of selection was to last for almost 500 years).

- The Keepers had power to charge rents, rates and duties in the town.

- They were to keep and uphold the ancient customs and laws and punish rebels and wrong-doers.

- With the consent of the burgesses they could make new laws and regulations for the town.

By 1376 a Keeper's fine for non-attendance was £2. They were expected to remain in the town during their term of office.

Rule by the Keepers was not always popular. In 1381 there was a revolt led by craftsmen who felt that they had little say in the running of the town where the twelve Keepers were elected from eighteen of the 'great and most sufficient burgesses' who had been selected by the previous keepers. In Beverley there was unrest against the hold over the town of the archbishop, the provost and the canons. When the canons rebelled against the archbishop the townspeople took the opportunity to play one off against the other.

In the elections in May 1381 the Keepers were replaced by two chamberlains: Thomas White, a tiler, and Henry Newark, a sanctuary man, both from humble backgrounds; and an alderman, Richard Middleton, who was a draper and thus from a richer background. Unlike the Keepers, these were paid posts, the chamberlains receiving £1 each and the alderman £5. These appointments and the salaries paid became a source of dissatisfaction. The dissidents accused the chapter underbailiff, Robert Butemond, of 'stealing' goods within the town. Another townsman under attack was Thomas Beverley, steward of the fees belonging to the archbishop, the provost and the chapter. Feelings ran high for the wealth of the town remained with the rich Keepers who, soon after the election, removed the town's documents concerning rights and privileges and money from the guildhall. Soon after the election the townspeople raided the guildhall in order to capture the borough's common seal. On 3rd June, Richard Middleton called an emergency meeting in the guildhall; in July William Haldene (who supported the new appointments) was attacked and his body was found in 'le Bek in Walkerlane' after his brains had been knocked out by John Ergham and others with a pole-axe, two battle-axes, six swords, two forks and other weapons. Richard of Boston, the leader of the revolt, was murdered and Richard Middleton was attacked. There then developed a policy of terror in which the 'less sufficient burgesses' (the craftsmen) went to the houses of the 'more sufficient' (the wealthy merchants) with an armed force and threatened to kill them and burn their dwellings if they did not provide them with bonds. By threats of force and fear of death they forced Adam Coppandale, Thomas Beverley, John Gerveys (a vintner) and William Dudhill and other worthy men of Beverley to make various bonds requiring large sums of money to be paid at specified times and under certain forms and conditions and then deliver them to Richard Middleton, late alderman, Thomas White, tiler, and Henry de Newark, late chamberlain. The merchants fled to London to make appeals to the royal courts and complained that they were followed by sixty men who had stolen horses from the common pasture at Beverley and had come to lodge at Tottenham and from there threatened Coppandale and his colleagues with violence, going through the streets of London with pole-axes and swords.

In the late summer of 1381 the king and his councillors demanded that the bonds taken by the men of Beverley, under forfeit of the sums mentioned in the bonds, should be sent to the chancery in London and that Thomas Manby, alderman, Simon Cartwryght and William Ithoun (chamberlains of the town of Beverley) should appear in person to show if they had or knew any reason why the these bonds ought not to be cancelled and annulled as documents made under duress and compulsion against the law of England. The reply was that Thomas de Manby, alderman and the chamberlains of the town of Beverley had no such documents, nor had they ever came into their custody.

Unrest in the town continued and on 16th April 1382 the bailiff of the liberty of St John of Beverley complained that, for fear of his life, he dare not arrest Henry de Newark, Thomas White and Richard Boston. In June, Archbishop Neville, with his brother John, Lord Neville of Raby (the sheriff of Yorkshire) and many other Yorkshire knights came to Beverley to try and establish political stability by taking pledges of good behaviour from 400 or more townsmen. By summer the bonds had been cancelled and a royal letter of pardon was granted to the men of Beverley on payment of a fine of 1,100 marks. In 1386 government of the town reverted to the twelve Keepers.

When in 1386 Neville was accused of treason Richard II took away his right to act as archbishop and confiscated all his goods. Two years' later Neville was proclaimed a traitor by Parliament and was forced to flee the country in disguise. The king and parliament, and even the pope, insisted that the Beverley vicars were to be reinstated. Neville became a schoolmaster at Luvain, France, and died in poverty in1392.

A New Constitution for the Collegiate Church of St John

In 1391 the new archbishop of York, Thomas Arundel, drew up a revised constitution for the collegiate church at Beverley. The constitution stated that:

> The number of the ministers in the church be the same as they were at the making of these statutes, viz. nine canons and prebendaries, the lord archbishop of York, who is a proper canon and prebendary, to be distinguished as president of them all when he

shall be present, including also the canon and prebendary which is called the eighth; also three officers, namely, precentor, chancellor and sacristy; and seven parsons, who formerly were called berefellarii; nine vicars, seven chantry chaplains, nine canons' clerks, one precentor's clerk and one charnel clerk; also seven clerks of the before named seven parsons, two thuribulars (who swung the incense burner during services), eight chorister boys; also two sacrists' clerks and two vergers, or bell-ringers.

The statutes state that in

processions the clergy are to keep their regular places and shall be personally present in their respective dresses; these shall include the clergy from the Minster together with the vicar of the chapel of blessed Mary, the clerks of the same chapel, the under master of the scholars, the chaplain of the altar of St Martin, the chaplain of the chapel of Ulbrigg (Hull Bridge) and Molescroft and the hospital of blessed Nicholas in Beverley as well as all chantry chaplains.

The provost of the Minster should pay to the treasurer of the Chapter, in the name of the nine canons, £10 in equal proportions four times a year. The precentor was to receive £10 while the chancellor and sacrist were to be paid as before. Each of the two clerks and the two vergers of the sacrist were to receive 6s 8d, the parsons £6 13s 4 each, annually. The nine canons, the chancellor and the precentor were to receive fifty-two quarters of oats every year. The nine vicars were to receive £8 annually and each week four bushels of wheat; the provost should assign to them two pits for digging peat in the turbary (the right to dig peat for fuel) of Leven and a proper place for drying the same. The provost should repair and properly sustain the houses in the Bedern, in which the vicars reside, and provide clothes for the table, and straw for the hall, logs for winter from time to time, from the vigil of All Saints to the vigil of Easter.

It is ordained that the provost abolish the corrupt and ancient custom of the King of Fools, both within the church and without.

The Feast of Fools was a countrywide practice in which members of the clergy took part in feasts with the intention of frightening or entertaining the onlookers. They would dress in ridiculous clothes and wear masks or blackened faces. The King of Fools might eat, drink or play dice upon the altar, sing indecent songs in the choir, practise the lewd airs of the lowest and most abandoned of their sex and after services expose themselves in a most unseemly manner! The harmless custom of the election from 6th December (the feast of St Nicholas) until Epiphany of one of choirboys as Boy Bishop continued.

Payment for attendances at services for the souls of Edward III, Queen Isabella or Queen Philippa, or Richard de Ravenser and John de Bentley was as follows:

> each canon to receive 8d, each officer 6d, each parson and vicar 4d, each chantry chaplain 3d, each clerk 2d, each chorister 1d. For the services for Lady Idonea Percy the ordination was to continue as before.

John de Ake - a Wealthy Merchant

By the end of the 14th century there was a belief, confirmed by the pope, that the prayers of chantry priests were effective in gaining a reduction of the time that a soul spent in purgatory. Masses would be said in chantry chapels for the soul of the founder and named people.

One of the twelve Keepers in the town in 1379 and 1380 was John de Ake. In his will of 1398, John de Ake left money to the two great churches and to the two friaries. All his lands and other property in Beverley he left to his wife Eleanor. After her death money was to be used for endowing a chantry chapel with a priest on Cross Bridge (the bridge which spanned the Walker beck) and to found the hospital of the Holy Trinity for twenty poor people.

By the end of the 14th century, despite rebellions and uprisings, Beverley was at the peak of the mountain of success. Sadly, the town was soon to begin its descent into the valley.

CHAPTER 7

1400-1500 – THE GRADUAL DESCENT

By the end of the 14th century Richard II had managed to alienate both his relatives and members of the nobility, and so was an easy victim to a contender for the crown. On 4th July 1399 Henry Bolingbroke, Duke of Lancaster, landed at Ravenspur (in Holderness) and claimed the throne of England. Richard II was deposed and died mysteriously the following year while in prison; Bolingbroke was crowned Henry IV. However, he was not accepted by all; first, Lord Percy, the First Earl of Northumberland, to whom Henry owed money, rose against him and a battle took place at Shrewsbury in which Henry was victorious and in which over 7,000 men died, including the Earl's son, Hotspur. In 1405 there was a conspiracy against the new king in which the Archbishop of York, Richard Scrope, took part. The rebels, with 8,000 men met on Shipton Moor, near York, where the archbishop made demands of the king for a free parliament, a reduction of taxation and the continuation of the war against the Welsh. The rebels were dispersed but Scrope was arrested and, after a semblance of a trial, beheaded. Shortly after his burial in York Minster miracles were reported at is tomb.

The days of the long rule of kings were over as first one section of the nobles and then the other fought for possession of the crown. The Wars of the Roses, referring to the white rose of Yorkshire and the red rose of Lancashire, were to last throughout the 15th century. However, throughout this time English society in general was relatively stable and prosperous – battles did not destroy the land, the towns or the sources of the wealth of those who fought.

Names of new streets in Beverley, entering the record books during the 15th century are:

- 1416 Wodeland (Wood Lane) from the west side of North Bar Within, opposite Hengate, to the wood (Westwood).

- 1433 Briddalmyddyng – street with a midden (dunghill). 1747 Burdet Lane; later Dog and Duck Lane after the pub.

- 1439 Podynglane – maybe selling offal. Off Ladygate and Cornmarket. 1556 Pudding Lane

- 1446 Wednesday Market – first use of name, previously known as Fishmarket. Also Cockpit or Cockpit Hill after the cockpit here during 18th century.

- 1449 Bulryng mentioned – west side of Cornmarket. By this stage the Cornmarket was divided into streets or lanes and named according to what was sold there.

Defences are Improved

Several factors including the instability of the monarchy, the execution of the archbishop (who was, of course, Lord of the Manor of Beverley) or the insurrection of the Percys made the people of Beverley consider the defences of the town. In 1409 the town bars were re-built; Newbegin Bar, Keldgate Bar (each costing £30 and both now demolished) and North Bar costing £96 0s 11d. Each of the bars, built in brick, had strong wooden gates which could be shut at night or during times of trouble. North Bar still retains the grooves in the walls of the gateway for the portcullis.

Beverley's lost gates. Above Newbigin Bar demolished in 1790 and below Keldgate Bar demolished in 1808

North Bar from the north. Built in 1409

Porches Added to the Minster and St Mary's

Early in the century the Minster and St Mary's both acquired new, covered entrances. A porch was important not only as a means of entry into a church but also as a place where penitents received absolution, women knelt to be churched after childbirth, babies were baptised, vows of marriage were exchanged, civil business was carried out, coroners held court, legacies were paid out by executors of wills, debts were collected and arguments resolved.

111

The East Riding Antiquarian Society Transactions IV give the Beverley Borough Account for 1409 – 10. The account was presented by the 12 Keepers and shows income and expenditure for the building of North Bar. Below is a selection of payments.

	£	s.	d.
For one tree bought from Peter Whitt with its carriage		18	
To William Rasyne and his helpers working there, and in the Guildhall, for the leaves of the doors of North Bar		5	5
To William de Wode for 3,000 wall-tiles (bricks)		10	8
On 2nd August for hurdles and other things necessary for the scaffold		5	5
On 9th August for 500 longspikes (spikes or nails)		22	
On 16th August to Agnes Tiler for 1,000 tiles		3	8
To John Elward for 1,000 squynchon (chamfered bricks) and 600 Wall-tiles		6	0
On 23rd August to Robert Newman, carter, for five days carting		5	0
To eight tilers and their servants, eleven labourers, with hurdles and other things brought		51	6
On 6th September to six bricklayers, three servants and eight labourers		43	3
To William Rasyne, senior, for one day			6
On 16th July to the labourers in the quarry		12	6
To John Ireland for 2.5 days		15	0
To five labourers at the Bar		10	0
To one carter for six days		6	0
To William Rolleston, mason, for spars		7	6

It is interesting to compare the size of the porches in the Minster and St Mary's. Previously the main entrance into the Minster had been at the north end of the north transept and when built, would have faced into the centre of the southern market. However, by the early 15th centre the main market was in the northern part of the town, houses had been built in Eastgate and Highgate, so that the new porch, facing towards Highgate, was merely an entrance into the church. It is said that in the room above the Highgate porch an official would watch for fugitives

St Mary's Porch

coming down the street seeking sanctuary. St Mary's was the church of the northern market and the large beautifully proportioned porch was a room in which people could congregate.

Hospitals and Anchorites

A number of new hospitals were built during the 15th century. Some hospitals were a form of chantry in which residents were expected to pray for the souls of those on whose charity they depended. Some were founded to help pilgrims or lepers. In Beverley two leper hospitals were provided, the first mentioned in 1394 was outside Keldgate Bar, the second mentioned in 1402 was outside the North Bar (probably the chief leper house of the town, for men and women). Two maisons Dieu (God's house) were funded by the churches - St Mary's hospital attached to the north side of North Bar (1434) and St John the

Evangelist in Lairgate (1467). The first mention of the hospital of St John the Baptist, in Fishmarket is 1454.

Several of these hospitals had anchorites – a religious recluse living a solitary life of silence, prayer and mortification. St Giles hospital had an anchorite enclosed in the churchyard of the church; St Nicholas hospital had an anchoress. A will of 1471 refers to Joan, the woman at the hospital and Gilliom 'the old women there'. In 14th and 15th centuries there was a hermitage outside North Bar on the road to Bishop Burton with a chapel dedicated to St Theobald – although a hermit is never mentioned. In mid 14th century a hermit is mentioned at St Thomas chapel outside Keldgate.

The Sanctuary Act Book of the Collegiate Church of St John at Beverley records that over a period of twenty-one years (1478 – 1499) 131 fugitives came to Beverley seeking sanctuary; fifty-two were from Yorkshire, fourteen from Lincolnshire, thirteen from the north midlands and eleven from East Anglia.

Margery Kempe

Margery Kempe, a mystic, was a follower of the Lollards (a Dutch word of derision meaning 'mumbler' or 'mutterer'). Lollards were evangelists who rejected priestly authority and encouraged poverty in imitation of Christ, and the studying of the scriptures in English. Lollards questioned the authority and power of the English church and so many people considered them to be heretics.

During the first half of the 15th century Margery Kempe travelled the country seeking forgiveness of her sins in the belief that the more she suffered the more she would be rewarded in heaven; as she travelled people would give her money and ask this holy woman to pray for them. Her book, written in 1436, tells of her travels and includes an account of her visit to Beverley.

Margery had travelled from Bridlington and as she was about to board a boat at Hessle, two Preaching Friars, believing that they would receive £100 as a reward, accused her of being a Lollard and managed to persuade two yeomen of the Duke of

Bedford to arrest her. She was brought to Hessle where people threatened to burn her at the stake. From there she was taken to Beverley and on the way men of the country called to her telling her to forsake the life she led and to 'go spin and card, as other women do, and suffer not so much shame and so much woe'.

On arrival in Beverley she was provided with a fair chamber and an 'honest' bed in the house of one of her captors. The man locked the door and took the key. Margery stood at the window telling passers by 'good tales' so that women wept sore and said with great grief in their hearts; 'Alas! Woman, why shalt thou be burnt?' The woman of the house, unable to enter her room because her husband had taken away the key, brought a ladder to the window in order to climb up and give Margery a cup and a pint of wine in a pot.

The following day Marjory was brought into the Chapter House of Beverley Minster before the Archbishop of York and many great clerks, priests, canons and secular men. The story of her arrest was told to the archbishop, and the Preaching Friar who had been present said that she depraved all men of Holy Church. The Archbishop listened to her defence and then told the friar that her words were not heresy. She was then freed and taken to a house where many priests went to her to see her and speak with her, and many people had great compassion that she was 'so evil fared with'.

Later the archbishop summoned her and she went to his hall where his household was at meat, and she was led into his chamber, even to his bedside. Once again accusations were thrown at her by a Preaching Friar who accused her of counselling Lady Greystoke to forsake her husband (as Margery herself had forsaken her husband) and spoke many other shrewd words. Margery replied that this had been before she had been to Jerusalem. The archbishop's steward and many others said; 'Lord, we pray you, let her go hence at this time, and if ever she comes back, we will burn her ourselves.' She then knelt, received the blessing of the archbishop and left his chamber. The archbishop's household begged her to pray for them.

However, the steward was angry with her for she left the chamber 'with right good cheer'. 'Holy folk should not laugh,' said the steward.

'Sir, I have great cause to laugh,' replied Margery, 'for the more shame I suffer the merrier I may be in Our Lord Jesus Christ.' She was then brought to the Water of Humber where she was left alone.

This story is interesting in what it reveals about a new questioning attitude of some members of the church and the disagreements with the friars.

Royal Visits – Henry V and Henry VI

On the day of the Battle of Agincourt, 25th October 1415, the day of the translation of St John of Beverley, the tomb of the saint was seen to sweat oil or blood throughout the hours of battle. Five years later, when travelling in the north, Henry V (1413 – 1422) diverted from York to visit Beverley and give thanks for the saint's intervention and support in his fight with the French. He ordered that St John was to become one of the patrons of the royal household and that his feast day, together with that of St George, was to be celebrated throughout England.

Whilst in the Minster the king would have seen the recently completed perpendicular style East Window, which replaced the single lancet windows of the 13th century. The window had been built as a result of £40 left in the will of Canon Waltham dated 1416. Today it has the only medieval stain glass of exceptionally high quality which remains in the Minster.

As is usual with a royal visit, great effort and expense was made to prepare the town to receive the king. A few of the expenses were as follows:

3s 6d paid to a man for carting dirt out of the Corn market for three and a half days preparatory to the arrival of the lord the king
2d each paid to two labourers filling the said carts with dirt for three days, plus a present of 4d.

In preparation for the visit the king's brother, the Duke of Gloucester, and the whole of his household stayed in Beverley for two nights at a cost to the town of £13 15s 10d. The Keepers of the town made a collection for a present to be given to the king which amounted to £72 18s 10d.

Henry V's son, Henry VI (1422 – 1461), succeeded to the throne in 1422 when he was only nine months old. He grew up under the protectorate of his uncles and great-uncles before being crowned in 1429 but did not assume his royal powers until 1437. He suffered from depression and bouts of insanity. During his minority Robert Rolleston was clerk of the wardrobe and after Henry assumed power he became a royal councillor and keeper of the great wardrobe. From 1425 he was preband of the altar of St Katherine in the Minster and from 1427 was provost of Beverley Minster until his death in 1451. Robert's brother, Roger, a merchant in Beverley, was regularly chosen as a Keeper in the 1430s and 1440s often heading the list of the twelve. When in 1448, Henry VI, on his only progress north, spent a week at the Earl of Northumberland's castle at Leconfield, it was Roger Rolleston who greeted him on his arrival in Beverley with the words:

> Most gracious Christian prince and sovereign lord, be welcome to your people and town of Beverley.

Whilst progressing round the town the king would have entered St Mary's church and seen the recently painted chancel ceiling depicting 40 English monarchs (finishing with his own portrait and details) and have, no doubt, been made aware of the boss in the centre of the chancel ceiling showing St John and King Athelstan holding a scroll saying, 'Als free make I thee as hart may know and eye may see' - a reminder of how kings had always favoured the town of Beverley. He commented on the imperfect state of the footpaths and gave the burgesses a patent to impose tolls for ten years to gain money for repairs.

Robert Rolleston founded a chantry at the altar of St Catherine's in the Minster and sought burial in the chapel. He bequeathed a new window whose stained glass depicted the life of St Catherine and the miracles associated with St Mary. On the exterior of this window, on the south wall of the south lesser transept the arms of Robert Rolleston can still be seen.

A year after the king's visit a fire at the Dominican Friary destroyed the dormitory and library. Henry VI gave ten marks (a mark being a third of a pound) 'for the relief of their great poverty and for the rebuilding of the said house'. This rebuilt structure, now considerably altered, is all that we see today of this once great complex of buildings.

The Twelve Keepers

The town continued to be governed by the twelve Keepers, who were in 15th century often referred to as 'aldermen', later as 'governors'. Their responsibilities included maintaining law and order in the town, controlling the use of wheeled traffic, overseeing the common pastures, scouring the Beck, looking after the banks and ditches which defined the boundary of the town, draining the common land, seeing to the defence of the town (providing a watch in times of danger), managing the town's finances, making leases of town properties and acting as trustees for charitable endowments.

To help in their administrations the Keepers had several paid officials. They included: a town clerk, a bellman who had four hand bells and was responsible for warning burgesses of council meetings (each day he made a daily progress from North Bar to the Beck to mark the official time when trading could begin), toll collectors who would be stationed at points of entry into the town and at the Beck. The town also had a 'furbisher' who was responsible for the armour kept in the town chest, which included body armour for six men. The Keepers also provided a supervisor of the corn and fish markets, a sweeper and raker of the market, a swineherd and shepherds for the pasture and carters who were paid for carrying wood and building materials from the Westwood. A shepherd of the Westwood was mentioned in 1436 and in 1438 the shepherds of Swine Moor and Figham who

St Mary's Chancel

received 2d for each of the animals in their care. By 1460 salaried officials were appointed, known as the 'herds', to supervise the Westwood and Figham,

The Keepers also gave gifts to powerful neighbours. They made regular gifts to the officials of the archbishops and when, in 1423, the Earl and Countess of Northumberland and their household watched the Corpus Christi festivities from the house of William Thixhill the Keepers paid for a dinner. In that year they also paid for paper, red wax, and red ink to make 'signs' for the feasts of Rogationtide and St John the Baptist.

The town was divided into wards, each ward being the responsibility of one of the Keepers. In 1436 ten townsmen were responsible for collecting enough money to equip one man-at-arms and his two archers. A tax was raised in each ward for contributions towards the wages of one archer.

The table below gives the number of people in each ward contributing towards the cost of one archer. This table shows Flemingate as having the largest number of people liable to pay tax while Norwood, which at this time was not fully developed, has the smallest.

Wards in 1436	No. of people contributing £1 towards the wages of one archer
North Bar Without	33
North Bar Within	40
Walkergate	36
Cornmarket (Saturday Market)	35
Alta Via	50
Fishmarket (Wednesday Market), Eastgate, Highgate)	44
Keldgate (Archiepiscopi)	
Provost's fee in Keldgate	54
Lathegate (now Lairgate)	41
Norwood	18
Flemingate	73
Barleyholme	41
Provost's fee at the Beck	38
Chapter Fee	22

By the beginning of the 15th century Beverley had lost its immunity from sending soldiers to the king's army. In 1405 recruits from Beverley were sent north to deal with lawlessness caused by the Earl of Northumberland and his followers. In 1445 archers were hired to guard the gates of the town. They were also positioned on the Westwood to protect the town during the Rogationtide procession against disturbances caused by the followers of the Earl of Northumberland and his family who were often at their castle at Leconfield.

In 1436 and 1449 six men-at-arms and twelve archers were sent to fight the Scots. There was no shortage of men wishing to receive soldiers' wages: one shilling a day for a man-at-arms and fifty pence a day for an archer. Equipping men for war was expensive and many soldiers from Beverley received at least part of their armour as a loan from the community. As soldiers from Beverley represented the town it was important, for the honour of the town, that they should be suitably equipped. In 1449 each man was provided with a heyke (similar to a livery jacket) of blue and white cloths costing 27s 4d. Red crosses were fixed to the heykes and embroidered. John Sixdyndale, a tailor in Beverley, was paid 7s. for assembling twenty-eight heykes for men-at-arms, archers, heynsmen and carriagemen. Only eighteen of the twenty-eight heykes made were for fighting men; the rest were for carriage men who controlled the baggage wagons which held supplies for the soldiers. In that year a blue and white banner with a silk fringe was provided with red cloth by which it was attached to the flagpole. Setting off for war was another colourful scene in the town as the men, their horses, their wagons and equipment assembled and rode off to join the king's forces.

The Merchants and Craftsmen

By the mid 15th century the wealth of the town began to decline as the centre of the cloth trade moved to the damper climate of the west of England. In 1439 the Keepers declared that because trade was 'greatly enfeebled' they were unable to lend money to the crown. By 1440 rents in Barleyholme (south side of the Beck), previously the wealthiest ward in Beverley, fell. Buildings became empty and property values declined.

In the mid 15th century family names such as Coppandale (the Coppandales held a moated manor house to the north of the town), Holme, Tirwhit appear repeatedly in the records and indicate the hold of certain merchants over the administration of the town. In mid 15th century some of these names disappear from the records and are replaced by new names such as Middleton, Gervays, Walkington, Brompton, Bewholme, Cockerill appear as people move from one area to another seeking employment.

Newcomers to the town often came from nearby. In earlier centuries the name Thomas de Ferriby or Henry de Snaith give the nameholders place of origin. When at the end of the 14th century English, rather than French, became the official language of the country the 'de' was dropped.

Wills and court records give a little information about the wealthy.

In 1428 John Rome, tanner, requested that one of two tenements in Flemingate be used for the free habitation of poor people.

1477 John Coppandale gave his servant Alice Sands the right to live in one of four houses he had built next to St Mary's churchyard.

1489 Robert Johnson, a dyer, in his will indicated that his house had a hall, a parlour, a summer hall and a high chamber. Furnishings included a flat piece of plate with white roses in the bottom and various soft furnishings including six cushions.

1494 William Rudd, tanner, requested burial in the north aisle of St Nicholas near the stall in which he was accustomed to sit.

Wealthy merchant families from Beverley at this time seemed to marry into the families of the county gentry. Agnes Creyke, a daughter and a widow of Beverley merchants, married Robert Hildyard of Winestead. A daughter of John Holme married into the St Quintin family of Holderness and a daughter of Thomas Frost (who died in 1496) married John Roos of Routh.

It is mainly only through marriages that we get information about the wealthier women of Beverley. For them there was little choice of partners and marriage arrangements usually started with a business meeting to discuss the dowry and land or riches which the two families would exchange at the marriage. After contracts had been exchanged there would be a formal betrothal ceremony in the church porch. Inheritance went to the male and women owned little property of their own.

Beverley merchants also traded with influential families; in his will of 1471 Henry Holme asks that two retainers of the Earl of Northumberland, Robert Constable of Flamborough and Ralph Hotham, should be his executors. Merchant families also intermarried within the town and left bequests to other families - the Coppandales, Creykes, Elands and Middletons.

As usual, information on the poorer inhabitants of Beverley at this time is sparse and women are barely mentioned in the records apart from Agnes Tiler who is mentioned as providing tiles for the building of the North Bar.

John Brompton, Wool Merchant

John Brompton, a Beverley wool merchant, was for two years a Keeper of the town though on one occasion was fined 5d for being away from Beverley when he should have been attending council meetings.

15th century East Yorkshire provided many dangers for wealthy merchants travelling with money. In 1441 John Brompton presented a petition in the House of Commons against John Hayton. He pleaded that when riding from York to Beverley with a small number of attendants he had been ambushed by John Hayton and twenty-four of his companions, several of whom were armed with bows and arrows and all of whom were masked. Many arrows had been fired, one of his attendants had been maimed and he and his attendants had been dangerously wounded. He said that on this journey he had been carrying a considerable sum of public money and complained that being in constant fear of his life his mercantile and other business had had to be suspended. He asked that the Chancellor of England, by the authority of Parliament, might issue a writ to the Sheriff of Yorkshire that John Hayton and his accomplices be brought to justice.

His will dated 9th July 1444 tells us much about his lifestyle. At the time of his death he was owed money by the Earl of Northumberland, a Hull merchant, John Bedford, and unidentified debtors listed in his 'little red book'.

His will begins by asking the whole host of heaven to receive his soul after his death and then goes on to describe his house which consisted of:

> A hall; a parlour, the great chamber, the forechamber, the withdrawing chamber, the servants' quarters and a waterhouse chamber, besides domestic offices.

He gives details of his enormous collection of plate and other luxury goods; his piety is revealed by his mention of:

> A standing piece of silver gilt ornamented with St Michael and the dragon, a bed of arras work with the picture of the Virgin Mary and the three kings, a great chair of Flanders work, and a chest carved with St George and other scenes.

He mentions three almshouses at the back of Hallgarth which he had founded and which he wanted to reserve for the use of the poor for ever. He made bequests to humble families in Langtoft and West Heslerton – perhaps this is where his origins were. He made bequests to religious East Riding houses.

He left his body to be buried in the Collegiate Church of the Blessed John of Beverley, near the body of his wife, Ellen, with instructions that,

> At his obsequies, thirteen poor men should carry candles and be clothed in russet, at his expense. A further sixty poor of both sexes were to be clothed in cheaper cloth.

He left £18 to be distributed among the poor as well as money for a meal for the poor and his friends. The codicil to his will states:

> Likewise, I give and bequeath to the building and adornment of the Parish Church of Eton, 6s 8d; of South Burton (Bishop Burton), 3s 4d; of North Burton (Cherry Burton), 5s; of Walkington, 6s 8d; of Cottingham, 10s; of Hess ill, 5s; of the Chapel of Swanland, 3s 4d; of North Ferriby, 3s 4d; of the Chapel of Melton, 3s 4d,; of Ellyngton, 5s; of Brantynghm, 3s 4d; of Ellerker, 5s; of South Cave, 5s; North Cave, 3s 4d; of the Chapel of Hotham, 3s 4d; Sancton, 3s 4d., etc.

The Merchant Guilds

The merchant guilds continued to control the lives of their members and to protect their crafts from newcomers. Towards the end of the century several guilds amalgamated.

The Guild of Tilers ordered that from Easter to 15th August work was to begin at 4 o'clock in the morning and finish at 7 o'clock in the evening - with short breaks in between. From 15th August to Easter work was to begin at the beginning of the day and finish when the light failed.

The Orders of the Drapers of 1493 quite clearly sets out the aims of the guild which involved religious observances as well as trade regulation:

a.   There should be a brotherhood for the maintenance of a wooden castle to be erected on Mondays in Rogation week. Every master of the craft should sit in his best clothes and apparel in the same castle at the coming of the procession of the shrine of St John. Anyone absent, if he was in the town, should pay 6s 8d to the community.

b.   The Drapers were to light a candle of wax before the image of St Michael the Archangel in the church of the Blessed Mary the Virgin burning Sundays and other feast-days throughout the year.

c.   The Drapers should perform on the feast of Corpus Christi a play called 'Dooming Pilate,' every year.

d.   The Drapers could make hose and keep apprentices and servants sewing in their shops.

e.   The twelve Keepers of the town and aldermen of the Drapers agreed that any burgess, who carried on the buying and selling of cloth by retail in the town of Beverley, should be in the brotherhood and livery with the said Drapers or pay £10 to the community.

f.   Anyone elected to the office of alderman of the Drapers and refusing to serve should pay to the use of the community and to the maintenance of the castle and pageant, 3s.4d to be equally divided.

g.   Drapers should elect from amongst themselves searchers to examine the accuracy of all yardwands (a yardwand was a yardstick i.e. a three-foot rod for measuring) and look out for other defaults or injuries pertaining to the craft or mystery of Drapers. If any injuries or defaults were found they were to be reported to the keepers.

Timber and Thatch

Grander houses of the 13th and 14th centuries generally consisted of a high central hall of one storey with an open hearth in the middle of the floor and smoke rising through a slatted ventilation set in the roof. Usually the house would be end-on to the street, although in an area with plenty of room it would front onto the street, with living quarters on the frontage and kitchen area at the rear. Most probably it would be built of timber with a thatch roof. Infill could be wattle (strong small interwoven branches of hazel) covered with daub (a form of clay plaster) or brick. In Beverley stone, which was expensive to transport, would only be used by the extremely wealthy.

Reconstruction of a Post and Cob Building

Changes in the structure of houses began in the 15th century when fireplaces and chimneys were set at the side of a room instead of the open hearth in the centre. Houses would now be of two or three storeys with attic roof spaces for domestic accommodation. Very often upper floors would overhang lower floors in order to provide extra space. If access was not available at the back there would be a passage way through the house. Only in the more opulent houses would there be glass; windows would be medium sized and protected with shutters or sacking.

No domestic buildings in Beverley today pre-date the 15th century, although parts of the houses in St John Street date from before that period. North Bar Within, the broadest street in medieval Beverley, has the best surviving timber-framed house of the 15th century at the entrance to St Mary's Court. This two storeyed house rests on a chalk foundation (houses up until the end of the twelfth century would have stood on the damp earth with the result that the timber would rot). It has a steep pitched roof suitable for thatch. The side, with its medieval mullion window, is jetted so that the upper storey overhangs the lower but the area beneath the jetty at the front has now been filled in.

Other 15th century buildings in the town include the Sun Inn and the Lord Nelson pub (with its extension which now faces the railway line) in Flemingate. A few interiors of this time remain in houses whose frontage has been altered to suit the fashion of the day.

Murder at Topcliffe

In 1480 the 4th Earl of Northumberland was perhaps the most powerful nobleman in England. At the battle of Bosworth, 1485, the Earl and his forces stood at the top of a hill watching how the battle proceeded. Richard III was killed. The new king, Henry VII, was displeased with the Earl for not supporting him and ordered that he should be imprisoned in the Tower of London. After his release the king, in 1489, gave the Earl the task of telling the people at Topcliffe (North Yorkshire) that, despite opposition, the king intended to impose further taxes. The mob stormed the Earl's house and killed him. Henry ordered that the burial of 'his most faythful servant' should be carried out with pomp worthy almost of royalty - all expenses to be paid by the Percys. In his will of 1485, the Earl had expressed the wish that if he died in Yorkshire he was to be buried in Beverley Minster.

The Earl's body was carried in procession from Topcliffe, to his castle at Wressle. From there it was taken to Leconfield and then on to Beverley Minster. The procession was led by twelve lords clothed in cloth of gold, twenty gentlewomen, sixty squires in gowns and tippets, 200 outfitted yeomen, 160 poor folk in black gowns and carrying torches, 500 priests, 1000 clergy and 100 grooms in livery. The Minster was draped with 400 yards of black cloth. Every poor person who visited the grave on the day of burial received dole of 2d, which was distributed to 13,340 souls; each priest present at the burial received 12d and each clerk 4d. The total cost of the funeral was £5,262.

The 4th Earl's eldest son, known as Henry the Magnificent because of his lavish lifestyle, built the Northumberland Chapel on the north east corner of the Minster to house the table top tomb which, until the 18th century, was surmounted by a battlemented

An Old House in North Bar Street Within altered in 1827.

Timber house on the corner of North Bar Within and Tiger Lane

canopy resting on tall, freestanding supports. The north window in the chapel, with its flattened Tudor arch, was built in memory of the 4th Earl who is shown in the stained glass window with his wife and their children, kneeling on either side of a shield bearing his coat of arms. Associated with the tomb was an altar at which five priests were to pray for the souls of the earl, his wife and their ancestors.

A tomb for the 5th Earl (died 1527) was also placed in the chapel and after the death of his wife in 1542 she, following her own wish, was interred with her husband. This tomb no longer exists.

The century ended with Henry VII on the throne and stability restored throughout England. This stability in Beverley and elsewhere was to be short lived for in the following century Henry VIII was to bring about a complete change to the town.

CHAPTER 8

1500 – 1600. DESCENT INTO THE VALLEY

By the beginning of the 16th century most areas of established beliefs were under scrutiny - the Renaissance (re-birth) was well under way.

In 1509 Hugh Goes received a licence from the magistrates in Beverley to establish a printing press in Highgate. Maybe from his press were circulated the thoughts of humanists centred round Erasmus of Rotterdam, the ideas put forward by Copernicus that the earth moved round the sun and not the sun round the earth as had previously been thought, or the discovery of Columbus, who in 1492 had sailed to the New World and home again, that the earth was round.

Purchase of the Guildhall

In 1122, Archbishop Thurstan had granted the burgesses of Beverley the right to have a hanse house, or guildhall, in which they could meet and discuss the administration of the town. The twelve Keepers of the town had met in a variety of places - the archbishop's hall in Saturday Market, property owned by St Mary's church, and in the merchants' guild hall in Walkergate, near Cross Bridge; a hall mentioned in documents but the exact site of which is unknown.

In 1501 a permanent meeting place was found which was to be the home of the borough council for the next 500 years. The Keepers bought from Edward Mynskip, for the sum of £73 6s 8d, a house which dated back to 1320 – described as a 'great messuage' in Cross Garths with a 'long chamber'. This great timber house, with its medieval central hall and 14th century screens passageway (uncovered in 1981) leading to the kitchens, was the following year repaired. A stone arched entrance with the Episcopal arms of the archbishop, which probably came from the guildhall in Walkergate, was placed at the entrance.

The merchants' guilds continued to have influence over the town and to protect Beverley traders from newcomers. Any newcomer to the town wishing to set up in business had to be accepted as a brother of the fraternity or pay a tribute to the guild. The drapers, like other traders, insisted that all who were involved in the buying and selling of woollen cloth should have served seven years at the trade. Strangers who brought cloth into the town were permitted to cut it only on market days; otherwise they were to sell by wholesale to registered drapers. Trade guilds were to be protected; no draper was to be a merchant or mercer and no merchant or mercer was to act as a draper. Drapers, on the other hand, were free to make round hose stockings for women and socks without making any financial contribution to the Tailors' Guild.

Each year, on the Sunday after Trinity, members of the merchants' guild met in the Common Hall to elect a warden, two stewards and two searchers. Fines for those elected but not taking up office were 40s (£2) for the warden, 6s 8d (33p) for a steward and 10s (50p) for a searcher. The duty of the searchers was to see that standards of trade were maintained – they were expected to ensure that weights or yards used as measurement were correct. Loyalty to the guild was expected and members were punished for slander and fined if they were disrespectful

Re-building the Tower and Nave of St. Mary's Church

On 25th April 1520, during a service, the west side of the central tower of St Mary's church collapsed, destroying the nave and killing men, women and children in the congregation. Sir Thomas More wrote that more might have died had not many townspeople been at a bear baiting. The rebuilding, which took four years, was mostly paid for by Beverley people. Sir Richard Rokeby, comptroller of the household of the archbishop of York, was in Beverley in 1522 when he was a commissioner for a muster of troops on the Westwood on the king's behalf. He died on 27th April 1523 and in his will left £200 for the repair of St Mary's church. Robert Halitreholme, rector of Bidenham in Bedfordshire, a native of Beverley, left 20s for repair of the church in his will of 1525.

Sponsors for pillars in the nave have a permanent memorial, for label stops between the pillars have carvings of benefactors and officials rather than angels and saints. On the north side of the nave, beginning at the west end, the inscriptions under the figures read:

'Xlay and hys wyffe made thes to pyllors and a halffe',
'thys to pyllos made gud wyffys God reward them',
'thys pyllor made the maynstrels.

On the last pillar stand five figures representing the Guild of Minstrels. Originally each figure carried a musical instrument, but only two instruments have survived. The central figure, representing the Guild's President, is shown wearing a badge of office, the 15th century medallion, which was presented to the town of Beverley in the early 17th century and is now part of the civic regalia. At Rogationtide, the Guild of Minstrels between the Trent and the Tweed met in Beverley to choose an alderman.

The figures on the label stops on the south side of the nave, according to the early 20th century architect for St Mary's, WCB Smith, were likely to be various officials. Starting from the east end there is:

An official with a square cap,
A civic dignitary with a flat cap,
Young Henry VIII,
The archbishop of York, Cardinal Wolsey,
An archbishop
Civic dignitary.

The Guild of Minstrels Musicians, St Mary's Church

In the first few months of 1530 William Leryfax must have known that he was dying. On the dark-grey Derbyshire marble font in St Mary's is an inscription which asks for prayers for the soul of William Leryfax, draper, and his wife who made this font at his own cost on the 10th day of March in the year of our Lord 1530. In his will of 22nd December 1530 he bequeathed a woman's damask gown to the prior of Watton and a damask tunic to the abbot of Meaux on the understanding that both were to take charge of his inheritance and oversee the bringing up of his son Robert.

Also around 1530 the present stone vault of the porch of St Mary's church was built completing the beautifully proportioned room that we see today.

Misericord Seats

Both St Mary's church and Beverley Minster have a set of carved misericord seats. Misericords, or 'mercy seats', placed in

St Mary's 'Elephant' Misericord Seat

the choir of a church, were a concession to members of the clergy who were expected to remain standing during long services, day or night. Each seat, when raised, provides a ledge on which the old and weary can lean. Beneath, these wooden seats are carved with a scene from everyday life of men or women surrounded by beasts and foliage; the animals shown often have symbolic meanings. Religious themes were not considered suitable for a seat which would be sat on.

St Mary's set of twenty-eight beautifully carved seats date to the mid-15th century. They were carved by the Ripon School of Carvers who were responsible for most of the wood placed in large northern churches and monasteries during the 15th and 16th centuries. Carvings under the seats include an ape as a doctor, a

St Mary's 'Preaching Fox' Misericord Seat

134

knight and two-legged dragon with a barbed tail (a wyvern), two green men, a knight and a boar, a king, a pelican, a fox and monks, an eagle and foxes, an elephant (clearly carved by someone who had never seen an elephant) and castle – this theme is also in the Minster carvings. The name 'Watton' is scratched on the back of the seats in several places which may imply that these misericords were originally made for the priory church at Watton but that after the dissolution they were moved to St Mary's church, Beverley. Until the late 19th century they were placed in the two chancel aisles before St Michael's chapel and St Katherine's chapel. When the Victorian architect, Gilbert Scott, rearranged the chancel in 1875 they were placed in their present position.

Beverley Minster has sixty-eight seats - the largest collection of medieval misericord seats of any church in the country, placed in the church in 1520. The makers are undocumented, although it is probable that these seats were also the work of the Ripon School of Carvers. A depiction of a fox dressed as a friar preaching from a pulpit to a congregation of seven silly geese, is a reminder of a 14th century stone carving in the north aisle of the Minster which tells the story of friars stealing members of the congregation. However, in the 16th century misericord the fox is shown being hanged by the geese as they get their revenge.

Struggles for Control of the Town

In 1535 an act of parliament stated that many houses in Beverley were 'in great ruin and decaye and specially in the pryncipalle and chief stretes'. In the 1530s vacant houses and plots are frequently mentioned.

Much of Beverley was still under the control of two ecclesiastical groups; the archbishop of York, Lord of the Manor of Beverley, and the provost and canons of the Minster. However, during the first half of the century the power of the archbishop was to be questioned for the Keepers would have preferred any fines or penalties imposed on townspeople to be added to the coffers of the Keepers rather than the pockets of the archbishop, provost or canons.

Cardinal Wolsey, already a privy councillor and soon to become lord chancellor of England, was at Henry VIII's suggestion, elected archbishop of York, an office he held from 1514 - 1530. As he never visited York, deputies performed his episcopal functions and his manor house in Beverley fell into ruin. Wolsey had expensive tastes and soon was short of money. Realising that monasteries were a useful source of income he procured a bull from the pope authorising him to bring about reforms; a later papal bull entitled him to suppress twenty-one religious houses whose revenues he then used to build his colleges at Oxford and Ipswich.

The Percys also had influence in the town of Beverley. Although by now the 5th Earl of Northumberland, Henry the Magnificent, had made his castle at Wressle his principal place of residence he continued to use his castle at Leconfield (the place of his birth) for entertainments and for hunting in the park. Borough records mention monies paid to Percy retainers and servants on several occasions. In 1502 the twelve Keepers of Beverley were invited by the Earl to breakfast at Leconfield Castle. In return for so distinguished a favour the Keepers, for the honour of the town, presented the Earl with 'ten capons, four swans, six heronwes, two bitterns and four sholands'. The Earl quarrelled with Cardinal Wolsey and was imprisoned in the Tower of London were, in 1527, he died 'a broken and trembling man'. His body was placed in a monument in the Northumberland Chapel in Beverley Minster.

A follower of the Percys was Sir Ralph Ellerker. From 1401 until the death of their last male heir in 1655 the Ellerker family held land at Risby, three miles south-west of Beverley. Sir Ralph and his three sons had all been knighted after the Battle of Flodden in 1513 in which the English army so decisively defeated the Scots.

In 1516 Sir Ralph Ellerker (who died in 1539) and his son, also called Ralph (who died in 1546), incurred the wrath of Cardinal Wolsey by hunting in the archiepiscopal deer park to the south of Beverley. When questioned, Sir Ralph admitted to kidnapping George Millet (keeper of the park) and imprisoning him at Cottingham.

In 1528 Wolsey's anger was directed towards the 6th Earl of Northumberland. He made a complaint to the Star Chamber (a London court set up by the Crown in late 15th century and so named because it was held in a room with a star painted ceiling) about the unruly activities of the Earl and his followers. Apparently the Earl had dismissed Wolsey's nominee for the office of Town Clerk of Beverley. The Earl, or his followers, had then beaten up the provost's bailiff for keeping company with the archbishop's nominated clerk. As the provost, Thomas Winter, was Cardinal Wolsey's natural son by Mistress Larke, who was herself sister of the canon of St James's altar at Beverley Minster, the Earl's actions seem a deliberate insult to Wolsey. The Earl's servants were also accused of threatening the life of Sir Robert Constable of Holme on Spalding Moor while he was at dinner in Beverley and of attacking and wounding William Buckbray, an armourer, while he was at work in his shop in the town.

The following year the Earl's supporters, armed with 'bows, bills and arrows' viciously attacked and beat up a servant of Sir John Hotham of Scorborough because of a boundary dispute between Sir John and the Earl.

In 1530 Wolsey fell from favour with the king and was apprehended by royal servants while at his palace at Cawood; he died on his way to London. The next year, Edward Lee, who was to support the king in his divorce of Catherine of Aragon and marriage to Anne Boleyn, became the new archbishop of York. Although generally conservative in matters of doctrine he encouraged the clergy in the reading of the Bible in English and the importance of preaching. From 1543 – 1548 his kinsman, Reginald Lee, was provost of Beverley Minster.

In 1534 Sir Ralph Ellerker (died 1539) bought a property in Beverley and thereby made himself eligible for election as a governor of the town; on 25th April he was duly elected. In December, in order to appease discontented townsmen, the archbishop restored some disputed privileges to them. Early in the new year the archbishop announced that the practice of existing

137

governors nominating thirty-four burgesses from whom the future governors could be elected had lapsed (blaming certain inhabitants of the town who had tried to control elections – presumably referring to Ellerker and his friends). The archbishop then nominated twenty-four councillors from whom the governors could be chosen at the next election. On 25th April Sir Ralph got himself re-elected together with seven other retiring governors. Archbishop Lee accused him of breaking the rules - for governors were permitted to serve for one year only - and also of kidnapping fourteen members of the opposition; the archbishop declared the election null and void and nominated commissioners to investigate. However, on arrival in Beverley they were unable to carry out their inquiries for Sir Ralph opposed them with a small army of 140 well-armed men stationed in the town.

The archbishop appealed to the Star Chamber which declared the election null and void and announced that there should be new elections on 20th December. Orders were issued that governors were not to serve in consecutive years and that those living outside the town were not to be governors or meddle in elections, even if they bought a house or land in Beverley. Ellerker, his son-in-law and several others were debarred from office.

At the same time, Sir Ralph Ellerker, his son-in-law and friends continued to poach in the archbishop's park taking buck and about 300 deer.

On 25th April, 1536, voting should have taken place. However, the archbishop, in order to avoid a repetition of the violence of previous years, postponed the elections. This led several inhabitants of the town to fear that if there was no election they might lose their rights so they decided to go ahead and hold the election on the usual day. When they arrived at the Common Hall (the Guildhall) they found it was locked against them. So they climbed onto the roof to ring the bell 'and thries did ryng the same bell with such violence and fury that they caused the same belle to be out of frame'. They broke into the hall and swore in twelve governors from amongst themselves forcing the elderly town clerk to enter the names in the record. The ringleader was

William Wyse who seems to have been a professional agitator who, before coming to the town of Beverley, had been expelled from several towns for causing strife.

Bishop John Fisher

In 1534, the Act of Supremacy, agreed to by Archbishop Lee, established Henry VIII as Supreme Head of the Church in England. One of the opponents of the act was John Fisher, Bishop of Rochester.

John Fisher was born in Beverley in 1469. His father, Robert, died in 1477 and in his will left money to churches in Beverley and in Lincolnshire (from where the family probably originated), the cathedral church in York, the two friaries in Beverley and to his family. After his death he was buried in St Mary's church.

John Fisher was one of four children. He was educated at the school in Beverley, situated in the south-west corner of the Minster graveyard, and Michaelhouse (later Trinity College) at Cambridge University. He was consecrated priest at York in December 1491. He returned to Cambridge and by the age of thirty-two had been elected vice-chancellor of the University. He later became chaplain to Margaret Beaufort, Countess of Richmond and Derby and mother of Henry VII. In 1504 he became Bishop of Rochester, resigned as Master of Michaelhouse and Vice Chancellor of the university, but was then immediately elected chancellor. He believed in the necessity of scholarship in the priesthood and accordingly did much to increase the standard of the study of theology at the university. With the financial support of his patron, Margaret Beaufort, he founded two colleges at Cambridge University: Christ's (a refoundation of an older Hall) and St John's (a refoundation of a hospital dedicated to St John the Evangelist). Both colleges are today linked with the name of Bishop John Fisher. Links between the bishop and Beverley were maintained for Robert Halitreeholme, who had attended Beverley Grammar School with John Fisher, established a Fellowship at St John's College to be held by a fellow born within the town of Beverley and in 1526 Lady Joan Rokeby, widow of Sir Richard, also endowed a fellowship to St John's College, Cambridge, for scholars from Beverley Grammar School. Further endowments from wealthy citizens of Beverley ensured that over the next three hundred years many boys from Beverley Grammar School were able to attend St John's College, Cambridge.

Bishop John Fisher believed in the authority of the church and was opposed to anything which might undermine the power of the pope. When Henry VIII precipitated a rift with the pope by seeking the annulment of his marriage to his Queen, Catherine of Aragon, Bishop Fisher upheld the validity of the marriage. Fisher refused to sign the Act of Supremacy which, in 1534, effectively annulled the marriage and accepted that Queen Anne was now the rightful queen; Fisher refused to swear the oath and, consequently, was imprisoned in the Tower of London. Later in the year a new act made it treason to deny that the King was Supreme Head of the Church in England. In 1535 Bishop John was brought to trial and executed on Tower Hill. 400 years after his death he was canonised by the Roman Catholic Church.

The Pilgrimage of Grace

In 1535 commissioners were sent by the king to assess the value of the smaller monasteries with a view to their being dissolved. Monks and nuns were questioned about their code of behaviour; dubious charges of immorality, indecency, promiscuity, homosexuality, and witchcraft were made, misdemeanours exaggerated and excuses found as to why a particular monastery should be dissolved.

The suppression of all religious houses valued at less than £200 a year occurred in 1536. Monks and nuns were forced to leave; most were given small pensions, monks took positions in other churches, nuns could return to their families.

Medieval hospitals also were suppressed, taken into ownership of the Crown and then sold or given away. Hospitals in Beverley were:

St Giles's Hospital which stood on the west side of Lairgate, to the north of Minster Moorgate. It was dissolved in 1536 and bought by Robert Gray. In 1753 it was sold to Thomas Pennyman and Lairgate Hall, was later built on the site.

St Nicholas's Hospital, with its chantry chapel, stood north-east of the Minster, near Chantry Lane. At the time of the suppression it was worth £5 6s 5d. In 1549 the Crown granted the house, chapel and three acres of land to Sir Michael Stanhope and John Bellow. Later the Wartons bought it. Part of a moat around the close still existed in the late 19th century.

The Hospital of the Holy Trinity stood in Toll Gavel, next to Cross Bridge. At the time of the suppression it was worth £3 12s. By 1556 it had been acquired by the corporation; for a time it was maintained as a maison dieu before being used as a prison. It was demolished in 1810.

St John the Baptist's Hospital stood on the east side of Butcher Row, close to Wednesday Market. It included a chapel with a chantry and was worth £7 8s 2d at the time of the suppression. In 1585 it was included in a Crown grant to the corporation and was maintained as a maison dieu.

St John the Evangelist's Hospital stood on the west side of Lairgate, near the southern end of the street. In 1585 the Crown granted it to the corporation which maintained it as a maison dieu.

St Mary's Hospital stood on the east side of North Bar Without, next to the bar. By 1557 it had been acquired by the corporation and was maintained as a maison dieu. It was demolished in the early 19th century.

Commissioners, employed by the king were instructed to value the possessions in parish churches; in Beverley they made a visitation to the Dominican and Franciscan friaries to assess their worth. People began to fear where this would lead.

In the autumn of 1536 much of the north of England rose in rebellion against the king's policies towards the lesser monasteries. The leader of the rebellion, known as the Pilgrimage of Grace, was Robert Aske from Aughton, a lawyer who claimed that the uprising was not a rebellion but rather a movement to defend the Church and impress upon Henry the shortcomings of his royal advisers. The rising began in Louth on 1st October and within a few days 'all Lincolnshire was up from Barton to Lincoln'.

On 5th October messages about the uprising in Lincolnshire crossed the Humber and were brought to Beverley. Knowledge of the uprising in Beverley comes from a record of the trial for treason of William Stapleton. In his defence William said that he, his elder brother Christopher, who was described as 'weak, crazed and impotent, lame in hand and foot', and their families, were staying at Greyfriars – the Franciscan friary.

Early in the morning of 8th October the town bell was rung in Beverley market place. William Stapleton, on his brother's behalf, ordered all members of their families to stay inside Greyfriars, while one of their servants went to the market place to see what was happening. The servant returned and told them that a proclamation had been made for every man to come in and take his oath to join the rebels on pain of death, and that Richard Wilson, a town governor, with a copy of the oath in one hand and a Bible in the other was swearing them in. Later a call was made for every man to appear at Hall Garth. After the proclamation every man appeared on Westwood green, near Greyfriars. There was a great noise, shouts and cries until the men were told to return to the Westwood the following day with such horse and harness as they had. As they departed Christopher's wife, despite her husband's injunction to stay indoors, went forth and stood in a close where a great number of the rebels were coming from either side of the hedge and said 'God's blessing have ye' and 'speed ye well in your purpose'. They asked where her husband and relations were. She replied, 'they are in the friary. Go pull them out by the head.'

When Christopher heard of this he became more confused than ever and wished that he were dead. He asked her what she meant by disobeying his orders and was worried that because of her behaviour he and his brother would be out of favour with the king and his heirs disinherited forever. She answered, 'It is God's quarrel.'

Later Christopher wanted to know the reason for the commotion and unrest. He was told that it was mainly revenge on old grudges and quarrels and dissention amongst the townsfolk, caused by the rift between the archbishop of York and the people for their rights. Some took the side of the archbishop and some the side of the town. One follower of the archbishop was almost slain on the Westwood.

Between the 8th and 11th October the rebellion centred on Beverley and there were daily assemblies on the Westwood for swearing adherents and the making of plans. William Stapleton's defence continued -

Everyman kept his hour on the Westwood and assembled there, all the town being sworn. Christopher Sanderson and Sir Ralph Ellerker (who were both involved in the uprising but had refused to lead the rebels) came to Greyfriars to ask Christopher whether he intended to join the rebels. He said that he was prepared to give them advice but not to be sworn in because he was sworn to be loyal to the king. They would not agree. When this was reported to the rebels on the green certain wild people felt that they should go and burn the friary down and members of the Stapleton family with it while others dissuaded them, especially because of Christopher's illness. Instead men were sent to Greyfriars and Christopher and two of his servants were sworn in. William, with the rest of the family, was taken to the green where between 400 – 500 rebels came towards them crying with terrible shouts. William saw the murderous gleam in those wild men's eyes and heard them shouting for him to be their captain. After much persuasion William Stapleton agreed to be their governor and they agreed to take his advice so long as it was not against the oath. He managed to calm their old grudges, restore friendship among them and gained an agreement that all old wounds were to be forgotten. They all agreed to go to Cottingham and Hessle and raise members of those towns to join them. That night some of them set off to fire Hunsley beacon; however as the beacon was not built they fired the hedges and haystacks instead. The chain of beacon fires spread across the Riding.

(From the trew confession of William Stapulton of the attempts committed and doon by hym against the kynges highness and the lawe)

The men of Holderness, Hullshire and Cottingham helped the rebels. From 15th – 20th October Hull was under siege, during which a sanctuary man from Beverley was soused in the river for plundering. Defence of Hull was under the leadership of Sir Ralph Ellerker (died 1546); Pontefract was also under siege. With a force of 30,000 men the rebels advanced from York towards Doncaster. Here, on 26th October they met the royal army of 11,000 men under the leadership of the Duke of Norfolk; a truce was negotiated and the armies dispersed. Aske believed that they had accomplished what they had set out to do, for the king had promised to right many of the grievances of the men and to hold a parliament in York made up of burgesses from northern towns, including Beverley. Aske received an invitation to present himself at court. He spent Christmas in London and then returned north to report the success of the mission.

In the north, however, rumours continued that a royal force was being gathered and suspicion of the king's intentions resulted in a second uprising. On 10th January, John Hallam of Cawkeld, near Watton, described as 'so fierce and cruel a man among his neighbours that no man durst disobey him', and Sir Francis Bigod of Settrington, went to Watton Priory. After supper, in the prior's lodging, although the prior, Robert Holgate, was away, in the presence of the sub-prior and two other monks sitting by the fire, they discussed how to pursue their quarrel with the King. After this meeting an army was gathered and on 18th January Sir Francis Bigod, with several hundred men, entered Beverley but the following day they were driven out by Sir Ralph Ellerker. This second rising in East Yorkshire, being opposed by Aske, was quickly stopped.

Once the rebels had disbanded Henry reneged on his promise of a pardon and 216 men were tried and executed. Aske was hanged at York, Hallam at Hull, and Bigod in London. The abbots of Jerveaulx and Fountains abbeys and the prior of Bridlington were hanged and in February 1537 the-sub prior of Watton Abbey was hung in chains at the abbey. The Duke of Norfolk reported to the King that on Sunday, 8th July 1537

On Friday being market day at Hull, Sir Robert Constable (governor of Hull) suffered, his body doth hang above the highest gate of the town, so trimmed in chains …that I think his bones will hang there this hundred year.

William Stapleton was pardoned. A general pardon, with the exception of Richard Wilson and William Woodmansey, was given to the people of Beverley.

Administration from London proved to be difficult. In 1538 the Council of the North was set up in the King's Manor, once the abbot's lodging of St Mary's Abbey in York, to act as a Star Chamber of the north.

Dissolution of the Friaries and Greater Monasteries

Uprisings and protestations did nothing to stop Henry VIII in his determination to break with the Church of Rome and gather for himself the wealth of religious establishments in England.

On 25th February 1539 the Dominican Friary in Beverley - also known as Black Friars - (with rents of just over £5 a year), its four-acre site and buildings (with a church as large as St Mary's, Beverley) was dissolved and claimed by the king. Its plate was sent to the royal treasury. Lead from the windows was melted down, reusable tiles taken away together with pipes and timber. The following day the Franciscan Friary outside Keldgate, on a seven-acre site, surrendered; it was demolished in the same manner.

Two monastic establishments which over the years must have contributed much to the wealth of Beverley were also dissolved in 1539. The great abbey at Meaux (annual income of £298) and the priory at Watton (annual revenue of £360) were dissolved. Following the king's visit to Hull in 1541, stone from Meaux Abbey was used to build a castle and blockhouses on the east side of the river Hull with the result that on the site where the abbey once stood, only a few earthworks and a ditch give an indication of the whereabouts of monastic buildings. At Watton, Robert Holgate, the prior, in return for surrendering the priory was permitted to keep the prior's lodgings and the refectory of the monastery as a private residence. He was also made archbishop of York. As at Meaux, undulations in the landscape indicate where other monastic buildings and cloisters were. The prior's lodging and the refectory remain as a private house.

The Dissolution of Religious Institutions

In 1540 the order of the Knights of the Hospitallers was abolished and the Holy Trinity preceptory in Beverley (at that time the richest commandery of the order) and land in the East Riding owned by the Knights was claimed by the king.

Also in that year, the Right of Sanctuary was abolished. Between 1500 and October 1539, when the last sanctuary man had been received at Beverley Minster, 365 sanctuary seekers had been registered, mostly from Yorkshire but others came from different areas of England and Wales. Most were accused of debt, homicide or other crimes. People accused of treason could claim the right of sanctuary - hence Henry VIII's wish to abolish it.

John Leland Visits Beverley

Around 1540 John Leland, keeper of the king's libraries, travelled through Yorkshire searching for ancient books and manuscripts in English monasteries and colleges. Below is a description of what he found in Beverley.

The Minster - the church of St John is 'of a fair uniforme making' – the 'prebendaries houses stand round aboute St John's chirche yard wherof the Bishop of York hath one motid, but al yn ruine. The fairest part of the provostes house is the gate and the front. There be besides yn the chirch of (blank) and the chirch of St Nicolas by the holm, wher the gut (stream) for the catchis is of St Mary's chirch, at the north ende of the toune, is larg, and fair, and crosse islid. In the toune were of late 2 housis of freres and 4 hospitales; St Giles' which belonged to the canons of Warter Priory. 'Trinite Hospital yet stondith yn the hart of the toun… Ther was a hospital of St Nicolas by the Blak Freres, but it is dekayid. Ther is an hospitale yet standying hard without the north Bargate…. Ther is an house also of the Trinite aboute the est side of the toune; and longgid to the order of the Knighttes of St John's

The toune of Beverle is large and welle buildid of wood. But the fairest part of it is by north, and ther is the market kept. Ther was good cloth making at Beverle; but that is nowe much decayid. The toune is not waullid: but yet be there there many fair gates of brike…..certain gates of stone portcolesed for defence. ….Ther is a great gut (the Beck) cut from the town to the ripe of Hulle Ryver, wherby preaty vesseles cum thyther. Ther cummeth owt of the Bisshopes parke, Westwoode, therby a little fresch broke to the town.

Leland commented that the archbishop's house is moated but all in ruin. It is likely that some of the prebendal houses might also have fallen into disrepair for by this time the canons of Beverley Minster seldom made an appearance in the town. They were generally politically ambitious priests who had received their prebendaries as gifts from Wolsey, who had little interest in the town or the traditions of the church, and merely collected payments from their prebends and from donations to the altars in their chapels in the Minster. The stipulation that senior clerics were to reside in the town for a specified number of weeks in order to receive their corrodies no longer existed.

By this time the population of Beverley is estimated at approximately 5,000. At the Minster it was the eight vicars and the fourteen chantry priests who had contact with the people of the parish and who carried on the daily services in the choir before the eight altars of the canons. The vicars continued to live communally in the Bedern. Testators of the parish continued to ask that they be buried in the Minster or its churchyard. People requested that they be buried before the statue of Our Lady of the Red Ark or before the images of St John the Evangelist and St Mary. Money was bequeathed to images of the saints and to the shrines – for example Cecily Lepington left 6s 8d to the shrine of St John, along with her blue girdle as well as her best bed covering to the Easter Sepulchre. William Leryfax ordered the purchase of two copes and a further two velvet copes with the images of St John of Beverley and St George, embroidered in gold, should he die without heirs (his prayers were obviously successful for he produced a son who was mentioned in his will).

Generally, trade and craft guilds continued to maintain candles burning before the altars of the guilds and the guilds and townspeople still took part in the Rogation tide procession of the shrine round the town. The Corpus Christi Day performance of the Mystery Plays had, however, lapsed.

In September 1541 Henry VIII, already gross in stature and with ulcerated legs, undertook a northern progress in order to demonstrate his authority to an area of the country where some of the old religious ways were still followed. With his new young wife, Catherine Howard, (who was already dallying with her lover Culpepper) and his retinue of followers he arrived in Lincoln on 9th August. Here the King and Queen retired to a tent in order to change their gowns of green and crimson velvet for cloth of gold and silver. They then entered the cathedral where a carpet, stools and cushions of cloth of gold awaited them and a service was held. From Lincoln they progressed to York and by mid-October moved to Hull. On the journey the King visited the home of Sir Ralph Ellerker (died 1546) at Risby and stayed at the Percy house at Leconfield. There are no records of a royal progress to Beverley but certainly the people must have been aware of the near presence of this powerful monarch.

In 1542 Archbishop Lee gave up the 600-year-old lordship of the archbishops of York over the town of Beverley. Under pressure from the king to relinquish some of the estates belonging to the archbishopric he handed over to the king the manors of Beverley and Southwell, together with other lesser properties, in exchange for some forfeited monastic lands of little value. This was merely a start in the king's design to limit the power and the wealth of the archbishops of York.

In 1545, Henry VIII was involved in expensive wars with the French and, consequently, became short of money. Commissioners were appointed to look into chantry endowments. Once they had reported their findings an act of parliament ordered the suppression of 'all chantries, hospitals, free chapels, fraternities, brotherhoods and guilds' seizing their revenues for the crown. There had been fourteen chantry chaplains at the Minster, four at St Mary's, one at St Nicholas and three others in the town's hospitals. The closing of the chantries began during the last year of Henry's life, closures which were to increase under the protectorate of the Duke of Somerset, during the reign of Henry's young son, Edward VI (1547 – 1553).

On Easter Day, 1548, the Church of St John the Evangelist at Beverley lost its collegiate status. Reports of royal commissions at that time show that Beverley Minster was the wealthiest ecclesiastical institution in the East Riding with an annual income of almost £1,000 a year (a labourer might earn under £5 a year) and with a staff of seventy-five. The staff consisted of the provost (who received a pension of £50 a year), eight canons, eight vicars, fourteen chantry priests, seven parsons, a sacrist, a master of works, a chamberlain, a precentor, a chancellor, two incense bearers, seventeen clerks, eight choristers and four sextons.

All the church plate was confiscated and we can only guess at the fate of the jewelled shrine of St John. Chantry chapels, chapels of the canons, statues, images and altars were removed. The only medieval exterior statues on the Minster which remain are the statues of St John of Beverley and King Athelstan on the exterior wall of the East Window and the statue of the 1st Earl of Northumberland on the north face of the West Tower. Perhaps the reason for so little damage being done to the angels and other religious figures on the Percy Canopy was an acknowledgement of the influence of the Percy family in the area of Beverley. All the Minster's properties and goods were forfeited to the Crown. Chapels of ease in the outlying townships of Storkhill, Theane and Molescroft, all in the Minster parish, were abandoned.

There seems to have been little opposition to these changes from the parishioners.

In 1517 Martin Luther, a German priest, had challenged the doctrine of the Catholic Church by proclaiming that leading a good and upright life, providing money for the church and following the dictates of the pope were no guarantee of eternal life; in order to gain salvation, the individual must believe in Christ. By the 1530s the views of protestant reformers were already becoming known. By 1538 copies of the Bible, translated into English had been placed in most parish churches in England; ideas that sacred images and holy shrines were superstitious relics were already gaining ground.

The Minster Sold for £100

The people of Beverley may have been willing to accept changes within the church but they were not prepared to lose the building itself.

After the dissolution the king gave church property to favoured courtiers and crown officials who then sold them to new buyers. In 1548 the Minster, the greater part of the former collegiate buildings at Beverley - the prebendal houses of St James, St Catherine, St Martin, St Peter and St Stephen, the houses of the provost, the chancellor, the precentor, the sacrist, and the seven parsons - were all given to Sir Michael Stanhope (the deputy governor of Hull) and John Bellow.

Sir Michael had already been given the archbishop's manor house in Hall Garth which he demolished and used the materials to build a new hunting lodge in Beverley Parks; he and his associate John Bellow decided to demolish Beverley Minster and sell the stone and lead for building materials. Fortunately, members of the town, led by a wealthy merchant, Richard Gray, objected. An open meeting was held in the Guildhall, attended by the twelve governors and 'all the honest men of the town' at which John Bellow declared 'that the King's Majesty had given the Minster of Beverley to Sir Michael Stanhope and that he had authority to pull it down'. Robert Grey and seven others then agreed to pay the £100 which was then given to Sir Michael. To raise money for this expense they demolished the Chapter House and the church of St Martin, which was attached to the south-west corner of the Minster, and sold the materials for £120; the residue was divided between them.

Sir Michael Stanhope was executed in 1552 having been charged with a conspiracy with the Duke of Somerset, the ruler of the country during the early part of the reign of Edward VI, to execute the Duke of Northumberland.

Because of its associations with the town the Minster survived as a parish church with a vicar and two assistants. The first vicar, Thomas Mitchell, who had been a vicar attached to one of the altars in the Minster, was elected together with two assistants, Thomas Dring (a previous vicar) and William Grigges (a chantry priest).

After the death of Edward, Henry VIII's eldest daughter, Mary (1553 – 1558) became queen of England and immediately began the restoration of Catholicism throughout the land. In

Beverley there seems to have been little enthusiasm for this process. Robert Thwing, previously a choirman at the Minster, had married. When brought before the chancery court to be admonished for taking a wife, he said that he would rather continue with his wife and live like a layman than be restored to the priesthood. During Mary's reign there were several Protestants on the council and those appointed as schoolmaster were usually Protestants. Testators no longer include the request for prayers for the souls of the dead; they no longer left money for the upkeep of the fabric of the church.

The responsibility for the upkeep of the Minster, St Mary's and the Grammar School and the appointment and payment of clergy and schoolmasters was now in the hands of the corporation. Members of the corporation, now called governors, pleaded poverty and as a result in 1552, Edward VI (1547 – 1553) and in 1579 and 1585 Queen Elizabeth (1558 – 1603) returned land and property in Beverley to the governors, the rent from which could be used to maintain the churches. Rather than lose rent while new building took place, property rented out was more likely to be patched and restored than to be demolished; a few of these half-timbered properties remain today and still retain their medieval timber frame. Little money seems to have been spent on the Minster and it is repeatedly described as 'decayed' and by 1590 the body of the church was said to be in great decay and the windows broken. Amounts spent on repairs on the Minster were limited: 1576/7 £1 8s, 1584/5 £30, 1590s less than £20 a year, 1602/3 £80.

In 1581 the governors of the town acquired the advowson of the churches, the right to appoint clergy (who in the case of the Minster clergy, until 1875, were usually referred to as 'perpetual curates'). The stipend of the incumbent at the Minster was increased to £21 6s 8d and in 1580 the number of assistants at the Minster was reduced to one so as to make it possible to increase the stipend to £40 in order to encourage graduate parsons to apply for the post. By the end of the century Protestantism seems to have had a firm hold on the people at Beverley Minster; long sermons were preached and ecclesiastical courts enforced attendance. In the following century, the Minster and the town were to become notable for puritan preaching.

Queen Elizabeth I's Charter

Throughout the later medieval period Beverley had borough status but was not a self-governing town. After the archbishop had relinquished the manor of Beverley to the Crown, and the collegiate church had been dissolved, control by the two church powers over the town, the archbishop and the canons, ceased. In 1573, at the request of the burgesses, and at a cost of £223 to the town, Beverley was incorporated by a Royal Charter of Elizabeth I. This meant that its burgesses now had powers to make their own laws for the government of the town. They could appoint their own mayor - although the charter stipulated that Edward Ellerker (great grandson of Sir Ralph Ellerker of Risby) was to be the first mayor - a town clerk, a recorder, and twelve governors; the names of the first twelve governors were given in the charter, thereafter they were to be chosen annually from twenty-six burgesses of the town who had been selected by the previous twelve governors - a process of selection which was to last until municipal reform in 1835. The corporation was permitted to appoint two people to represent the town in Parliament – of those appointed some were governors but most were from outside the town. The corporation had its own prison, was entitled each Monday to hold its own court of records, and the mayor was to be clerk of the market and have control over the price of bread, wine, ale and other victuals, fuel and wood.

The mayor was to be elected on the Monday before Michaelmas and be sworn in seven days later. The outgoing mayor, who could not be re-elected until five years had elapsed, together with the governors and the burgesses, would choose the next mayor from the governors. The mayor was expected to attend divine service every Sunday and on special occasions he wore a gown trimmed with fur and with a velvet tippet. Individual governors wore their own uniformed robes which signified their office.

The Poor get Poorer, the Rich get Richer

By the beginning of the 16th century the number of pilgrims visiting Beverley had greatly decreased. This in itself must have resulted in considerable unemployment in the town. After the Reformation and the demise of religious institutions both within and without the town there must have been a further reduction in opportunities for work.

The economy of the town continued to decline with the falling off of the wool and cloth industries. Beverley increasingly depended on trade which took place in its markets and much business was done with Londoners. By 1560 the nine-day Cross Fair, held in Highgate, not only attracted people from many parts of the north of England but also from London and merchants stayed in Beverley during the time of the fair. In 1560, two drapers, Thomas Whip, from London, in his will asked to be buried in St Mary's church and left bequests to the poor of the town and Richard Ferrant, also from London, was buried in the Minster (where his inscription remains) and left to his wife, mother of his twelve children, the house he leased in Beverley.

Income to the town included tolls on goods sold at markets and fairs, the sale of trees on the Westwood and from tradesmen employed with clothing and equipping soldiers recruited for military service.

The poor, who before the reformation had been helped by religious institutions or wealthy benefactors, now became a burden on the town authorities. Outbreaks of the plague in 1576 and 1590 in no way helped the situation. In 1599 Beverley was discharged from payment of money to the crown because of the poverty into which the town had fallen. 400 houses were said to be decayed and uninhabited and the town paid £105 year in relief to the poor and needy, many of whom were unemployed, and eighty orphans.

Nevertheless, while some became poorer, others became richer. Church properties were available at low prices - the Constables of Burton Constable and Halsham bought the site of the Holy Trinity – previously the home of the Knights

Hospitallers - (which was later sold to the council). Robert Gray, bought the Hospital of St Giles property previously owned by the collegiate church, and took on the lease of the manor of Beverley.

Towards the end of the century two families, whose forebears had been merchants in Hull, settled in Beverley and were to be influential in the town for many years - the Wartons of Beverley Parks and the Gees of Bishop Burton.

Lawrence Warton (1523 – 72), a Hull merchant and mayor in 1570, acquired former monastic and Church properties in Hull and East Yorkshire and the lease of the manor of Beverley (which included Beverley Parks, the former deer park of the archbishops of York). On his death, his son, Michael Warton I (1549 – 1590), married to Joan, daughter of John Portington whom Leland describes as 'one of three gents in most fame in the locality', inherited the estate. In 1573 Michael took over from the crown the lease of the manor of Beverley, became a member of the Town Council and assumed the lucrative posts of steward and bailiff. In 1586 he became one of the two representatives for Beverley in Parliament (the Wartons were to continue to represent the town for the next 150 years). His will of 1590 describes him as of Beverley Parks; he left to his wife 'my house in Beverley where I now do dwell, called Blackfriars, for life' (the Dominican Friary).

The Gees were a merchant family who originated in Leicestershire. William Gee, was a wealthy Hull merchant, mayor of Hull in 1562, 1573 and 1584, and it was he who endowed the Old Grammar School in Hull. His son, William (1561 – 1611), was a recorder of Hull and Beverley and secretary of the Council of the North under Elizabeth I and her successor, James I. He was knighted in 1603 by James I on his royal progress from Scotland to Westminster. A brass plaque to his first wife, Thomasina, is in the choir of Beverley Minster. Thomasina was born in 1570, the daughter of Matthew Hutton, Archbishop of York (1595 – 1606). Hutton had accepted the Calvinistic theology but when he became archbishop realized that he had to uphold a church with bishops and archbishops. He became tolerant towards Catholics as well as extreme Puritans. Thomasina had three children, Thomas, Jane and Susan. After the death of Thomasina, William Gee married Mary Crompton, daughter of one of the Queen's auditors, whose family owned land in Bishop Burton. He built High Hall which was to be the main residence of the Gee family until the death of Roger Gee in 1778. Sir William died at the age of 50 in 1611 and his handsome memorial, with effigies of his two wives and five children in an attitude of prayer, is in the south aisle of York Minster. The Monument records that he was a man 'illustrious for

Queen Elizabeth I

piety, integrity and beneficience'. His will contains many puritan sentiments and offers thanks for his elect status 'on the knees of my heart'.

Opposite is a transcription from the Latin of the writing on a brass plaque in the choir of Beverley Minster. Here is no appeal to the saints to pray for the soul of Thamasina Gee, as would have been written in pre-reformation times, but a simple puritan approach expressing sadness at her early death but joy at the assurance that she was in heaven.

The 16th century was a time of enormous change in the fortunes of Beverley. Gone was the prosperity of the previous 300 years when trade and religious institutions flourished; instead disputes with the archbishop, the dictates of the king and changes in trade must have dominated the thoughts of the inhabitants. Hull, with its control over entry into the river Hull and its strategic significance as a port from where military supplies could be sent as arguments with the Scots continued, had overtaken Beverley in size and importance.

156

Epitaph on the death of the most saintly, chaste and truly noble woman, Thomasina Gee, late wife of William Gee, Esquire.

To her who lies beneath this mass of stones I offer my verses; alas!
The Muse had preferred to render her this service while she lived.
She succoured multitudes of the needy with her hospitality – a sacred duty – and now, herself a noble guest; she drinks the waters of eternity.
The ruler of Heaven has blessed her with a threefold reward; justice, eternal life, and a throne.
She bore aloft a torch – all her dutiful love – (as an example) to mothers; may Heaven now bear before her a torch that will never be extinguished.
Although her body sleeps quietly in the dust, yet her spirit sees the faces of the Eternal (Trinity), and she awaits the day when all shall be changed, when this corrupt and burdened (body) is restored like a second crop.

Does an unexpected fate so rob little daughters of her who bore them, and a husband of his wife, and strikes a mother?
Does grim death so bring old age upon her sorrowing parent, while it harshly takes away her life?
Does she whom we lament, thus over-hastily mock her relatives and her beloved friends with the length of their lives?

(My) voice celebrates a housekeeper of blameless life –
To her beloved husband she was a faithful wife, to her servants a kindly mistress; whoever you may be who read these words, you have her name and example.

She died on the 23rd day of the month of December in the year of the Incarnation of the Word 1599, and in the 29th year of her age.

157

CHAPTER 9

1600 – 1700. THE SLOW CLIMB OUT OF THE VALLEY

Queen Elizabeth, after a reign of forty-five years, died in March 1603. Having no children she was succeeded by her cousin, the great-great-grandson of Henry VIII, James VI of Scotland. When he was just a few months old, after the execution of his mother, Mary Queen of Scots, James had became king of Scotland. After inheriting the English throne, at the age of thirty-seven, he made a leisurely progress south to assume his new role as James I, king of England, Scotland and Ireland. On his progress south he stopped in York and, after dining with the mayor, knighted several Yorkshire gentlemen including Sir William Gee of Bishop Burton. In Scotland he had been used to a more autocratic rule and when he became king of England a struggle between king and parliament developed. For most of the century there was little toleration between the Anglican, the Roman Catholic and the Puritan religions. James I died in 1625 and was succeeded by his son Charles I.

In Beverley the 17th century did not begin well. The Parish Register for the Minster records that between August 1604 and June 1605 there were four times the usual number of deaths; 130 deaths in the parish of St Martin's alone. In 1610 the Parish Register for St Mary's records that twenty-three bodies were buried while forty were 'shuffled into graves without any readings over them'. Plague was to be a repeated occurrence during the century.

The corporation took measures to prevent the spreading of infection. Booths (and later a pest house) were erected in the Trinities, where the Knights Hospitallers once had their commandery, whose moated site made it possible to keep people isolated from the rest of the community. In 1637 severe steps were taken to prevent the disease spreading from Hull to Beverley. Anyone from Beverley wishing to go to Hull had to obtain a licence from the mayor; goods and visitors from Hull were banned, public gatherings were banished and no more than ten persons were permitted to attend childbearings.

These restrictions had an adverse affect on trade. During the first half of the century the town was not wealthy and in 1626 was given remission for the payment of taxes because of its continued poverty.

Puritan Influences in School and Church

Beverley Grammar School from the North East

In 1609 the medieval school on the south west corner of the Minster graveyard was replaced by a new stone building, on the same site, which was to serve as the Grammar School for the following 200 years. The control of the Grammar School, the employment of its masters, most of whom appear to have been puritan in outlook, and the payment of their salaries was the responsibility of the corporation. Close links were kept with St John's College, Cambridge and a number of Beverley boys went there once their schooling in Beverley was completed. Several students from Beverley who attended St John's College became puritan preachers during the Civil War. Maybe this was as a result of religious persuasions acquired while at school in Beverley.

By the beginning of the century Beverley Minster, now a parish church, served the united parishes of St Martin's (which covered the area within the borough) and St John's (which included settlements outside the borough but within the liberty of Beverley).

Beverley gained a reputation for providing religious services which stressed the importance of the spoken word rather than the administration of the sacraments. To be appointed a preacher in Beverley seems to have been a coveted position for when in 1632 Revd James Burney applied for the post of preacher at the Minster he had to compete with six other candidates. At times religion and politics seem to have been mixed for there are recorded cases of parishioners who had criticised the government of the town, or who had been imprisoned for assault on the town's officers, being arrested for moral offences.

Puritan preachers were also appointed to St Mary's. In 1632 Revd Nicholas Osgodby became curate, and in 1637 vicar. He was a friend of Revd Ezekiel Rogers, vicar of Rowley (three miles south of Beverley), who in 1638 went with many members of his congregation to America and founded Rowley, Massachusetts.

There was a small number of Catholic recusants in the town centred round the household of the Warton family.

The Civil War Comes to Beverley

Between 1639 and 1643, Beverley was once again caught up in national events, not because of its importance as a town but rather because of its proximity to Hull.

Charles I, and his archbishop of Canterbury, Laud, had antagonised the Scots when he tried to impose the rites and disciplines of the Anglican Church rather than allow the Scots to follow their own brand of religion – Presbyterianism. A Scottish

Charles I

army entered Yorkshire and war looked inevitable. In March 1639 the King and his two young sons, nine year old Charles and six year old James, were warmly received by the mayor and corporation of Hull when they arrived in the town to inspect the munitions stored in the garrison. It is likely that the royal party came to Beverley en route from Hull to York.

In October 1640, in order to raise money for a war, the king was forced to recall Parliament which had been dissolved ten years before.

When parliament was summoned, the twelve governors of Beverley appointed two people to represent the town. In the 17th century most MPs were men of puritan persuasion. Such names as Sir William Gee, Sir Christopher Hildyard, Sir William Alford of Meaux and Sir John Hotham of Scorborough (elected in 1625, 1629 and 1640) appear in the list of those selected. In 1640 the mayor and corporation of Beverley invited Sir John Hotham of Scorborough and Captain Michael Warton, eldest son of Sir Michael Warton II of Beverley Parks, to represent the town.

As disputes between king and parliament continued unease descended on the town and by January 1642 each of the governors was instructed to watch his own ward in case of unrest. On 23rd April 1642 Charles I and 300 of his followers left York early in the morning and rode to Beverley Gate, the north gate of

Hull, to demand that it be opened so that the king and his troops could enter the town. Sir John Hotham, governor of Hull, stood on the town wall and told the king, who stood below, that as much as he would like to obey the wishes of his sovereign, he must heed those of the Commons whose members had instructed him that he was not to allow the king to enter. The mayor of Hull appeared on the walls, fell on his knees with tears rolling down his cheeks, and said that he would like to do as the king asked but the soldiers who had been stationed in the town stood ready to kill anyone who opened the gates. At four o'clock the king retired to a nearby house to consider his position and to give Sir John time to change his mind. When, an hour later, King Charles returned to the gate he was again refused admittance; two of the king's heralds proclaimed Sir John a traitor and all who obeyed him guilty of high treason. The king and his followers then rode to Beverley where they stayed at the house of Lady Gee, the widow of Sir William Gee of Bishop Burton, who lived in a house at North Bar. As the king entered the town of Beverley the bells of St Mary's church greeted his arrival.

The following morning two of the king's heralds returned to Beverley Gate and once again asked that the king be admitted into Hull. The reply came that Sir John had perused all his papers and orders of Parliament and found that he was unable to permit anyone entry into the town without betraying the great trust which had been laid on him by Parliament. When the heralds returned to Beverley, and delivered Sir John's message to the king, Charles sent a message to Parliament complaining about Sir John's behaviour. He and his followers then returned to York. This was the first occasion on which the king had received a rebuff as a result of instructions from Parliament.

Nicholas Pearson, at this time clerk to the parish of St Mary's, wrote in cipher in the Parish Register his political opinions interspersed among the entries of baptisms, marriages and burials – each entry being accompanied with a sketch of a hand adorned with ruffles. In March 1642 (when without warning, the king had entered parliament and attempted to arrest five of its members) he wrote 'England's destruction looked for.

Danger of present destruction. Death in the pot.' On 23rd April he wrote: 'to ringer when the king came in and went eleven shillings and eight pence'.

In May the King summoned the loyal gentlemen of Yorkshire to meet him at York in order to form a bodyguard of 200 loyal subjects. Sir Michael Warton II, now aged 69, joined the king's muster and offered £20,000 to the king's cause – a princely sum even in those days.

As hostilities between king and parliament increased the people of Beverley were caught between the royalist dominated area to the north and west of the town and the parliamentary controlled town of Hull to the south. Trade was affected and it was important that Beverley, which now had Royalist troops stationed in the town, maintained good relations with Hull, only eight miles away.

There was distrust between individual people. Mr Beckwith, a friend of Sir John Hotham, lived in Beverley. Fourteen men, one wearing a visor which covered his face, came to his house and discussed with Mr Beckwith how members of the garrison at Hull could be bribed to open the gate and allow the king and his followers into the town. One of the men present, Mr Beckwith's son-in-law, Mr Fowkes, returned to Hull and told Sir John of the plan. A council was held and while some wanted the plan to go ahead so that they might kill the intruders, Sir John forbade the spilling of blood. He sent a message to the king at York telling him that the plan had been discovered; he also sent a message to Parliament reporting what had happened. Mr Beckwith was declared a 'delinquent' (a term used during the Civil War to describe those who had offended against the wishes of parliament; often resulting in the confiscation of land) and fled to York for safety.

On 8th June, the same year, the London merchants arrived in Beverley for the Cross Fair. As usual, they asked permission of the mayor, Mr Netherthorpe, to trade. The governors met and held a heated debate: they feared that the presence of Londoners with parliamentary persuasions would upset the Royalists in their midst. However, the need to trade won the argument and permission was granted.

The Council also decided that as the defences of the town were inadequate the Bars should be repaired, the gates locked at night and ditches made across lanes leading to the Westwood with bridges only wide enough for foot-passengers.

On 3rd July, at about the 'shutting up of the day', King Charles and his two sons once again rode through the North Bar into Beverley, this time with thirty-three members of the nobility – dukes, marquises, earls, barons and gentlemen – and stayed at the house of Lady Gee. The King's purpose was to oversee the first royalist siege of Hull. (Nicholas Pearson writes: 'king came to towne. Hull mills burnt on the 11th day'). Whilst in the town many messages went to and fro between king and parliament. The townspeople must have been well aware of these royalist intruders; indeed many homes had soldiers billeted on them. The streets must have been full of the King's followers and soldiers on horseback and no doubt, for a time, local trade revived as the needs of the royalists were accommodated. The King, four foot eleven inches in height, and his courtiers attended a service in the Minster –they were met at the door of the church by Revd James Burney and the sermon, in an effort to prevent war, was preached by one of the archbishop's chaplains – his text Hebrew 10, verse 24 'And let us consider one another to provoke unto love and to good works'.

Towards the end of the King's three-week stay in Beverley a group of parliamentary soldiers broke into the town whilst the King was at supper. Charles realised that the town could not be defended and left, leaving behind a small garrison of soldiers. After the king had departed, parliamentary soldiers from Hull drove out the royalist soldiers who had remained in Beverley. (Nicholas Pearson wrote: 'King's war hot at Beverley').

During the early years of the Civil War a paper war was conducted in which each side wrote newsletters and pamphlets trying to discredit the other. One such letter, even allowing for exaggeration, gives the flavour of the difficulties facing the townspeople:

Upon Tuesday, 2nd August 1642. Forty of the Cavaliers came to Beverley commanding the Towne to raise all the force they could, to go presently with them upon some plot they had in agitation against Hull; and swore God dam them if they did refuse to go with them, and they would beat down their houses about their ears, and make them examples to all the Country, but the Townsmen not fearing their great threatenings answered them that they would not stir a foot, for they had enough to do to look to their own Towne, and not go against (as they think) their best friends. Those Cavaliers seeing they could do no good there, went away in a great rage from thence

Between March and June 1643, parliamentary soldiers were billeted in the town at a cost to Parliament of £5,000. There were many disputes about payment of these costs. Prisoners were kept in the town jail in Cross Street (previously Holy Trinity Hospital). There were many reports of both royalist and parliamentary soldiers plundering and burning surrounding villages.

On the morning of 28th June, 1643, Captain Boynton, a relation of Lady Hotham, was parading 800 parliamentary troops in Saturday Market. From the southern end of the market appeared a horseman who, when he entered the square, tried to take over the leadership of the soldiers. The rider turned out to be Sir John Hotham.

Sir John and his eldest son, Captain John Hotham, had both become disenchanted with the parliamentarians and had decided to join the king's cause. Parliament, suspecting this decision sent out instructions for their arrest. Captain Hotham had been detained the previous day but Sir John managed to escape from Hull and, fearing pursuit, avoided the road to Beverley and rode to Stoneferry intending to cross the river into Holderness and so reach his house at Scorborough. Unfortunately, the river was too deep and the current too strong for him even to attempt to cross. He rode to Wawne ferry only to find that the ferryman was not there. Accordingly, the only way to reach his house was to ride through the town of Beverley.

When Sir John entered Saturday Market Captain Boynton recognised him. Aware of the instructions for Sir John's arrest, he rode up to him and seizing the horse's bridle placed him under arrest. Sir John made a dash for freedom, spurring his horse into an open lane leading from the market place but a soldier knocked him from his horse and he was captured and led to the house of Lady Gee. The following day Captain Boynton took him under heavy escort to Hull where he was imprisoned in the garrison with his son. Captain Boynton quickly returned to Beverley for fear of a royalist attack once the capture of Sir John became known. This came late in the afternoon when sixty mounted dragoons, lead by Sir Hugh Cholmley, entered the town. They were soon driven from the town with great loss. (Nicholas Pearson wrote: 'A great scrimmage in Beverley yesterday and God gave us the victory, at that time. Ever blessed be God. War in our gates. Thirteen slaine men in ye king's ptie was buried ye 30th day'). Sir John and Captain Hotham were taken by boat to London and imprisoned in the Tower. Their goods and property were confiscated. Seventeen months later they were both executed on Tower Green.

A month after the arrest of Sir John in Saturday Market there was further violence in the town. (Nicholas Pearson: 'Now all our Lives are at Stake.' God deliver us')

Lord Fairfax had been made governor of Hull and his son, Sir Thomas, was in charge of troops stationed in Beverley from where the cavalry made forays into the surrounding area. Towards the end of August, the royalist Earl of Newcastle, with a company of 12,000 foot soldiers and 4,000 horse left York and advanced on Beverley. Sir Thomas, knowing that Beverley was 'an open place' and could not be defended, asked permission from his father to withdraw. Permission was refused. 'Retreat I may not; defend the town I cannot' was his comment. (Nicholas Pearson: 'Great fear of the Lord of Newcastle. Great danger of destruction')

On the evening of 29th August Sir Thomas Fairfax led his soldiers to the Westwood and waited for the royalist army to approach from York. Early the next morning the first scouts were seen and Sir Thomas gave orders for the foot soldiers to retreat to Hull, and the cavalry withdraw to Beverley. There was heavy fighting outside the town but eventually the remnant of Sir Thomas' army passed through North Bar and the gates were shut firmly behind them. The Earl of Newcastle, leader of the Royalist soldiers, waited until the remainder of his army arrived before advancing towards Beverley. At two o'clock Sir Thomas held a council of war at which it was decided that his soldiers should retreat to Hull as Beverley could not be defended. Before the retreat could take place the royalists broke through the gates and there was much fighting in the streets. Both sides fought with much bravery but by four o'clock Sir Thomas's cavalry had been driven out of the town and was being pursued to the gates of Hull by the Earl of Newcastle's royalist troops.

For a few hours there was a nervous quiet in the town, but then the royalists returned and vented their wrath on the people of Beverley who had sheltered the parliamentarians. A parliamentary Civil War tract states that shops were destroyed, houses stripped, the clothes ripped of men and women and people imprisoned. All cattle were driven from the town and surrounding area towards York. Even crueller than the soldiers, says the tract 'were the women who followed them. With hideous faces they followed the men in their dreadful acts of violence, sparing none. They even robbed women in childbirth of the very linen they lay on. They showed no pity or mercy'. The Council claimed that £20,000 worth of damage was done that day.

In October, during the third siege of Hull, royalist troops were once more stationed in Beverley. After the failure of the siege as the kings' troops passed through Beverley on the way to York, they caused further destruction. After that, the arsenal having been taken from Hull, the actions of the Civil War moved away from the East Riding of Yorkshire.

In 1645 new members were needed to represent the town in parliament after the execution of Captain Hotham and the death of Captain Warton who had, in 1645, been killed by a canon ball at the siege of Scarborough. The new representatives, James and John Nelthorpe had both served in parliamentary armies.

From 1646–1648 parliamentary troops were at times stationed in Beverley and there were constant complaints by the corporation about lack of reimbursement of billet money. The corporation allowed alehouse keepers three shillings a man above the sum paid by the soldiers themselves. It also granted pensions to lame soldiers and to soldiers' widows. Other complaints were about interruption to local trade, loss of money to the people, non-attendance at Council meetings and the refusal of townspeople to hold municipal office.

The Wartons of Beverley Parks

Dominican Friary

Several families in Beverley suffered as a result of their royalist sympathies and had their lands sequestered (seized) for a time. One such family was the Wartons.

Michael Warton II inherited the estate from his father in 1590 and, like his father, lived at Blackfriars. Soon after his marriage in 1592 to Elizabeth, the heiress of Ralph Hansby of Bishop Burton, he made a number of additions and alterations to the house and grounds. He demolished the prebendal buildings of St Michael, thereby increasing the size of his garden - and rebuilt the friary, adding an extension to the west. The east section of the house is of stone standing on 14th century footings and has a 14th century doorway but it is likely that the late 16th and early 17th century brick additions, which include the west wing and the porch, were built by Sir Michael Warton II and may have been added after his marriage to his second wife, Everilda Maltby (nee Creyke), a Roman Catholic. Inside, the Great Hall has 17th century oak panelling and part of the original hammer beam roof. Adjoining this room are wall paintings showing birds, which almost certainly represent the Creyk family crest, a black crow with wings elevated. The brick and ashlar precinct wall has a late 16th, early 17th century brick gateway which once had a shaped gabled top. After the death of Sir Michael II the Friary, with eight hearths, was tenanted by Sir Francis Cobb who died there 'by his own hand', on New Years Day, 1675. Thereafter little is known about its occupants until it was sold in the late 18th century by Lord Yarborough (related by marriage to the Wartons) to Robert Whiteing who, in 1827 lived in part of the building and rented the remainder to tenants.

Sir Michael became High Sheriff of Yorkshire in 1616 and was knighted (at the same time as Sir John Hotham) the following year when James I visited York.

In 1628 he bought Beverley Manor (which included Beverley Parks) from the Crown for a bargain price of £3,592 – in 1642 the annual rent alone from this estate amounted to £1,197.

Sir Michael was a Catholic and both his wives were accused of being recusant.

As a result of his royalist sympathies his lands were sequestered and in December 1644 his house, chamber and stable were searched while he was confined; he was released the following day. In September 1646 a parliamentary fine was fixed at £4,000, later reduced to £3,920 (he had previously complained that lost rents and destruction of his property had cost him £30,000) and his lands were restored.

Michael Warton II died in 1655, aged 81, having during his lifetime considerably added to his inheritance. As his eldest son,

Captain Michael Warton III, had been killed it was his grandson, Michael Warton IV (1623 - 1688), who inherited the estate at the age of thirty-two.

Political Divisions Within the Council

The political affiliations of the town during the Civil War are difficult to unravel. Closeness to Hull and traders from Holland with Calvinistic ideas may account for the large number of puritans in the corporation at Beverley. At the Minster, Revd James Burney, was both a puritan and a royalist. Nicholas Osgodby at St Mary's was similar – in 1644 he was ejected for his opinions, and joined the king's army; Joseph Wilson, a Presbyterian preacher was appointed in his place; in 1653 Joseph Wilson left for a living in Hessle. The Council had a number of parliamentary governors and yet they elected the royalist Robert Manby as mayor for two consecutive years. Later he was accused by seven of Beverley's governors of absconding with the town's plate, the mace and money from the public treasury to the royalist stronghold at York. In August 1644, after the city had been overtaken by parliamentarians, the Standing Committee set up in York ordered Robert Manby's removal from office. In November the Standing Committee stated that Thomas Clarke, William Elrington and Edward Grey (re-instated after the Restoration in 1660) were unfit to serve as governors and ordered that they should be removed from the Council at Beverley. They were replaced by William Forge and William Wade who became the new mayor in 1646 (both men were removed as governors in1662), John Johnson and William Newcombe.

The Commonwealth

On 30th January 1649 Charles I was taken to the scaffold outside the Banqueting House in Whitehall and beheaded. Parliament, led by Oliver Cromwell, was now the undoubted ruler of England. During the ten years of Parliamentary rule the Puritans ordered that all alehouses were to be closed on Sundays, and theatres and race meetings were to be abandoned. Cockfighting and duels were forbidden. People found guilty of immorality or swearing were punished and rowdy language and superstitious behaviour was suppressed. Dancing round the Maypole was forbidden.

Puritans visited churches throughout the land and destroyed all that symbolised idolatry. In Beverley they entered St Mary's church, ripped up the brasses, destroyed stained glass windows with pictures of saints and destroyed the books relating to the old religion. In Hull they lit a bonfire in the street and threw the books on – there are no records of such a happening in Beverley but perhaps it did occur. Although the Minster had been damaged during the Civil War as a result of military action remarkably little damage seems to have been caused by Puritan enthusiasts. Statues of angels and saints remained. One of the reasons for so little destruction may be because the Percys prevented damage to the church which housed the memorials of their ancestors.

On 7th December 1651 George Fox, leader of the Quakers, preached in Beverley Minster. George Fox was born in 1624 and between the age of nineteen and twenty-three struggled in a search for spiritual truth. In his diary he records that when, at last, he realized that no help was to come from a human source he heard a voice saying "There is one, even Christ Jesus, that can speak to thy condition and when I heard it my heart did leap for joy'. After this experience he travelled around the country meeting groups of people and speaking in churches. Several times he was imprisoned for his beliefs and it was two months after his release from gaol in Nottingham that he first came to Beverley. He stayed at an inn in the town and records in his journal that 'the next morning my clothes were sore wet'. He went to the Minster where John Pomfrey, the Puritan schoolmaster of the Grammar School, was preaching. George Fox was then invited to speak and afterwards the mayor, Thomas Hudson, came to him and took him by the hand, reasoning with him and dealing with him moderately.

After his departure a group of people met together and formed the first Quaker Meeting in Beverley. Quakers, also known as the Society of Friends, met in each other's houses for they believed that they had no need of churches for grouping together before God was sufficient. Quakers were unpopular with the Established Church for they refused to pay tithes, church rates or money for church repairs. A member of the Friends in Driffield refused to remove his hat when appearing before the magistrate saying that he would bow only before the authority of God. The magistrate was so enraged by this discourtesy to the rule of law that he ordered the man to be sent to the House of Correction and to be whipped till the blood ran down at his heels. The Friends in Beverley also suffered persecution. In 1654 Thomas Gargill, a prominent Quaker in Beverley spent six months in prison at York, with 239 other Quakers, for speaking in the church at Swine; next, he was in 1678 imprisoned for five years for refusing to pay towards church repairs. There was little improvement after the restoration even though Charles II, as Cromwell had done, promised religious toleration. As Quakers made no effort to hide their religion, often meeting in the open, they were an easy target for a corporation which viewed them with suspicion. They were imprisoned, beaten or had their goods removed. In 1661 Elizabeth Dawson, Elizabeth Brown, Jeremy Burton and Christopher Weatherill were committed to Beverley gaol for religious meetings at the house of Thomas Hutchinson and for refusing to promise to cease such meetings. In 1665 a tanner of Beverley, Thomas Waite, was committed to prison at York for non-payment of tithes.

On 3rd May, 1667, Thomas Waite leased a piece of land in Beverley for use as a Burial Ground for 'protestant Dissenters commonly called Quakers.' – Friends were not permitted to be buried in the consecrated burial grounds of the Established Church. The land was fourteen yards in length and twelve yards in breadth and its western boundary was Lairgate. After the passing of the Toleration Act in 1689 a Meeting House was built.

The Restoration: Alteration in Anglican Churches

In 1660 the bells of the Minster and St Mary's rang out to welcome the restoration of the monarchy and the accession of Charles II to the throne. The Royal Arms were placed over North Bar – the Commonwealth arms being removed. Nicholas Osgodby was reinstated as vicar of St Mary's church.

Changes were made in the Minster to restore the church to Anglican worship. The old pews were sold off and a new pulpit and pews for the mayor, recorder and aldermen purchased. Plate and flagons were returned to the church from the safekeeping of the corporation. A table of the Creed, the Lord's Prayer and the Ten Commandments was set up in the chancel. The pillars and other parts of the interior were 'dressed and beautified'. The royal coat of arms of Charles II was hung in the church where it still remains.

In 1664 workers re-discovered the tomb of St John of Beverley. In the centre of the Minster they found a vault of squared free stone, fifteen feet long and two feet wide at the head and one foot at the base. Encased in a sheet of lead were found ashes, six beads (three of which crumbled to dust when touched – the remaining three were cornelian), three great brass pins and four large iron nails. On a lead plate was found the following inscription:

> In the year from the incarnation of our Lord, 1188, this church was burnt in the month of September, the night after the feast of St. Matthew the Apostle (22nd) and in the year 1197 the 6th of the ides of March, there was an inquisition made for the relics of the blessed John in this place, and these bones were found in the east part of this sepulchre, and reposited, dust mixed with mortar was found likewise and re-interred.

The coffin was re-interred in the position where it had been found in the centre of the church and its place marked with a brass plate.

Memorial to Sir Michael Warton, 1573 - 1655

After the Restoration divisions within the church in Beverley seemed to grow. The official nominee for the post of curate at the Minster was Elias Pawson. However, a group of parishioners, including some aldermen, wanted to appoint Joseph Wilson, who had been ejected as vicar of St Mary's. He was a man described by his opponents as being 'so scandalous in his life, factious and seditious in his practice in what concerns the civil government and schismatically as to the ecclesiastical that he hath scarce his equal'. When Pawson tried to enter the church, Wilson's supporters disturbed the congregation by banging on the chancel doors in an attempt to gain access to the pulpit. Eventually, Wilson preached as an unlicensed minister in the town and many members of the congregation broke away and formed a dissenting Presbyterian congregation.

The Minster, St Mary's and St Nicholas were all in urgent need of repair. In 1667 the parishes of St Nicholas and St Mary were united and the church of St Nicholas was left to deteriorate; the stones may well have been used to fortify the defences of Hull and for building elsewhere. Nothing now remains of that medieval church.

The Corporation Test Acts of 1660's and 70's insisted that all office holders in local and central government must be members of the Anglican Church. Four members of the corporation, who belonged to a Presbyterian congregation, were displaced. The Wartons, who had remained Catholic, converted to Anglicanism and from then on became firm supporters of the Minster where they have several magnificent memorials. One of the first acts of Michael Warton IV was to install a memorial to his grandfather, Sir Michael Warton who died in 1655, in the retro-quire of Beverley Minster. This monument shows the kneeling figure, in alabaster, of Sir Michael between two black columns, and with a pediment surmounted with his heraldic arms.

The Plague Returns; Population declines

By 1650 mortality rates appear to have become even higher than earlier in the century, perhaps as a result of fever or typhus. Between 1651 and 1670 2,750 burials are recorded in the Minster and St Mary's and between 1650 and 1700 there were approximately 600 more burials than baptisms in each church.

In 1665 the plague spread throughout the country. In order to contain the infection the corporation imposed restrictions on the movements of people: visitors and goods from infected places, especially Hull, were excluded from the town, a regular watch was kept for any strangers and all public meetings were banned. All cats and dogs, believed to be carriers of the disease, in the area of Highgate and Eastgate, were ordered to be killed (as cats kill rats perhaps this was an unwise move) and the town gates were shut between nine o'clock in the evening and six o'clock in the morning. By the following June precautions had been relaxed but there was obviously still unease - when three students returned from Cambridge, where the disease still was, they were ordered to stay out of the town for some weeks. With the lack of movement of people, trade suffered.

In the 16th century the population of Beverley had been approximately 5,000; hearth tax returns for 1672 suggest that in Beverley the population had dropped to a total of between 2,480 and 3,100; perhaps the decrease in population was because of disease or as a result of economic changes in the town which resulted in people leaving to seek work elsewhere. These returns show that areas with the highest number of wealthy households, those with four hearths or more, were Saturday Market, Hengate, Walkergate, Norwood and Wednesday Market. The house, probably that which had been lived in by Lady Gee who died in 1649, now owned and lived in by the Wartons at North Bar had twenty hearths.

Charitable Gifts

The poor seem to have been present throughout the town. In 1680 Sir John Hotham and Michael Warton gave £20 as Christmas Dole to be distributed to various wards in the town, no person to receive more than one shilling. Shelter and medical help for the deserving poor was provided by the corporation in the maison dieu which remained after the Reformation. During the 1670s £40 to £50 were distributed annually. In the 1680s this sum was reduced to £30. In 1684 £5 was given to the poor after a storm.

Private charities provided by John Dymoke, Margaret Ferrer and Thwaites Fox gave dole to the poor, trained apprentices for work and gave help to craftsmen. In 1636 Thwaites Fox gave cottages in Minster Moorgate as a hospital for four poor widows endowing them with £10 a year from rents of land outside Beverley, to maintain the hospital and make payments to the occupants. The Wartons encouraged industry by setting up a school to teach bone-lace making and stocking manufactory – an important industry when knee breeches were in fashion. Educational charities provided free schooling and attendance at university. In 1653 the will of Dr Robert Metcalfe, who had attended Beverley Grammar School and been a lecturer at the university of Cambridge, instructed that land he owned in Cambridgeshire, which yielded £47 rent annually, should pay £10 a year to the town's lecturer (preacher), £10 to the schoolmaster and that £20 should pass to his sister Prudence for life. After her death it was to be used to send three scholars from the grammar school to Cambridge. He also left £450 for the corporation to buy land yielding £22 10s rent so that £20 might be distributed to the poor.

In August 1666 there was a great fire in London in which much of the centre of the city was burnt. In November 1666 the corporation of Beverley, aware of the danger of close packed timber houses, ordered that two dozen leather buckets and two fire 'houkes' or 'clamps' were to be provided for the public use in case any 'scath' fire happens'. The streams running through the town provided water with which to put out fires.

Building in brick rather than timber was another precaution against fire. Brick making had continued from the 13th century along Beckside and Grovehill. There is no evidence of building in Beverley between the Reformation and the Civil War but between 1660 and 1670 Number 56-58 Flemingate was built of brick in the Artisan Mannerist style – a style much used in the Low Countries – with its elaborate brickwork, ornamented pilasters and pediments. The doorway of another such building can be seen today in the alleyway beside the Monks' Walk Inn (previously named the George and Dragon) in Highgate.

The Gentry Come to Town

After 1680 brick houses became the norm for affluent townsmen. Nos. 14-16 Newbegin was built in 1689 for Charles Warton, a younger son of the Warton family. This was the first in

Charles Warton's House, 14-16 Newbegin

a series of country style houses, set in magnificent grounds, built in Beverley by the wealthy. Symmetry was all important at this time and this house with its seven bays, two storeys, dormer windows, strong cornice and hipped flat tiled roof is typical of the period. Behind, the grounds to the north originally stretched to Wood Lane. A similarly handsome late 17th century house is 54 Keldgate which was built 1696 for the Constable family of Wassand, later known as School House, which also has an extensive garden.

In 1674 Joseph Lambert became the master of the fifty boys at the Grammar School and under his guidance the reputation of the school was to rise. County families such as the Boyntons, the Constables, the Gees of Bishop Burton, the Hildyards sent their sons to the Grammar School at Beverley and built impressive houses in the town. Sons of yeomen and clergy also attended the school.

The two parliamentary representatives of the town after the Restoration were Sir John Hotham, who had inherited the estate after the execution of his grandfather in 1645, and Michael

Warton IV. The families of these two men were to be influential in the town during the 17th and early 18th centuries.

Sir John Hotham married Elizabeth, the only daughter of Sapcote, 2nd Viscount Beaumont of Swords in Ireland. Of their seven children only two survived till adulthood. In 1661 he and Michael Warton were appointed to represent Beverley in parliament and agreed do so at their own expense. After representing the town for twenty-three years, which necessitated his spending much time in London 'to,' he claimed, 'the prejudice of his health and fortune,' Sir John expressed resentment that he had received no payment from the corporation. Throughout his life he was a believer in the protestant succession and the power of parliament. He was an energetic supporter of the Bill of Exclusion; which meant that only a member of the Anglican Church could succeed to the throne.

In 1683 there was a plot, known as the Rye House Plot, in which certain Protestants planned to kill the king and his brother, James, as they returned from Newmarket. The corporation in Beverley wrote an address of congratulation to the king for his safe deliverance from this plot. All members signed the address apart from two. The corporation then handed the address to Sir Ralph Warton, brother of Michael Warton IV (died 1688), with the intention that he would deliver the letter to the Duke of Somerset who in turn would hand it to the king. For this and other benefactions to the town, Sir Ralph was made a freeman of Beverley and at the next election became one of its parliamentary representatives.

Sir John Hotham was implicated with this plot and the king's ministers received an anonymous letter which said that a store of arms and saddles was at Hotham's House at Scorborough. The letter also suggested that Edward Grey, a governor of Beverley, had entertained burgesses and the 'fanatic party' and organised secret meetings with non-conformist clergy, in order to provoke feelings against popery and thereby promote the candidature of Sir John Hotham at the next election. John Dymoke, another governor and perhaps the anonymous informer, said that he and others had been abused over the loyal address and that he disapproved of Grey's activities.

After the accession of James II, who was reputed to be a Catholic, Sir John Hotham fled to the court of the Prince of Orange in the Netherlands and remained there until the Glorious Revolution of November 1688 in which King James and his catholic queen vacated the throne and the protestant William and Mary became king and queen of England. Sir John was promoted to the rank of general and, like his grandfather before him, made Governor of Hull. Early in the 1689 Sir John returned to Yorkshire. The whole countryside turned out to greet him and the gentlemen of Yorkshire rode out from Hull to escort him into the town where, despite heavy rain, the streets were full of people cheering his return. From there he rode through Beverley and so to his home at Scorborough. Within a few days he fell ill and on 6th April 1689, at the age of fifty-seven, died. His handsome memorial is in the church at South Dalton.

Michael Warton IV (1623 – 1688) was educated at Beverley Grammar School, St John's College, Cambridge and went on to study law at Gray's Inn, London. At the age of twenty-three he married the Hon. Susanna Poulett, daughter of Lord Poulett of Hinton St George in Somerset. They had four sons and three daughters – all but one of whom lived to adulthood. The memorial to their second son, John, who died at the age of six, hangs in the retro-quire of the Minster.

In 1656 he acquired the largest house in the town at North Bar. What that house was like we can only imagine. It may have been a large medieval timber house or it may have been rebuilt by the Wartons. All that remains today is the wall and gate piers to the north of the property on York Road. However, the inventory taken of his possessions, made by his servant Robert Cook after Warton's death, tells us much about this house. There were seven rooms on the ground floor, which included three guest rooms and two family rooms. On the first floor was an elegant drawing room with olive wood furniture, a dining room with long, oak tables and benches, three children's bedrooms, a best chamber and a small blue room with magnificent pictures. The garret had five bedrooms and a large area for storage. The furnishings were of the latest fashion and well designed. There were plenty of presses, cupboards, chest of drawers, portraits and landscape pictures. The family owned an exceptional collection of silver.

Michael Warton rebuilt the hunting lodge at Beverley Parks. It had been restored by Sir Michael Stanhope a century earlier and named New Lodge and Samuel Buck's sketch of 1720 shows the building as a handsome two-storeyed house, with seven bays, set in a walled enclosure; by 1667 Michael Warton had enlarged the park. Like his forebears, Warton bought land and property so that by the late 17th century he owned 12,500 acres of land in Yorkshire. His estates were farmed efficiently and each year cattle from his farms were specially shod before their eleven-day walk from Beverley to London for sale at Smithfield Market. In 1696 Abraham de la Pryme, vicar at Holy Trinity, Hull, wrote in his diary that Michael Warton was 'frequently called the rich Warton, because he was the richest man for to be a gentleman only (i.e. untitled) that was in all England for he was worth £15,000 a year'.

In August 1688 Michael Warton died, at the age of sixty-five, in lodgings in London. His body was brought to Beverley, a six-day journey during which the cortège stopped at the George at Stamford, at inns at Newark, Bawtry and Boothferry. His funeral took place in Beverley Minster. It must have been a solemn affair with the funeral coach and the pillars of the Minster draped in black cloth, the coffin bearers and his servants dressed in black and his house at North Bar hung in deep mourning. The total cost of the funeral was £519.13s.8d

Sir Michael Warton V (1649 – 1725), his eldest son (who had been knighted in 1662) inherited the estate at the age of thirty-three and it was he who arranged for memorials to each of his parents to be placed in the Minster. They were carved by William Stanton of London and placed on either side of his grandfather's memorial in the retro-quire. They were moved in the 19th century to their present position between the retro-choir and St Katherine's chapel. It is some measure of the esteem in which he was held by the town that the heraldic arms of Michael Warton, impaled with those of his wife, Susanna, are displayed over the entrance to Beverley at North Bar.

Michael Warton's estate consisted of land, money, furnishings in New Lodge and North Bar House; books, saddles, pistols, guns, wagons, coaches, horses, a gold striking watch, a tobacco box, jewels, silver plate (worth £2,000), deer and asses. All other livestock was to be sold. Sir Michael's brothers, Ralph and Charles, who were executors of the will, each received £5,725; Money to the value of £33,336 15s 6d was deposited in various places in North Bar House, there being no banks at this time, in cupboards, chests, Ralph Warton's 'privacy', closets, gun room and even in the summerhouse.

Money was also left to Sir Michael's three sisters: Mary, who was unmarried, received the most and in July 1690 she requested her share of £5,000. This was counted out by her brothers in North Bar House and packed into five trunks and five hampers, placed in a wagon and taken to her sister's house in Lincolnshire. By October 1692 she had handed the money over to Sir Thomas Pennyman of Ormesby Hall as part of the marriage settlement between herself and his eldest son, James.

Sir Michael Warton V divided his time, when in the area, between his houses at Beverley Parks and North Bar Within; though as a member of parliament he would have spent much of his time in London. He had first represented Boroughbridge, then Hull but after the death of his father he represented Beverley until ill-health forced him to resign in 1721.

An Improvement in Trade

For most of the 17th century Beverley was not a rich town and there were no surplus funds for costly municipal buildings. The corporation maintained the common pastures and gained an income from fines for breaches of the regulations, sale of timber and leases of fishing and fowling. Freemen of the town continued to keep animals on the pasture. There was no predominant manufacture, although a small amount of cloth making continued; but commerce was in many small handicrafts and trades.

The guilds had lost much of their power over the trade of the town. Such control as remained rested in the hands of about twelve guilds, some of them amalgamations of previous guilds. Some of these guilds amended their rules at the beginning of the 17th century and placed more emphasis on preventing newcomers coming to the town and taking trade away from townspeople than on the quality of workmanship.

The town authorities took more responsibility for business, however, and set strict rules on how it was to be conducted. A bell would be rung in the market place and trading would begin. The mayor and governors would pass through the markets and see that no misdemeanours occurred and no traders charged illegal prices. In the previous century butchers had been forbidden to slaughter bulls between Pentecost and Michaelmas unless they had been openly baited. In the second half of the 17th century more rules and regulations are recorded in the corporation minute books.

If any merchant brings corn on horseback into either market, the corn to be set on market hill, and does not immediately take his horse into some stable or backyard he will be fined twelve pence.

The town beadle, Lawrence Knowles, is no longer to have his annual salary of forty shillings but instead is to be supplied with a coat and four pence for every person he shall whip.

The streets are to be cleared of wandering pigs and 'jolly bitches'

No person coming to live in Beverley is to be a freeman until he can prove that neither he nor his family will be a burden on the parishes but will have means to support themselves.

No blood, guts, garbage, horns of filth is to be cast into the public streets or lanes.

No meat is to be sold between ten o'clock on Saturday night and four o'clock on Monday morning.

John Carlin chosen swineherdsman at a salary of forty shillings per annum, and a coat every Christmas; to continue in office as long as he shall behave himself carefully.

If butchers sell swine flesh which is bad the punishments are as follows:
First offence: a fine
Second offence: set in the pillory (recently re-built in the southern part of Saturday Market);
Third offence: imprisoned or fined
Fourth offence: banished from the town.

If meat is not sold at the agreed prices the punishments are;
First offence: £10 fine or 20 days imprisonment in the town gaol with a diet of bread and water;
Second offence: £20 fine or standing in the pillory (an uncomfortable experience as townspeople released their pent up feelings by throwing bricks and stones as well as rotten fruit and eggs);
Third offence: £40 fine or stand in the pillory and the loss of an ear.

The majority of trades were connected with agriculture - such as malting, oat-meal-making, tanning and some corn milling. However, after 1660 there were new occupations: bookseller, clockmaker, coffeeman, gunsmith, linen draper, milliner, physician, soapboiler, tobacco pipe-maker, and vintner - perhaps an indication of returning wealth. A close watch was kept on incomers setting up in competition with already established trades.

Important to the town's economy were the twice-weekly markets and the Cross Fair. This fair, held in Highgate and Flemingate, continued to attract dealers from many towns in the North of England. It also attracted merchants from London who brought grocery, haberdashery and textiles and occupied houses in Highgate (then known as Londoner Street). Edmund Gibson, a writer and later Bishop of Lincoln, in 1695 commented on the Cross Fair in Beverley which began: 'about nine days before

Ascension Day when the Londoners bring down their Wares, and furnish the Country-Tradesmen by whole-sale'.

Towards the end of the 17th century the Cross Fair declined in importance. In 1673 the corporation ordered that on Ascension Day, 24th June and 25th October the cattle fair should be held in Norwood, the horse fair in North Bar Within, and the sheep fair in North Bar Without.

In 1685 a new charter was obtained from James II which set the pattern for the way in which the town's local government was run for the next 150 years. The chief details were:

The Corporation or Common Council was to consist of the mayor, twelve aldermen and thirteen capital burgesses (councillors), who were to meet in their guildhall and had the right to hold lands and dispose of property.

The Council could inflict punishments, charge fines, and choose the mayor.

The burgesses (freemen) were to choose the thirteen capital burgesses out of a list of twenty-six burgesses prepared by the Council.

There was to be a recorder (judge of the local court of law), a town clerk, constables and other officers.

The town was to have a prison and a Court of Record (law court) every Monday.

All freemen had to be sworn in before the mayor.

There was to be a weekly market on Wednesdays.

There was to be a fair held on the Thursday before 14th February each year of livestock and mixed goods.

The Corporation could buy property.

The town was to elect two MPs to Parliament.

The mayor, recorder and aldermen were to be Justices of the Peace.

Fairs benefited from the increasing number of people who attended meetings of the quarter sessions in Beverley. The corporation encouraged the gatherings of the militia in the town, as these brought more customers, and before the end of the century the aldermen encouraged prosperous farmers, professional men, and the gentry by supplying amenities such as a bowling green and organised race meetings on the Westwood on the area now known as The Gallops (the track encircling the ground where Black Mill now stands).

William III hired mercenaries from Denmark to serve in his campaign against Ireland. In late 1689 a large troop of Danish soldiers arrived in Hull and were stationed in Beverley awaiting orders. A plaque on the south wall of St Mary's Church tells the story of a beheading which took place in Saturday Market. A cartload of sand was brought into the marketplace to cover up the blood after the execution:

> Here two young Danish soldiers lye
> The one in quarrel chanc'd to die
> The other's Head by their own Law
> With Sword was sever'd at one Blow
> December the 23rd 1689

1697 Celia Fiennes Visits Beverley

In 1697 the intrepid traveller, Celia Fiennes, on her grand tour of the north on horseback, describes Beverley thus:

There are three or four large streetes well pitch'd, bigger than any in York, the other lesser Streetes about the town being equal with them; the Market Cross (ie the medieval market cross) is large. There are three markets, one for Beasts, another for Corne and another for Fish, all large. The town is serv'd with water, by wells walled up round or rather in a Square, above halfe ones length, and by a pully and weight lets down or draws up the bucket which is chained to the beame of the pully - there are many of these wells in all the streetes. It seemes its in imitation of Holland, they being supply'd with water so. The buildings are new and pretty lofty.

The Minster has been a fine building all stone, carv'd on the outside with Figures and Images, and more than 100 pedastalls that remaine where Statues has stood, of angels and the like, ... Earle of Northumberland's and Lady's Monuments; his is very plaine only a marble Stone raised up with stone about two yards high, his name (by means of his great achievements in the Barrons warre) Great Percy Earle of Northumberland is monument enough to posterity; his tombe was a little fallen in and a hole so bigg as many put their hands in and touch'd the body which was much of it entire, of the bones the skull was whole and the teeth firme tho' of so many years standing......there are four good monuments all of marble of the Warton family, in the middle of the Church is the tomb of St John with a brass inscription on the pavement, and at a little distance they shew'd us the wearing of the pavement with the obeisance of his votarys this being St John of Beverley..... There is another church called St Mary's that is very large and good. I thought that had been the Minster at first entrance of the town; there is the prayer every day and it's used on all acounts and so the other is neglected. This has a quire in which they were preaching when we were there.

There is a very good free schoole for boys, they say the best in England for learning and care, which makes it fill with Gentlemens Sons beside the free Schollars from all parts; provision being vary cheape here.

17th century Beverley had seen many troubles but by the end of the century the town was on the road to recovery.

187

CHAPTER 10

1700-1800 - THE GENTEEL SLOPES

From Saxon times until the 18th century the system of farming in England had remained more or less the same. Open fields, some of which encompassed as much as thirty acres of land, were divided into strips. The strips would then be allocated to the Lord of the Manor and his tenants. Most tenants lived in villages and daily walked out to work on their strips of land. In order to increase farming efficiency, a change began to take place. In certain areas the strips in the open-fields were redistributed and the land was enclosed with hedges and fences. The major part of the land went to the lord of the manor, other areas went to tenants who then built farm houses in the centre of their land rather than in the village; poorer farmers, who were forced out, sold their land and moved into the towns to seek work.

This process, which began in a small way, was to greatly increase from mid-18th century as improved farming methods led to an increase in the production of food which could then be taken to industrial towns to feed a fast rising population. New roads were built from farms to join old roads, canals were dug and rivers maintained so that food could be transported more easily. At the end of the century the process speeded up as war with France meant that food could not be imported. To enable more food to be grown at home more open fields were enclosed.

Barbara English in her book 'The Great Landowners of East Yorkshire 1530 – 1910' lists, at various intervals, the names of the ten wealthiest landowners in the East Riding from 1530 – 1910. The list for 1720 includes the names of several families who were associated with the town of Beverley: the Bethells of

Rise, the Constables of Burton Constable and of Everingham, the Hothams of Scorborough, the Stricklands of Boynton, the Boyntons of Burton Agnes, the Wartons of Beverley Parks and the Gees of Bishop Burton.

The processing of agricultural products and the transport of goods was to bring wealth to the town. Beverley, with the Beck and the river Hull, had a good water route to the Humber and thus to developing town such as Sheffield, Leeds and Hull. After the middle of the century efforts were made to improve roads leading to and from the town.

Beverley was the County Town of the East Riding. Other busy market towns nearby were Pocklington, Howden and Market Weighton but none of these reached the same level of importance as Beverley. Hull was a large and prosperous town whose markets served Holderness and the villages to the west. Beverley was the judicial and administrative centre of the East Riding and it was here that people gathered during meetings of the quarter sessions of justice and where, increasingly, landowners built their houses so that they might stay in the town and enjoy the entertainments provided. During the century lawyers and professional men increased in number and they too needed accommodation. The militia was several times stationed in the town and needed housing, feeding and entertaining.

All these factors contributed to the rise in prominence of this ancient market town. During the 18th century the face of the town was to undergo a change for the Georgians had no qualms about pulling down old timber houses and replacing them with the latest fashion in building; many of the brick houses we see today were built during the 18th century. One wealthy resident of Beverley in the second half of the 18th century was John Courtney. His diary gives us a vivid insight into life in the town at this time.

During the first third of the century improvements in the town became evident. A gentleman travelling from London to Scarborough in 1733 recorded in his journal;

Beverley is as handsome a town as any in the whole county of York, and I believe exceeded by few in England: the High-Street is a dry long, wide, noble Street, well paved, with Shops stock'd with all sorts of Goods on each side. About the middle of this stands the Market-House - a very grand Cupola, supported by eight stone pillars, with a Statue of Justice on the top. They have a good School here, and a very fine Sessions-House, but what the Town chiefly values itself upon, are her two churches, perhaps the finest private churches in England; they are both built Cathedral-wise.

An Increase in the Population

An analysis of registered baptisms gives an indication of the size of the population of Beverley. In 1721 the population of Beverley is estimated to have been 2,939 – still considerably lower than the level of 5,000 reached in 1377. Diseases still stalked the town at the beginning of the century and parish records show burials exceeding baptisms so that any increase in population was the result of migration rather than a decline in the death rate. Soon after the middle of the century, however, the population throughout England began a steady increase – this trend was reflected in Beverley – an estimated 3,500 in 1764 to 5,401 in 1801.

The Grammar School and Charity Schools

By 1710 the number of students attending the Grammar School had risen to 140 thanks to the appointment of Joseph Lambert. During the first half of the century the Grammar School maintained its high reputation and was well attended by sons of the local gentry.

In 1701 Joseph Lambert bought the site of the medieval house of the Seven Parsons, in the street which from the early 19th century was called St John's Street, and built a house which is now Nos. 9-11. Excavations in 2003 have revealed that there has been building along this street frontage for over 1000 years.

After the retirement of Joseph Lambert in 1716 the number

of pupils declined but was to be revived after the appointment of the Revd John Clarke twenty years later. Clarke remained master of the school until his resignation in 1751. The Grammar School maintained its links with St John's College, Cambridge and between 1700 and 1750 150, pupils, both boarding and day-boy, having completed their education in Beverley went on to study at Cambridge.

There were several dame schools in the town. A school had been set up in 1693 to teach children of six to eight years to read and make bone-lace. Sir Michael Warton in his will of 1688 left £10 'for carrying on the business of bone-lace making in the Charity House'. Education for the poor was mostly financed by charity and given to children who came from what were deemed to be reputable families.

Changing attitudes to the poor, accompanying the evangelical revivals of the early 18th century, influenced several worthy residents of Beverley to organise a charity school. Advised by the Society for the Promotion of Christian Knowledge (SPCK) the Revd Thomas Mease (Vicar of the Minster 1716 – 50), John Moyser (MP for Beverley 1705-08), Francis Boynton (Recorder for Beverley 1723-39) and Alderman George Davies (an apothecary – mayor of Beverley 1701 and 1721), in 1709 organised a fund raising scheme for a new charity school in Beverley and within a few months subscriptions amounted to nearly £200 a year. On 1st August, 1710, the Charity School, known in 19th century as the Blue Coat School because of the blue coat with brass buttons worn by its pupils, opened with twenty-six boys and four girls. At first the school was run by subscribers but later the corporation took over the responsibility of the management of the school. The school, a boarding school for poor children, provided its pupils with shelter and free instruction in the skills of reading, writing and accounts, food and clothing. The Corporation gave £100 for fitting up the school in buildings behind the Guildhall. Funds for the upkeep of the school were raised by donations being placed in a collection box at the entrance to the school and by some of the girls being employed to spin wool.

The Revd Thomas Mease on 6th June, 1713, instructed that all children at the school should be taught to say private prayers twice daily so that 'it would imprint an early and awful sense of the Divine Majesty upon their hearts'. The school was expected to preserve the prevailing social structure in which a carefully regulated degree of poverty had a vital part. The Revd Samuel Johnston (vicar of St Mary's 1720 – 76) in his sermon before the Mayor and Council on 10th October, 1725 pointed out that:

> Without the assistance of the poorer sort, the merchant and tradesman could not raise an estate, nor be master of one, nor live with comfort and pleasure if he was not kept from the meaner offices and drudgeries of life.

By 1743 the number of pupils had been reduced to twelve and the following year the school moved from the Guildhall; by 1774 it was held in the Dominican Friary. At the beginning of the 19th century it was moved again, probably to No. 38 Highgate (a mid 18th century house, belonging to the Minster, facing south)

Influential Families

At the turn of the century the Wartons were still one of the richest families in the East Riding and the most influential family in the town of Beverley. In 1702 Sir Michael gave the corporation £10 to drink the health of the new queen, Queen Anne. The medieval market cross, which was large enough to allow a wagon to pass through, had greatly deteriorated and between 1711 and 1714 a new market cross was built in Saturday Market funded by Sir Michael and his fellow MP, Sir Charles Hotham. Completed in the last year of the reign of Queen Anne, it bears the heraldic arms of the Queen, Beverley Borough, Sir Michael Warton and Sir Charles Hotham. It remains today, classical in style, with eight Doric columns supporting a roof on which is a cupola topped by a square glazed lantern with an obelisk and weathervane on top. The vases were added in 1797. Part of the

The Market Cross

reason for this generous gift to the town was to ensure the benefactors' re-election to Parliament.

Sir Michael was pre-deceased by his two younger brothers. Charles Warton had been educated at Beverley Grammar School, St John's College, Cambridge and Gray's Inn. Towards the end of the 17th century his large, red-brick house had been built in Newbegin. It was he who managed, successfully, the considerable estates of the Warton family in the East Riding. By 1689 Charles Warton, as a result of property and money left to him in his father's will, had built a hospital for six poor widows in Minster

Moorgate. Shortly before his death in 1714, at the age of fifty-seven and unmarried, he gave two cups and a paten to St Mary's Church. In his will Charles bequeathed the hospital in Minster Moorgate to trustees, together with the 201-acre Killingwoldgrave farm in Bishop Burton, the rent from which was to pay for the running of the hospital; £40 a year was to be paid to the occupiers of the hospital as an allowance which included clothes and coal, and, after paying for the maintenance of the hospital, a sixth of what remained was to be distributed to the poor of Beverley, £1 1s was to pay for a sermon in St Mary's church and the rest to be used to bind poor apprentices. Twelve years after his death £250 from the estate was used to enlarge the hospital in Minster Moorgate and buy lands to support the running costs.

In 1696 Sir Ralph Warton, Sir Michael's uncle, gave an alms dish and flagon to St Mary's church. He died in 1700, aged 72, unmarried.

Memorials to Charles and Sir Ralph are at the west end of the south aisle of St Mary's church (originally these two memorials were between the windows of the South Choir Aisle but were removed in the 19th century to make room for further memorials). Ralph Warton, Sir Michael's youngest brother, also educated at Beverley Grammar School died 1708, aged 53, unmarried, and his memorial is in the South Transept of St Mary's Church. All three memorials, similar in style with a large piece of drapery hanging from a circular canopy, are attributed to William Woodman the elder from London.

In 1723 Sir Michael wrote to a friend, the first Earl of Oxford, that 'a distemper in the guts....tyrannises over the poor remains of life my fever has left'. On 25th March 1725, aged 76, Sir Michael died, unmarried. In his will he left instructions that his body was not to be opened but decently carried down and 'laid by my dear mother in our vault' in Beverley Minster, and that a decent monument was to be put up by his nephew and executor of his will, Michael Newton, to whom he bequeathed all his personal estate. His memorial stands under the East Window of the Minster. It was designed by the celebrated sculptor, Peter

Scheemaker, with an urn on a sarcophagus and seated allegorical figures. Written beneath is a list of charitable gifts named in Sir Michael's will:

£10 to Charity School to encourage bonelace making
£100 to the poor of each parish
£1,000 to the hospital built by Charles in Minster Moorgate
£500 to the repair of Beverley Minster
£4,000 for maintenance of Beverley Minster
£1,000 to each nephew and niece who were unmarried

The gift for the maintenance of the Minster was placed into a fund, the New Fund (the Old Fund being money given by Queen Elizabeth I). The Old and the New Fund have now been amalgamated and money from this fund is still used today to maintain the fabric of the Minster. Another benefit of the New Fund was to the town itself. The Corporation was responsible for the maintenance of properties belonging to the Minster; rent from these properties was used to pay for the maintenance of the fabric of the church and the payment of the incumbent. Because the New Fund provided money for the church, the rent from properties could be used to repair individual houses. Thus several Minster properties which might otherwise have decayed, although altered, remain today.

There being no male heirs, the Warton estate was divided between Sir Michael's three sisters – Elizabeth, Susanna and Mary. Elizabeth was the widow of Charles Pelham, who died in the same year as Sir Michael. Her son inherited, and later became MP for Beverley. He died in 1763 with no issue. Susanna (who died in 1737) had married Sir John Newton. Their only son, Sir Michael Newton, died in 1743 with no issue - so the inheritance passed to his nephew, Michael Archer, who took the name of Newton. Mary (who had died 1727) had married Sir James Pennyman. They had six children.

Judging from memorials in both the major churches in Beverley members of the Warton family remained in the town throughout the 18th century. Initialled brass plates in the floor of the retro-quire of the Minster mark where members of the family were buried.

Another wealthy member of the town at the beginning of the 18th century was John Moyser (1660 – 1738), and it was he who, towards the end of the 17th century, built one of the largest houses in the town (now replaced by St Mary's Manor) on the east side of North Bar Within with grounds stretching back to Pighill Road (now Manor Road). An anonymous visitor to the town in 1724 wrote in his journal a description of the garden of Mr Moyser's house;

> Four acres of Ground contained a great variety of Avenues of Firrs, of Parterre of Statues; and also of Arbours, Seats and Vases in Trilliage Work; besides two seats one of Ionic pilaster, the other of Doric Pillars.

In April 1705 John Moyser, after becoming a burgess and a freeman of Beverley, presented the town with a new mace (still in use today) which was carried on official occasions by John Jackson, macebearer and chamber clerk for fifty years. On his retirement in 1709 John Jackson presented the corporation with an oval snuff box which remains in the town's collection of silver. The old mace was sold in 1724.

In May 1705 John Moyser was elected as a member of parliament for Beverley with Sir Charles Hotham. In 1714 John Moyser was instrumental in raising money so that work could begin on the badly needed restoration of Beverley Minster. He and his son James (1693 - 1751) were amateur architects and part of the social circle of the Earl of Burlington with his large house and estate at Londesborough and would have been well aware of the latest architectural trends. On the death of James Moyser the considerable estate was divided between his three daughters, Mary, Diana and Sarah. The following year his daughter Diana, who had married William Strickland, bought out Mary and Sarah's shares in the North Bar Within house, and she and her family moved in. William Strickland was to represent the town of Beverley in Parliament from 1741 – 1747.

A third influential family at this time was the Hothams. During the 17th century three Sir John Hothams had represented the town in Parliament: the first was executed 1643, the second died in1688 and his son died three years later leaving no male heir. The estate then went to Sir Charles Hotham, the grandson of the executed Sir John. Charles Hotham's father in 1662 had been deprived of his fellowship at Oxford for having dabbled with the occult and had gone with his family to Bermuda where he gained a post as a minister of religion. Charles had been born the following year but in 1671, after the death of his father, he was sent to live with relatives in England. He studied classics at Cambridge and then entered the army. At the age of twenty-two he married Bridget Gee, whose mother (daughter of Sir John who died in 1688) at the age of twelve had married William Gee of Bishop Burton. In 1691, at the age of twenty-eight, he inherited the Hotham estates. Sir Charles liked to live in a highly fashionable style despite the relative poverty of the Hotham estates. He was a soldier who served in Spain and Portugal and, in 1710, was promoted to Brigadier-General and made colonel of a new regiment, his own having been disbanded.

In 1705 the Hotham's house at Scorborough was destroyed by fire and for several years the family lived with the Gees at their hall in Bishop Burton, in a rented a house in Hull and another in London. Perhaps it was for political reasons that Sir Charles decided to build a new, and extremely costly, house in Beverley. In 1713 he leased from the Corporation land in Eastgate which adjoined land which he already owned. The following year he took out a 100 year lease from the Corporation on land on both sides of Eastgate. After the purchase of further closes with properties, which he then demolished, he had acquired a large enough area to build his house. In 1716 he was granted special facilities for making bricks on the Westwood. His new palatial house was designed by Colin Campbell, a Scottish architect who, in 1717 had published, with the help of the Earl of Burlington (a promoter of the Palladian style), his 'Vitruvius Britannicus' which contained his design for the Hotham House in Beverley. No expense was spared on this neo-palladian house, one of the first in the country. The staircase and chimney pieces alone cost over £1,000; William Thornton of York was paid £1,000 for interior fittings - the final cost of the whole house was £7,000. Work was completed in 1721, two years before the death of Sir Charles.

The fact that Sir Charles spent so much of his time away from his estates may have contributed to his unpopularity among the electorate of Beverley. Three times he was defeated before, in 1703, with the aid of bribery and the entertaining of voters, being elected MP.

Bribery at elections was not uncommon in the 18th century, and candidates would often pay to keep public houses open for days before and during elections. Sometimes there was violence at elections. On one occasion Sir Charles' opponent was more popular with the people than he. Both candidates were standing on the hustings in Saturday Market when members of the crowd seized Sir Charles's son and attacked him with fury. As no effort was made to quell the rioters Sir Charles, drew his sword, seized his rival by the collar, pointed the sword at his breast and said: 'Sir, stop your mob and order my son to be released for, by the God who made me, this sword shall pass through your body the very moment he falls'. His order was obeyed! After the election he represented the town in Parliament until his death in 1721.

Sir Charles was succeeded by his thirty year old son, also Sir Charles, the 5th baronet, who seemed to prefer London to Beverley. He became MP for Beverley in his father's place but in order to keep the seat he was forced to spend liberally within the town and particularly on the freemen who were the electorate. In London he moved in court circles and in 1728 bought a house in Piccadilly; he became Groom to the Royal Bedchamber of George II, a highly lucrative post. The new house in Beverley was never lived in and the books and furniture were moved to his house in Piccadilly, for Sir Charles, who had married Lady Gertrude Stanhope, daughter of the Earl of Chesterfield and who is said to have spent £724 on furniture for his bride's bedroom, felt that it was unbecoming for a person of his standing to reside in a busy market town like Beverley. However, he continued to invest in property and land in the town.

With more efficient farming, the Hotham estates recovered in value. In the 1730s the gardens at his country villa at South Dalton were laid out and in 1770s building on Dalton Hall began. In Beverley Sir Charles provided further benefits to his constituents, by giving money to the poor, subsidising two schools, donating money towards the building of new assembly rooms and giving £50 towards the cost of a new pulpit for St Mary's. He erected a magnificent military monument to his father which lies on the north wall of the north choir aisle in Beverley Minster – originally this memorial was taller but in 19th century was truncated to its present height. Sir Charles died in 1738 and was succeeded by his son, Sir Charles Hotham (died 1755).

In his will Sir Charles stated that the house at Beverley was to be sold within 15 years of his death for £2,000 or upwards and the money was to be used for buying land. It did not sell quickly and in 1758 the remains of the furniture and fittings were sold at a public auction in Beverley, many pieces being bought by Thomas Wrightson, a builder, who also bought the shell of the house for a token sum. Today, parts of the details from the house can be seen around the town; a staircase in the Cross Keys Hotel, Lairgate; doorcases in Nos. 26 and 28 Eastgate (built by Wrightson). A carved oak cornice, containing the monogram of Sir Charles Hotham, was placed in the Nag's Head public house in Grovehill. In 1928 the pub was demolished and the oak cornice was removed to its present position in Beverley Art Gallery (above Beverley Library).

Parliamentary Elections

The 1685 Charter stated that the two parliamentary representatives from Beverley were to be chosen by the freemen of the town rather than selected by members of the corporation. In 1727 809 freemen voted; 688 of these were freemen who were resident in Beverley which amounted to 20% of the population, making Beverley one of the largest electorates in the country.

18th CENTURY PARLIAMENTARY REPRESENTATIVES FOR THE TOWN OF BEVERLEY.

(Until 1868 Beverley sent two representatives to Parliament)

1722	Sir Charles Hotham,	Michael Newton,
1727	Charles Pelham,	Ellerker Bradshaw
1734	Sir Charles Hotham,	Ellerker Bradshaw
1741	Charles Pelham,	William Strickland
1747	Charles Pelham,	Sir William Codrington,
1754	Sir W. Codrington,	John Tuffnell,
1761	Michael Newton,	George Forster Tuffnell
1768	Hugh Bethell,	Charles Anderson Pelham
1772	Sir Griffith Boynton,	In the place of H. Bethell
1774	Sir James Pennyman,	George Forster Tuffnell
1780	Sir James Pennyman,	Francis Anderson
1784	Sir Christopher Sykes,	Sir James Pennyman
1790	John Wharton,	Sir James Pennyman
1796	William Tatton,	N.C.Burton
1799	John Wharton,	General N.C Burton

Not all elections were contested. After the retirement of Sir Michael Warton in 1722 and the death of Sir Charles Hotham in 1723 the dominance of these two families declined; after 1738 no Hothams represented the town in parliament. However, the 'Bar Interest', i.e. the Warton heirs – the Newtons, the Pelhams and the Pennymans - continued until 1796 although they were usually opposed which resulted in increasing sums of money being spent by the candidates to ensure election. A useful source of income to publicans and voters! In 1722 Michael Newton spent £131 on freeman at twenty-six inns in the town and in 1784 Sir Christopher Sykes, opposing the 'Bar Interest, spent £2,830 as follows:

£703 general expenses
£753 on innkeepers services
£672 cash payments
£513 ribbons
£83 on voters' freedoms
£53 on his own freedom
£53 to his agents

Success depended on the purse rather than the politics of the candidates.

The Restoration of Beverley Minster and St Mary's Church

Deterioration of the fabric of the Minster had continued. In 1704 the Archbishop of York, John Sharp, secured a Royal Brief which gave the corporation authority to make a national appeal for funds for the repair of Beverley Minster. Permission was granted for stones from St Mary's Abbey, York, to be used in restoration work. £100 were received from the King's and the Archbishop's charities. Collections in the town raised £57 12s 6d from St Mary's parish and £24 9s 6d from the Minster parish (a poorer area of the town). Local gentry also contributed but by far the largest single contribution was the £500 given by Sir Michael Warton. By 1731 the trust formed by James Moyser to raise and administer funds and contributions had raised £6,132 15s 5d.

In 1716 Nicholas Hawksmoor, a London architect, was invited to come to Beverley and give advice on the restoration of the north wall of the north transept, which was in such a bad condition that it leaned four feet into the street. The roof of the north transept was removed and a wooden cradle, designed by a York joiner, William Thornton, was placed on the exterior and interior of the north wall; over a period of eleven days the cradle, by the use of ropes and pulleys, was raised and the wall was gradually brought back to an upright position. Included in the Minster restoration programme was a new stone floor in the nave and aisles, a fine marble floor (with geometric designs) in the chancel, the rebuilding of the central tower, on which was placed an onion shaped dome which was removed 100 years later. Apart

A Georgian Brick House in Newbegin

from the nave most of the medieval beams in the roof were replaced. A treadmill was placed above the boss of the central tower and materials were hauled up into the roof by someone walking inside the wheel. Today the wheel is still in working order but for health and safety reasons has been replaced by a mechanical pulley. New iron gates were placed at the entrance into the chancel (in 19th century moved to the North Choir Aisle) and a new cover was hung over the font. The wooden West Doors were carved by William Thornton, and included figures of the four Evangelists together with their symbols of the lion, the ox, the angel and the eagle.

This extensive renovation programme, which involved 400 craftsmen, women and children, was completed by 1730 and cost £7,500. Daily payment to those working in the Minster was as follows:

Masons	2s – 3s
Plumbers	2s
Joiners	1s 0s 8d
Men / apprentices	10d
Women	6d
Children	2d – 4d

The restoration of the Minster included the intrusion of Classical elements – wooden ionic pillars supported galleries; a new heavily carved stone archway over the chancel entrance; and a huge, stone, Corinthian-column (higher than the adjoining Percy canopy) was fixed to the west side of the reredos. These classical adhesions to a Gothic building were not appreciated by all. Arthur Young, the agriculturalist and writer, visited Beverley in 1769 and in his journal wrote about the exterior of the building:

The Minster, for Gothic architecture, is a very light and beautiful building, and kept in good repair; but its modern decorators appear to have had ideas of neither beauty nor propriety; for, with true taste, they have given the venerable pile just such an entrance as you would imagine for a cake house; a new-fashioned iron rail, and a gate handsomely adorned with gilding, and a modern stone wall with two urns of white stone, which, with a few reliefs cut on them, would do tolerably well for the decoration of a shrubbery.

He then goes on to describe the interior:

But these gentlemen, not content with this stroke of genuine propriety, have carried their Grecian ideas into the very choir of a Gothic cathedral. At the entrance, under the organ, they have raised some half dozen ionic pillars and pilasters; and built an altar-piece in the stile of, I know not what. It is an 'imperium in imperio'; the bird of Jove certainly flutters her lofty wings to command the attention of the spectator, and call it off from the barbarism of Goths and Vandals to fix curious fluted Corinthian pillars, raised merely to support the pedestal whereon appears the king of birds. You will not quickly meet with a more capital piece of absurdity; and yet (if you could support a use for it) this altar-piece, as high as the cornice of the pillars, has something light and well proportioned in it, but rendered heavy and unpleasing by the eagle's pedestal. Behind the altar-piece is a modern one, by Scheemakers which is in a heavy unpleasing taste.

Grecian style pillars and galleries were also installed in St Mary's church. In 1754 a local builder, William Middleton, was given the task of pulling down an old loft and replacing it with two new galleries over the north and south aisles of the nave. In 1784 seating was still found to be insufficient and the churchwardens were granted permission to enlarge lofts and increase income by selling off the pews. On 11th February 1788 a local resident, John Courtney, wrote in his diary complaining about a summons he had received from the churchwardens demanding that he came to the vestry and produce documentary evidence showing his right to his pew. Apparently, Colonel Cruger, Major Roberts, Mr Hudson and Mr Hunter had recently applied for pews. John Courtney pointed out to the churchwardens that he had sat in his pew for fifty years and that as all but Mr Hunter were newcomers to the town it seemed very odd that the churchwardens should wish to turn out the old inhabitants from their pews – the next attempt might be to turn them out of the town!

Non-Conformists

The number of non-conformists grew in the 18th century. While the Society of Friends remained a small group, by 1715 the Presbyterians numbered several hundred followers including leading tradesmen and members of the corporation.

John Wesley was born on 17th June 1703 at the rectory at Epworth where his father was rector. In 1729 he and his brother, Charles, belonged to a group in Oxford which resolved to conduct their lives and religious study by 'rule and method' – hence they became known as 'Methodists'. By 1738 they began travelling the country and preaching their message. They laid emphasis on repentance, faith, sanctification and the privilege of full, free salvation for all. Although the leaders of the movement were ordained as ministers of the Anglican Church, their evangelistic methods were unpopular and they were generally banned from preaching from the pulpits of the established church. Instead they would talk to the people in barns, houses or open fields.

John Wesley records his visits to Beverley in his journal:

14th July 1759. I preached at eight (am) in Mr Hilton's yard, near the great street in Beverley, and was surprised to see so quiet and civil a congregation where we expected nothing less. All the men were uncovered, and the whole audience was attentive from beginning to end; nor did one person give us a rude word while we rode from one end of the town to the other.'

Thursday 17th July 1766. Pleasant ride (from Hull) to Beverley. Preached at 6 in a room as warm as an oven, and the people tolerably attentive.

Saturday 19th July 1766. I took a view of Beverley Minster, such a parish church as has scarce its fellow in England. It is a most beautiful as well as a stately building, both within and without and is kept more nicely than any cathedral I have seen in the Kingdom; but what will it be when the earth is burned up and the elements melt with fervent heat.'

Over the next thirty-one years John Wesley was to visit the town fourteen times. In 1764 an old cock-pit in Wood Lane was bought by the Methodists and became their chapel. By the time of Wesley's last visit in 1790 he had a thriving band of followers.

Administration of the Town – Income, The Beck, Punishments and the Spa.

In 1724 the mayor and aldermen included eight tradesmen, one apothecary and three attorneys. Later in the century aldermen were increasingly from the gentry and professional classes as members of the gentry took an interest in the government of the town.

Each year, on the Monday before Michaelmas, the mayor was elected from amongst the aldermen by all the freemen. His swearing in, two weeks later, was celebrated with music, bell-ringing, gunfire and bonfires and the distribution of apples. A bull was baited in Saturday Market or in front of the new mayor's

The Tiger Inn, North Bar Within

house and the gentlemen of the town were entertained to dinner at the Blue Bell Inn (re-built and renamed the Beverley Arms in 1794) or the Tiger Inn (built 1740) both in North Bar Within.

As the town prospered the income of the corporation rose from £331 in 1710 to £760 in 1760.

Income came from:

Rents - the income from rents was to steadily increase in the second half of the 18th century from £290 in 1740, to £400 in 1770, to £549 in 1790

Admission fees and the sale of freedoms. The cost of buying the 'freedom' of the town rose from £85 in 1700 to £125 in 1740, to £242 in 1778. Strict control was still kept on those wishing to reside in Beverley, and only freemen could set up in business. Parliamentary candidates were usually non-resident and the Corporation insisted that they should buy their freedoms before they could stand for election. The fee was set at 100 guineas in 1791.

Fines from those freemen who refused to take office as mayor, alderman or capital burgess.

Tolls from markets and fairs which were paid to the corporation. In 1706 this yielded £40, in 1740 £50, in 1770 £72 and in 1790 £86.

Tolls from entry into the town, either through the bars or from the Beck. The Beck was still a profitable part of the town as is evidenced by some of the 18th century houses remaining in that area. Tolls from the Beck amounted to £119 in 1725, £100-£200 in 1750 to £300 later in the century.

Sale of property.

Expenditure was mostly on:

The building and repair of property.

Maintenance of streets – pavers were continually at work and in 1735 the main streets were paved with cobbles brought in large quantities from Holderness. In 1751 some watercourses were covered over and pumps replaced wells.

Salaries for employees.

Dredging and cleaning the Beck.

The Beck continued to be an important link between Beverley, the North Sea and the fast developing towns in West Yorkshire. Standing at the Beck and looking over the flat fields which lay alongside the river Hull there would have been the constant sight of the tall masts of sailing ships following the contours and curves of the river before they entered the Beck or continued on to the staithes at Grovehill. At this time there were no lock gates into the Beck and the rising and falling of the tides caused much destruction of the banks and the silting up of the channel of water through which the ships could move. The Beck was in great danger of being choked and warped up by sludge and soil brought in by the tides and by earth falling in from the banks. An Act of Parliament was passed in May 1745 for more effectually cleaning, deepening, widening and preserving Beverley Beck, repairing the staithes near the Beck and the roads leading from the river to the town, cleaning the streets of Beverley and regulating the carriages to and from the Beck and the river Hull. The Act pointed out if the banks were not supported by piles and other expensive work was not carried out the Beck could not be kept open. As this work would be a continual expense and would cost more money than could be raised by the duties granted by the previous act, the Act outlines new charges which should be made on any ships, boats, keels, wherry or any other vessel which pass up or down the Beck or the River Hull in order to load and unload goods or merchandize at public staithes at Beck End or Grovhill.

In the table opposite it is interesting to note the kind of merchandize coming in and out of the town. (A farthing was a quarter of an old penny).

The Act stipulates that tolls were to be paid to the mayor, aldermen and capital burgesses of Beverley. All carts travelling into Beverley or the surrounding area were to have wheels which were nine inches broad. If owners or occupiers of houses, lands or tenements within the town did not clean the streets, lanes and public places before their respective houses, lands or tenements and carry off the dirt, filth and soil thereof they would be fined

Another responsibility of the corporation was the administration of punishments. In 1735 the corporation ordered three new stocks to be set up. One was to be near the Pillory House (built 1679, demolished 1761) in Saturday Market – the stocks would be kept in the pillory house and set up when needed.

Beverley Minster 1220-1425

St Mary's 1150-1524

North Bar 1409

15th Century House in Flemingate

Norwood House 1760

The Court Room in the Guildhall

Saturday Market from a Postcard dated 1908

New Developments at Beckside

For every Quarter of oats, barley or malt - one farthing
For every Quarter of wheat, rye, beans, peas, rapeseed, hempseed linseed or any other kind of seed or grain - one farthing
For every hundred weight of flour, - three farthings
For every hogshead of salt - four pence
For every ton of salt, in bulk - two pence
For every three hogsheads of sugar, tobacco, or any other goods packed in hogsheads - eight pence
For every four hogsheads of wine or rum - twenty pence
For every hogshead of brandy or other spirits - four pence
For every eight barrels of soap, raisins, or tar - four pence
For every butt of currants - eight pence
For every two pipes of Smyrna raisins - eight pence
For every 16 bags of nails - four pence
For every 32 firkins of butter - four pence
For every twenty hundred of cheese - seven pence
For every ton of timber or stone - two pence
For every two bags of hops - eight pence
For every quarter of oatmeal - one halfpence
For every hundred of pipe staves - three halfpence
For every dozen of cinders or charcoal - one halfpence
For every twenty sheep skins - one farthing
For every quarter of bark - one farthing
For every pack of wool, or other goods - one penny
For every 12 dozen of bottles - one penny
For every four bushels of roots or fruit - one halfpenny
For every ton of hemp, line or flax - seven pence
For every quarter of fern ashes - two pence
For every small cask, box or parcel not exceeding 112 pounds - one farthing

Another form of punishment was the ducking stool, a chair suspended over a pond. The offender (usually a woman accused of gossiping) was strapped in and the chair was lowered, none too gently, into the pond until the offender was submerged – this would be repeated two further times before the offender was permitted to go free. The pond, to the west of North Bar, could be reached by walking up Cuckstool Pit (now Tiger Lane) which at that time extended as far west as the town ditch. This system of punishment was abandoned in 1761.

The drinking of water from wells, water which was believed to have medicinal properties, became popular in the 18th century. Since the end of the 17th century water from a well on Swine Moor, dedicated to St John of Beverley, had been drunk for medicinal purposes. In 1695 Edmund Gibson wrote:

> About a mile from Beverley to the east in a pasture belonging to the town is a kind of spaw, though they say it cannot be judg'd by the taste whether or no it comes from any mineral, yet taken inwardly it is a great drier and, washed in, dries scarbutick scurf and all sorts of scabs and also very much helps the King's Evil (a form of scrofula formerly held to be curable by royal touch).

In 1745 the corporation let the well to a grocer, John Hornby, on condition that he would build a new building there which would include a tea room, ball room and a pump room. This was not done and so two years later the corporation built a new well house. From 1772 until their disuse in 1816 the wells were in the charge of a keeper employed by the corporation. The spa in Beverley never seems to have been popular.

Traders and Retailers

Trade in the town was mostly concerned with the processing of agricultural products and, as in medieval times, providing services for visitors and residents. Daniel Defoe's 'Tour Through the Whole Island' was published in 1720. In it he describes Beverley as 'a large and populous town, though I find no considerable manufacture carried on there'.

By 1700 two mills on the Westwood are recorded which, along with two water mills on Mill Dam drain, dealt with the increasing amount of grain brought into the town. By 1791 there were fifty-four corn factors and a number of oatmeal dealers and millers trading in corn. Shops would provide goods for the farming community and blacksmiths, wheelwrights and craftsmen sold harnesses, rakes, ploughs and other agricultural implements and replacement parts.

Tanning remained an important industry throughout the century. In the years 1715-1734 the names of twenty-eight different tanners are mentioned in the records. The brotherhood of tanners in 1788 consisted of ten tanners, eleven skinners and two leather dressers. Five tanners are reported in Flemingate which, of course, had access to the Beck and streams which provided the water needed for leather processing. It was also near the river Hull from where skins were transported to other parts of the country or abroad. Other yards were in Keldgate, St John Street, Lairgate, Walkergate and North Bar Without.

Between 1715 and 1734 123 shoemakers are mentioned and thirty glovers (both offshoots of the tanning industry), thirty-seven weavers (much reduced in number from before and working mostly in linen) and nine dyers with dye works along the south side of Keldgate. The textile trade still remained in the 18th century but on a very small scale.

Shipbuilding continued along Grovehill. In 1763 Richard Hopwood was granted permission by the corporation to build boats there.

Maltsters were still a wealthy and influential group at the beginning of the century with twenty-eight malsters mentioned between 1715 and 1734 but by 1774 there were only nine and many malt kilns about the town had fallen into disuse. The number of brewers increased towards the end of the century. Most beer was brewed by individual landlords in inns and ale houses which in 1724 numbered forty-eight. There was plentiful accommodation for visitors; in 1756 there were 222 guest beds and stabling for 361 horses.

The greatest number of job opportunities must have been in the building trade. Perhaps some of those skilled craftsmen who had worked on the restoration of the Minster in the first half of the century remained in the town to build the many new houses needed for an increasing population.

Local craftsmen-retailers often owned shops in the main streets in which goods, made in workshops at the rear, would be displayed for sale in the windows. Crafts included - tailors, breechmakers, a goldsmith, a silversmith, a coppersmith, a coach maker, a gunsmith, a cutler, a wigmaker, a tobacconist and a watchmaker. External wooden shutters would protect the windows at night. Other services were offered by a scrivener, a translator, a bookseller, a dancing master and several musicians and by 1740 there was a circulating library.

Fairs and Market Days

In the middle ages fairs were usually held at the time of religious festivals, but by mid- 18th century the number of fairs in most market towns had been reduced and were occasions when livestock was bought or goods were sold. In Beverley accounts of fees received for carrying Londoners' goods from the beck to Highgate, where the Ascensiontide Fair had been held since 1174, show a decline; 1673 - £13 6s 8d, 1701 - £4, 1730 - £1 10s. Gradually, as the sale of livestock increased and caused congestion in narrow streets, fairs were moved to the edge of towns. By 1731 the fair had been moved to Norwood, a wide street to the east of the town, and sheep pens were set up along each side of the street while cattle were tethered to posts.

Fortnightly cattle markets were also held in Norwood. Rings which held bars to prevent cattle straying into the gardens of nearby houses can still be seen in the gateposts to Norwood House (built 1760). Pigs were sold on the north east part of Saturday Market in an area known today as Sow Hill.

Market days were important occasions in Beverley. People, as always, came to town from the surrounding districts to sell their produce, purchase goods, meet up with friends and discuss business with colleagues. Grain was brought into the market place – either a sample sack or by the cartload - and sold direct to the merchants, millers or maltsters. Wagons, having deposited their loads, would be moved to the yard of a nearby inn. Farmers and dealers would meet in one of the inns to exchange news on new developments in farming, firm up on deals or settle debts, with lawyers present, and discuss trade. Mid-afternoon dinners would be arranged in the local inns.

After the cessation of trading in Wednesday Market in 1751 Saturday Market became a thriving market. In order to contain the area in which meat and fish were sold a butchers shambles was built in 1753 with forty-five stalls on the east side of the market between the Dings and Ladygate (between 1774 and 1830 the number of butchers in the town was to rise to 60), and in 1777 a Fish Shambles was built.

Road Improvements

The Stage Coach passes through North Bar in the early 19th century

Successful markets depended on well paved roads for people and goods to travel along. Since the time of Elizabeth I roads had been the responsibility of the parishes and by the 18th century many had fallen into a bad state of repair. John Courtney writes of roads in which his horse fell into holes almost up to his neck; he comments that the road from Beverley to York took four hours and forty-five minutes to travel 'being very bad roads'. The land to the east of Beverley was still marshland and travel in the winter was limited until an act of parliament permitted drainage to take place. The area to the east of Norwood was often flooded during winter and until the early 19th century flat-bottomed boats would come up the dykes as far as Norwood.

In the mid 18th century turnpike trusts were established which took over from the parish authorities the responsibility of maintaining the principal roads. These trusts, which were supported by local landowners who wanted to move produce from their farms to the towns, had wide powers to borrow capital which paid for the upkeep of the road. The road from Beverley to Molescroft and Leconfield was turnpiked in 1766. The first toll bar was at 'galley end', the end of Gallows Lane in New Walk (so named because in medieval times the archbishop is believed to have had his gallows here). At first the turnpike was a bar of tapering iron or wood which pivoted on a central pillar to allow traffic through. Later the bar was replaced by a gate, with a side gate for pedestrians who travelled free. At the toll house was a board which displayed a list of charges and a weighing machine to determine the weight of heavily laden vehicles – a typical toll was a farthing a head for cattle and sixpence for a carriage and horse. In the following century the toll gate was moved to where the Molescroft roundabout now stands for it was found that farmers were going up Pighill Lane (Manor Road) to reach Molescroft without paying tolls at the toll gate.

Each stretch of road would have its own turnpike trustees and meetings of the trustees of roads round Beverley often took place in the Tiger Inn. In 1744 the road from Beverley to Hull was turnpiked; in 1761 the road from Beverley to White Cross, Leven, was turnpiked (however, stormy winter weather of 1763/4 caused the banks of the river Hull to break and the road was for some time under four feet of water); and in 1764 the road from Beverley to Kexby Bridge and then to York was turnpiked.

Once roads improved, goods could be transported by wagon rather than by pack horse. By mid-century carriage springs had been improved, coaches could travel at a faster pace and people in greater comfort. Towards the end of the century high-speed coaches travelled from Beverley to Hull or York and, eventually, to London. Coaching inns were the Blue Bell Inn, the Tiger Inn and the King's Head, which all had adequate stabling behind, and until the advent of the railways this was a profitable trade. Horses stabled in North Bar Within would be washed in the dyke outside the Bar.

Travelling by coach gave the opportunity for conversation with strangers. John Courtney, who lived in Newbegin House, wrote on 16th May 1805 about an intelligent Scotsman who travelled with him in a stage coach from Hull:

> Who is concerned in a new manufactory of Cotton in London and gave me a sample of some very fine and nicely rolled. I arrived at the Tyger Inn at Beverley about 7 o'clock and walked home with Timothy my servant who followed with my portmanteau.

John Courtney – an 18th Century Gentleman Living in Beverley

One member of the town who observed these changes and was much involved in their administration was John Courtney (1734-1806) whose parents had been married in the church at Walkington. John Courtney was educated at Beverley Grammar School, under the tutorship of Revd John Clarke. His final year of schooling was at Wakefield, to where Clarke had moved in 1751, and from there he went to Trinity College, Cambridge. His father had made a fortune in the East India Company, which the twenty-two year old John Courtney inherited on his father's death on 1st November 1756. Each year, in his diary, he remembers with sadness the anniversary of his father's death. John Courtney's business life was concerned with organising his finances and, after the death of his uncle, the finances of his Aunt Featherstone, who lived in North Bar Without. He and his widowed mother occupied a house in Walkergate, on the site where Walkergate House now stands, where he continued to live after his marriage in 1768 and until the death of his mother in 1770. In that year Sir Warton Pennymnan Warton (son of Sir James Pennyman and Mary Warton), owner of Newbegin House, died and the following year John Courtney bought the house. He bought some cottages on the other side of Newbegin so that he could enlarge his garden; in order to view the land he had iron railings put into the boundary wall along Newbegin. Here he and his wife brought up their seven children and occupied the house until their respective deaths in 1805 and 1806. They are both, as are also his parents and his aunt and uncle, buried in the chancel of St Mary's church.

John Courtney's journals give an insight into the life of the wealthy living in Beverley at the time. Vols. I and II cover the period 1759-1768 and are mainly concerned with his pursuit of a wife; many times he seems to have been refused (perhaps the smallpox which he had had as a young man had left him sadly disfigured, perhaps, although wealthy, he was not of sufficient wealth or social standing for a society concerned with heredity and status). The volume ends with his marriage to Mary Smelt of Hull.

No diary exists for the years 1768 – 1788. Vol. III 1788-1797 gives much information about his children, his life in the town, his dinners at the Tiger Inn and his visits to the Guildhall. He writes about his concerns with Turnpike Trusts and his social involvements in the town at the Assembly Rooms, the theatre, the race course and the giving of private concerts and dances.

Vol. IV 1798-1805 covers a time when the town was much concerned with the French wars and when many of the military were stationed in Beverley, his social life, travel by stage coach, and his family. The diary finishes a year before his death.

The Country House in the Town

By 1740 the principal houses of the town, with their large landscaped gardens, were Newbegin House, Hotham House in Eastgate, and the Moysers' house in North Bar Within. Two new houses were to be added to this list – Lairgate House (later known as Lairgate Hall) and Norwood House in Norwood.

For the last forty years of the century members of the Pennyman family lived at the Hall, Lairgate. The Pennymans were landed gentry whose roots lay at Ormesby in Cleveland. In the late 17th century the third baronet, Sir James Pennyman, married Mary Warton and for the next 100 years the family was to be closely associated with Beverley. After the death of Sir James in 1745 his son, William, inherited the estate. He died in 1768, childless, and his brother, Sir Warton Pennyman Warton, who had married Charlotte, daughter of Sir Charles Hotham, became the new baronet. He and his wife lived in Newbegin House. They had one son and nine daughters, most of whom were christened in St Mary's church, and who married into local gentry families. After the death of Sir Warton in 1770, his only son having pre-deceased him, the inheritance passed to his cousin, Sir James Pennyman who had been baptized in Beverley on 6th December 1736. Sir James was the son of Ralph Pennyman and Bridget (Gee). Their memorial is in St Mary's church, 'erected as a tribute of filial affection by their daughters Charlotte Bethell, widow of William Bethell Esq. and Dorothy Worsley, widow of Revd James Worsley of Hovingham.'

In 1745 Sir James's uncle, Thomas Pennyman, bought a house which stood on the site of the medieval hospital of St Giles, in Lairgate. Here in 1760 he built a large brick house. Thomas was unmarried and after his death in 1765 Sir James Pennyman purchased the property. Sir James was described as 'a good sort of man, with a thumping landed property in Cleveland, who is exceedingly anxious to get into parliament'. He married Elizabeth, daughter of Sir Henry Grey of Howick, Northumberland and they had ten children. Sir James was a man of fashion who enjoyed spending money and following the latest trend in architecture. His great passion was gambling and so keen was his addiction that he is said to have invited friends at his house to gamble as to which raindrop on the window would reach the sill first.

Sir James employed John Carr from York to re-design Lairgate House in Beverley and also Ormesby Hall, his house in Cleveland. Lairgate House was extended to the west by a dining room and a drawing room so that the main rooms of the house faced onto his landscaped gardens which stretched as far as the Westwood. The stucco ceilings of both these rooms are probably

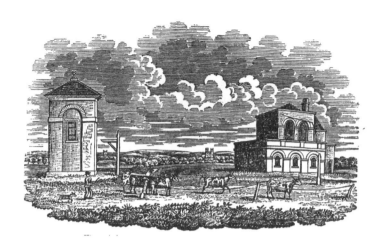

The Grand Stand on the Race Course

the work of Carr's plasterer, Henderson, and closely resemble ceilings which he was working on at Thirsk Hall. In addition the hand painted Chinese wallpaper in the dining room, some of the panels of which duplicate those at Nostell Priory, which was also being worked on by Carr, was the height of fashion at that time. Both rooms have mahogany doors and finely carved marble chimney pieces. The cantilevered staircase leading up to the central dome was re-decorated to make an imposing entrance to the house.

When in 1765 money was needed to build a stand at the racecourse Sir James contributed generously, supervised the building of the grandstand (also designed by John Carr) and was a steward at the races. In 1772, in his role as MP for Scarborough, Sir James had helped Beverley in its opposition to a Bill for bridging the river Hull at Stoneferry and 'for his assiduous attention' was granted the freedom of the borough and became its mayor. In the 1774 parliamentary elections he was returned (as a descendant of the Wartons) 'in the Bar interest' and was to continue to represent the town for the next twenty-two years.

Another important house in Beverley was Norwood House. It was built in 1765 – 70 for the wealthy lawyer Jonathan Midgley on the site of a house and three acres of land he had bought in 1751. Norwood House is referred to by Nikolas Pevsner and David Neave in their book on buildings in the East Riding, as 'Beverley's best Georgian house' with an 'uncommonly fine drawing room'. It had a landscaped garden stretching to the north. After her husband's death in 1778, Jonathan Midgley's widow continued to live in Norwood House until her death in 1791. She and her husband had two daughters, Anne and Mary, but no sons. Anne and her husband, Lord Grantly lived in the house for four years but after the death of Anne in 1795 Mary inherited the house and lived there with her husband, William Beverley, and their four children. After the death of Mary her husband continued to occupy the house.

Other gentry families with town houses were James Gee, younger brother of Thomas Gee of Bishop Burton, who in 1746 built No. 10 Newbegin (set slightly back from the road – re-fronted in early 19th century), members of the Sykes family who occupied Ash Close (built 1732) on the east side of North Bar Without (the Sykes were newly entered into the landed gentry and in 1751 they began the building of their house at Sledmere; the farming skills of Sir Christopher Sykes were to change the face of the Wolds); and the Constables from Burton Constable occupied No. 10 Hengate.

18th Century Brick Buildings in Beverley

A typical early 18th century house in Beverley would be of a pale reddish brown brick, had two storeys, two dormer windows, and a steep pitched roof with overhang (there being no guttering). There were plenty of thatched buildings in Beverley but from the beginning of the 18th century new houses had pantiled roofs. When houses were re-roofed, pantiles might be used but more fashionable (and more expensive) would be plain flat tiling on those parts of the roof visible to the public (see the house adjoining east side of North Bar). More expensive still was Westmorland slate (Lairgate Hall, Norwood House). The house would have a simple unadorned front door in the centre with sashed windows (sashed windows had become popular by the 1720s), which had thick glazing bars and small paned glass on either side. Above would be three sashed windows, two dormer windows in the roof and a chimney at either end of the house. Such a house is No.35 North Bar Within built in 1740 by William Wrightson. Newbegin Bar House (built by the corporation in 1745 at a cost of £315) is similar but as the town ditch ran along the front of the house the front door is at the side of the house and would thus have been inside Newbegin Bar which once stood at the top of Newbegin.

Cornices under the roof were often in brick. Tumbling was much in use – a system from the Netherlands whereby bricks on the end gable of a house were slanted in order to provide extra strength. As the century progressed ironwork was used. Servants' quarters projected into the garden behind. By mid-century shops often had bow windows which allowed greater visibility for goods on sale. Early 18th century houses would have external shutters (White Horse Hengate) but later wood shutters would be inside the window and folded back during the day. As the industrial revolution progressed and cotton material became available curtains began to replace shutters. Another feature of early 18th century houses in Beverley is the patterning of brick cornices projecting from the wall under the roof.

The principal rooms faced the street; the ground floor would have the dining room and common parlour, while the first floor would have the drawing room and 'best chamber'. Day rooms would be panelled. Single storey cottages with attic windows were plentiful but sometimes an upper floor was added (14 Hengate). Many of these 18th century houses in Beverley retain their original features, including the internal cornices, staircases, fireplaces, windows and doors.

New housing was built in Highgate after 1751 when, after the fair had moved to Norwood, the Londoners vacated their houses. Shops in the street were no longer needed and so the area

The Hall, Lairgate

was developed for private occupation. Some properties were demolished and three storey houses built in their place, others, like No 30 Highgate and the George and Dragon (now the Monk's Walk) were re-fronted. This applied throughout the town and was particularly common in shops where trade or rent could not be interrupted while re-building took place. Some other streets where mid-18th century houses were built are Walkergate, Flemingate, North Bar Within, Hengate and Newbegin.

In the last quarter of the century styles changed again. The houses were basically the same shape but now often three-storey (with servants' accommodation in the attics). They were reasonably priced and built for a growing number of professional people, retired military personnel, returned colonists or people who wanted to enjoy the amenities of this elegant County Town.

Lairgate House (now a hotel) had been built in the 17th century. Its walled-garden stretched up to Slutwell Lane (originally known as St Giles Gardens, in 1773 recorded as Slutwell Lane because of a well called Slutwell in the gardens; in 1896 changed to Albert Terrace). In 1780 an extra storey was added to this house. Inside is a fine main staircase, stucco ceiling and fireplaces of the 1780s and a good secondary staircase of

1690. In 1776 the owner of Lairgate House, Mr Lockwood, built a single storey office in his garden, on the corner of Lairgate and Grayburn Lane for his legal practice which in the 19th century became Crust, Todd and Mills.

William Middleton – Builder and Mayor of Beverley

The town was fortunate in having two enterprising speculative builders, William Middleton and Thomas Wrightson. William Middleton married and had two sons, both of whom predeceased him, and five daughters. In 1753 he became a freeman of the borough and was four times mayor of Beverley. His portrait hangs in the Guildhall.

William Middleton acquired brickyards in the east and the south of the town. He was to spend much of the 1760s working for the corporation and in 1761 he built the new Assembly Rooms in Norwood, to the designs of John Carr. These rooms, with the central pillared ballroom and side rooms for cards and afternoon tea were to be an important part of the social life of Beverley for over 200 years.

The following year his plans for remodelling the Guildhall were accepted. The Guildhall, a 14th century building, had been little altered since it had been bought by the corporation in 1501. Its main room was the Great Hall which by 1756 it had so deteriorated that it was necessary to hang matting on the walls to soak up the moisture. The mayor's triple bench, dated 1604, and the treasurer's table with its space below lifting lids in which documents could be kept (both these pieces of furniture are both now in the Magistrates Room) were originally in the hall. William Middleton rebuilt the hall into the courtroom we see today with its Royal coat of arms and ceiling (in the centre of which is the figure of Justice, without a blindfold) decorated by the Italian stuccoist, Giuseppe Cortese – who was working in Yorkshire at that time. In 1764 the corporation ordered William Thornton, the York woodcarver, to make six arm chairs at twenty-five shillings each and six common chairs at seventeen shillings each and Edmund Foster was engaged to carve a timber mayoral dais - designs for all these came from Chippendale's Directory. In this room the justices met and corporation meetings took place. William Middleton enlarged the building by adding the Magistrates Room in which small meetings took place and which for the following 200 years justices of the peace and members of the corporation used as a retiring room.

In 1769 William Middleton was employed to build the grandstand on the race course designed by John Carr. Thereafter Middleton's work gave Beverley its distinctive appearance, which we see today and his houses can often be recognised by their elaborate, Adam style pedimented door cases which were so popular towards the end of the century. Walkergate House built about this time was probably designed by William Middleton, although there is no documentary evidence to prove this, is a handsome three-storey building. Sadly, its small paned Georgian windows have been replaced with large paned glass, thus altering the visual proportions of the building. William Middleton and William Wrightson kept up-to-date with changes in fashion with the help of architectural pattern books. Middleton and Wrightson's clients were mostly wealthy aldermen and tradesmen who disliked ostentation and overspending and who wanted reasonably sized houses.

At the beginning of the century Beverley, being still confined within its medieval boundaries, had inexpensive housing in closely built up lanes and yards behind existing buildings. But an increased need of space for new and better housing meant that the town was to open up. Development could not take place to the west and east of the town because of the common pastures so new building took place to the north. In 1780 the corporation encouraged the laying out of New Walk as a formal promenade with gracious houses alongside. In 1792 a committee set up by the corporation decided to develop the site immediately north of North Bar. An old blacksmiths shop and the maison dieu were demolished and Middleton built Amphion House in their place and constructed a passageway beside the Bar.

Providing for the Poor and Infirm – Ann Routh

Ann Routh's Almshouse

Since the late 16th century the care of the poor in Beverley had been the responsibility of each of the parishes in Beverley with the exception of St John's parish which consisted of townships outside the town. Some of the poor lived in charitable hospitals which had been provided since the days of Elizabeth I and as trustees, the corporation ran Thwaite Fox's Hospital and Sir Michael Warton's Hospital, maintained town almshouses in Butcher Row and the maison dieu which remained in Lairgate and outside North Bar. The parishes distributed out-relief to paupers in their own homes. However, in 1726 the parishes of St Mary, St Martin and St Nicholas united to build a workhouse on the west side of Minster Moorgate for it was felt that it would be more convenient and more economical to provide for the poor under one roof. During the remainder of the century there were usually about thirty paupers in the workhouse, the majority of whom were adults; in the 1750s and 1780s almost half the inmates were children. Over the last quarter of the century expenditure by the three parishes on poor relief multiplied three and a half times – 1776 - £224, 1785 - £370, 1803 - £808. In 1795 the union was dissolved, possibly because of these rising costs, and each wing was administered separately.

Each year the corporation distributed a Christmas charity made up of money from various 17th century bequests and other sources. In 1797 the Poor and Strangers' Friend Society was founded 'for the sole purpose of doing good to the distressed, diminishing the number of street beggars, and relieving at their own habitations, such persons as were found on observation and inquiry to be 'proper objects of benevolence'. During the century artisans and craftsmen, who in medieval times would have been supported by their guilds, began to make their own provision for times of sickness and death. Various friendly societies such as the Brotherly Society, founded in 1776 and the New Friendly Society founded in 1789 were set up.

Throughout the 18th century a number of individual benefactors, left bequests to aid the plight of the poor and the infirm.

One of these was Ann Routh, born in Beverley in 1662 as Ann Truslove. She came from a wealthy family who had been connected with the town since Tudor times. The family held property in the area of the Minster and paid rent to the Corporation for a tenement, garden and orchard in Eastgate which contained one acre of land. They also owned shops and land at Barleyholme. After the death of her father, Mayne Truslove, when she was eight years old, Ann was placed in the care of her uncle who had moved to Pocklington. At nineteen she married

Christopher Moore, a successful businessman and landowner, one of a group of mercers and grocers in Pocklington. They had three children (one died young; the other two pre-deceased Ann). Her husband died in 1699.

Six months after the death of her first husband, Ann, now a wealthy widow, married Thomas Routh. There were no children of this marriage. Ann continued to live in Pocklington but in 1703 moved to a newly built house, No. 65, in Toll Gavel, Beverley (now a tea room). In her will, dated 15th December, 1713, she included an annuity, or rent charge, of forty shillings from her house in Toll Gavel to the minister of the Minster to preach a sermon every 30th September which was the day of the death of her son. Another annuity of £4 was, at the discretion of the mayor and aldermen, to be distributed to the poor of the same parish through the winter months. She ordered that funds were to be raised from her properties to buy land for the building of an almshouse large enough to accommodate twelve poor old widows. Each of the widows was to have an allowance of two shillings a week and be provided with a blue coat on which was sewn a silver badge, engraved with her name and the date of her death. In a codicil to her will in 1721 she left rents to the mayor and aldermen of Beverley and the Minster to pay thirty shillings yearly to the boys of the Charity School in Beverley (the Blue Coat School), the rest of the rents to be given to the poor of the Parish who attended the church.

A memorial to Ann Routh hangs on the pillar to the south of the organ screen in Beverley Minster. After her death the corporation gained possession of all Ann Routh's considerable properties in Yorkshire as well as her house in Toll Gavel. In 1734 the Corporation bought an orchard in Keldgate for £53 17s 0d on which they built the almshouse (at a cost of £387 11s 6d.), designed by James Moyser – the idea of the arcaded theme at the front of the almshouse possibly came from almshouses built with a similar theme designed by the Earl of Burlington - and was formally opened in 1749. Above it, as instructed in her will, were placed the heraldic arms of Ann Routh and her first husband, Christopher Moore.

Memorials in the Churches

A walk round St Mary's Church and the Minster gives glimpses into the lives of the people in the town who could afford to have their names recorded in memorials. A memorial in St Mary's church notes the death on 13th July 1729 of Jane (aged 81), wife of Thomas Ellinor, bricklayer. They had borne two sons, both of whom pre-deceased them; one of their sons, Thomas, died in Jamaica. His will of 1726 decreed that after the death of his parents his real and personal estate was to go to charitable uses within the town of Beverley. This included rent, from two messuages and a stable in Toll Gavel, which amounted to £27 a year; one guinea a year was to be paid to the vicar of St Mary's for a sermon to be preached on Easter Sunday and the remainder of the money, after paying for repairs to the properties, was to be given to the churchwardens to distribute on Good Friday, each year, among poor persons of the parishes of St Mary's, St Nicholas and St Martin. By a codicil to his will of 1728 he ordered his executors to transmit all his money, outstanding debts, and personal estate in the island of Jamaica to his executors and trustees in England. However, this money was never forthcoming.

The Revd George Davies, by his will dated 1764, bequeathed £100 to the corporation of Beverley to be placed out at interest, and laid out in meat, 'to be distributed to the poor of the parish of St Mary's Beverley, annually, upon Christmas day, for ever'. Mrs Frances Pinckney died in 1788 and in her will bequeathed £100 to be applied in the same manner.

A memorial to Robert Wride (a woollen draper, alderman and three times mayor of Beverley) and of his wife lies in the north aisle of St Mary's church. They had nine children, seven of whom pre-deceased them. Their memorial was put up by their two surviving children, Walter and Ann. Ann Wride, recorded on her tomb as 'spinster', died in 1779 aged 82.

In St Mary's church there are several memorials to members of the Grabury/Grayburn family who gave their name to a street,

AN EXTRACT FROM THE WILL, DATED 1778, OF MRS ANN WRIDE

Mrs Ann Wride bequeathed £800 to be invested in some good security, in the name of the vicar and churchwardens of the parish of St Mary, who are directed to apply the interest in the following manner.

'To eight poor women of the said parish, who regularly frequent the church, shall be given 20s each, on Easter Sunday, immediately after divine service, in the chancel of St Mary's; and to each a new gown of grey stuff, and other necessary articles of apparel to the value of 20s each.

To eight poor men shall be given at the same time and place, and under the same circumstances, the sum of 10s each; and the clerk, sexton, and wand-bearer of that church shall always constitute three of the number.

The further sum of £5 shall be annually distributed amongst the poor of this parish on Christmas-day, in the proportion of 2s 6d to poor families, and a shilling each to single persons.

To eight poor persons inhabiting the Maison-dieu, near the North Bar, shall be given on the last mentioned day the sum of 10s each.

And, I do also order that the sum of one guinea shall be paid to the vicar of the said parish of St Mary, and his successors for the time being, on every Easter Sunday, in consideration of the trouble he may have in seeing the said charitable trusts duly performed according to my will;

and I desire that the two first verses of the 2nd Psalm may be always sung on Easter Sunday and on the Sunday next after my decease, in the morning service.'

Annual income, £30 1s 0d.

previously called Catfoss Lane, running off the west side of Lairgate. William Grayburn, merchant and alderman of the town, died in 1688. His son, Richard, died in 1720 at the age of 31, described as a dutiful son, an honest tradesman and a pious Christian.

Charles Moss died 1731 aged 41. His wife warns:

Thou that comest to take a view of one gone into eternity beware thou tread not rudely upon learned ashes for thou now standest at the tomb of Charles Moss, Doctor of Physick, a Gentleman well learned in languages, arts and sciences but chiefly incomparably skill'd in the theorick part of physick, and in the practick part gave place to none.

Towards the end of the 18th century Beverley seems to have become a retirement place for army officers. The Minster has a memorial recording the death of Oliver De Lancey, Brigadier General in America who died in 1785 at the age of 69. A native of the Colony of New York, he possessed valuable estates in North America which, because of his loyalty to George III at the outbreak of the War of Independence in America, he sacrificed. At the start of war he raised a brigade of three regiments and continued in command until the end of the war. Once the war was over he and his family were compelled to seek asylum in Britain. He lived in No. 25 Highgate. Memorials to his two granddaughters, Charlotte Child and Anna Maria Lawson are also in the Minster.

Law and Order

In 1708, as a result of an order from the East Riding Magistrates, the first Registrar's Office, one of the first in the country, was built near Well Lane (now Champney Road) and the area to the east of the building, and north of Cross Street, became known as Register Square. Here all public records of deeds, conveyances and wills were to be kept.

In mid-18th century, meetings of the East Riding Quarter Sessions were held in a building in Hall Garth. The borough JPs had their own petty and quarter sessions gatherings in the Guildhall. Offences involving loss of life were heard at the twice yearly assizes at York.

A right to have its own prison had been given to the town in 1573 and offenders were imprisoned in the medieval maison dieu at Cross Bridge in Toll Gavel. This was repaired in 1730 but by the 1770s only one or two prisoners were confined there and in

1792 it was said to be in a poor condition. Prisoners were also kept in the East Riding House of Correction attached to the Guildhall.

Generally Beverley was a peaceful town but along with the rest of the country there were times of unrest. In 1748 a mob, objecting to the raising of tolls on the river, killed the toll collector at Grovehill and burned down the gates there. In 1757, at the time of the outbreak of the Seven Years War, there was a riot in Beverley against the imposition of the Militia Act. This act sought to raise a territorial army in order to defend the country against the threat of a French invasion. Several hundred people from the surrounding area entered Beverley, demanded money from the resident gentry and threatened to burn the town. The money was given and the rioters left.

The East Riding Militia

Members of the militia were often stationed in the town. In 1745, 1750s and 1760s there had been up to 800 soldiers in the town seeking accommodation. Since an Act of Parliament in 1660 each county had a militia under the control of the Lord Lieutenant who could commission a number of deputy lieutenants and militia officers. To be Lord Lieutenant, Deputy Lieutenant or a commissioned officer a man needed to own property of which at least half was in the county in which he served. The higher the rank the more property was required – a colonel needed an estate producing £400 a year, an ensign an estate producing £50 a year. No soldier could expect promotion unless he held the necessary property required for the higher rank. The Militia Act of 1757 gave the country a properly organised efficient militia force of 32,000 men. Each county was expected to provide its quota of men and in order to organise this, in 1762, each parish had to provide a list of all able-bodied men between the ages of eighteen and forty-five.

In 1759, when England was at war with France, there was a real fear of invasion. The East Yorkshire Militia Regiment was formed, divided into ten companies, with a colonel, a lieutenant colonel, a major, seven captains, ten lieutenants, ten ensigns and one adjutant – plus a surgeon, a quarter-master, twenty sergeants, twenty corporals, twenty drummers, and 400 privates.

After the uprising in France, in which many members of the nobility were executed, a proclamation was issued by the revolutionaries in November 1792 which offered the assistance of France to all peoples who would rise against their rulers. After the execution of Louis XVI England was once again under threat of invasion and war was declared. The East Yorkshire Militia was reviewed by the Lord Lieutenant of the East Riding, the Duke of Leeds and his son the Marquis of Carmarthen. They arrived in Beverley on Thursday 27th December and on 28th, it being winter, they reviewed the militia in the Minster. The organ played 'God Save the King'. On 31st December there was a muster at Beverley and the people of Beverley were asked to subscribe to clothing for the men; £560 was raised.

By March 1793 a new Militia Act empowered the Lord Lieutenant to raise volunteer companies and the Duke of Leeds called a meeting of lieutenants at Beverley. In April, meetings were held at the Guildhall of the 'Noblemen, Gentlemen, Clergy, Freeholders and Yeoman of the Riding to consider plans to be adopted for the internal defence of the Riding'. Five troops were formed based on Hull, Beverley, Driffield, Bridlington and Hunmanby. On 14th May John Courtney was at a General Meeting of the Lieutenants of the East Riding at the Beverley Arms:

> I never saw so many. There was the Lord Lieutenant, the Duke of Leeds, and twenty-four Deputy Lieutenants; Major General Lord Mulgrave, General of the District and Major General Lenox. The Duke of Leeds was in the Chair. We dined forty-eight. The table reached from the top to the bottom of the Great Room above stairs. I sat near the bottom, my son at another table. Major Garforth was at the top – about sixteen gentlemen. Colonel Maxwell and Major Pitts sat in a group, the officers of the staff at another group at the top of the room. In going away I was obliged to disturb them by looking for my hat and stick. The Duke spoke to me, and Colonel Mulgrave too, and advised me to take a good one.

The militia stayed in the area and by November 1803 Lord and Lady Mulgrave (who were staying at the hall at Bishop Burton) became part of the social scene attending assemblies and dining with John Courtney at his house in Newbegin.

The presence of the military in the town was welcomed by traders and innkeepers, and no doubt, also, by mothers, who like Mrs Bennett of 'Pride and Predjudice', had unmarried daughters. Other mothers might view the soldiers with fear as their less virtuous daughters viewed them with delight!

Entertainment in Beverley

There were several cockpits in the town including a large round building in Wednesday Market with seating for 600 people, smaller pits in the Globe Inn and near the King's Head in Saturday Market, the Blue Bell Inn (Beverley Arms) and in a building in Wood Lane.

Betting men often spent the evenings of horse race days at one of the cockpits in Beverley where cockfighting took place. The Sporting Register in 1747 quotes:

> At Beverley in the Whitsun week last, Mr Norris fought the gentlemen of Hedon for four guineas a battle and in forty of the said main (a main being a match between fighting cocks), which consisted of nineteen battles, ten were won by Mr Norris and nine by Hedon.

One of the first musical festivals in the North of England took place in 1769 with a concert of Handel's music to celebrate the placing of a new organ in the Minster, built by John Snetzler who was one of the most prominent organ builders of the day. St Mary's church acquired a new organ in 1792.

Assemblies had been held in Beverley since 1732 and from 1745 were held in rooms in North Bar Within. In 1762 the wealthier members of the town subscribed to the building of new Assembly Rooms on the corner of Norwood. Here assemblies for dancing and cards were held on alternate Wednesdays beginning in late September, continuing throughout the winter months and throughout the whole of race week in June. A flavour of the time is given in the journals of John Courtney:

> Wednesday 25th May 1763 - This evening the new Assembly Rooms were opened by a ball given by the officers of the East Riding militia. Sir Griffith Boynton opened it with Lady Legard. There was a very splendid appearance of ladies and gentleman and the rooms were also very elegant as well as the entertainment.

By 1790s regular assemblies began in mid October to coincide with the annual meeting of lord lieutenant and deputy lieutenants for the East Riding and the military added a glitter to grand occasions. John Courtney wrote of one such occasion which took place on 15th June 1798.

> My wife and my sons, John and Septimus, and my two daughters were at the Assembly. As Mr B. (Bethell?) was not come I was obliged to be the manager. Lady Charlotte Lennox came and sat down at the bottom of the room. I went to ask her to permit me to lead her to the top. She said that she should wait for her mother, who, soon after coming in, I went to her and desired I might have the honour of leading Her Grace to the top of the room. I, accordingly, handed the Duchess of Gordon up to the top of the room, and soon after I spoke to all the great people and managed that Major General Lord Mulgrave and Lady Georgiana Gordon were the first couple and Major General Lennox and Lady Mulgrave the second. At tea the Duchess sent a gentleman to me to desire I would sit down at their table and talked to me and was extremely affable and polite. We all came away about two o'clock

For many centuries horse racing had taken place in Beverley but from 1690 regular meetings were held on the 'tan gallop' west of Newbegin Pits; in 1712 races took place in September, in 1750 at Whitsun. In 1764 the racecourse was moved to its present position on the Hurn and in 1767 the grandstand, designed by John Carr (who had also designed grandstands at York and Richmond) was built by William Middleton. Money for the stand was raised by special subscription. By 1770 Beverley had its Gold Cup race. John Courtney celebrated the opening of the new race course:

> I was three days upon the stand in the race ground
> and danced every night at the assembly.

Race meetings were held on three consecutive days in June. In 1771 a merchant from Hull, RC Broadley, spent five days at Beverley at a cost of £5 18s of which 17s 6d was spent on subscriptions to and expenses at the assemblies.

> £1 1s at the races
> 2s 6d for a concert
> 2s 6d for theatre
> 10s 6d for lodgings

Theatrical entertainment was also popular. By 1730 Beverley was included in the circuit of a principal York theatrical company. In the 1750s a playhouse was built in Walkergate; it was replaced by another in Register Square. In 1766 Tate Wilkinson became manager of several Yorkshire theatres and with his players visited Beverley. In 1771 his lease of the theatre had expired but was not renewed and he was ordered out of town by the mayor for being about to put on a 'naughty play'. Later he was to write that:

> Beverley is not a town of trade, but, like York, is chiefly supported by the genteel private families that reside there in a continuance; I cannot boast of any permanent intimacies with superior persons at Beverley, beyond a kind of summer friendship that with the least gust drops off.'

By 1788 the town had become part of the Richmond circuit when members of the Butler family from Richmond came to Beverley for four or five weeks in August and before the Hull season began in October.

John Courtney comments on the plays he and his family saw:

1797 5th May - 'A Cure for the Heart Ache' – the play was a new and very good one and a merry one from beginning to end and in general well acted'.

15th June - 'Duplicity and Love a la mode' – badly performed'.

17th June - 'Everyone has his Faults' – very full house and very hot'.

1798 10th June – 'My sons John and Septimus were on the race stand. My wife and daughters were at the play to see 'The Castle Spectre''.

John Courtney frequently refers to concerts and parties with dancing in people's houses. In 1788 Charles Dibdin, a dramatist, novelist and song-writer, undertook a musical tour of the East Riding and Hull. Of Beverley he wrote:

Beverley is a town of much spirit and respectability' with its water link with Hull 'there is a perpetual bustle and business going forward; which mixed with the appearance of affluence in the residences of gentlemen of independent fortune, many inhabitants of which it boasts, render it a place of very considerable importance. The sessions for the East Riding are held at this place and there is an office for publicly registering wills and deeds for that division.'

The Close of the Century

Towards the end of the century the interests of three influential families living in the town were to remove elsewhere.

In 1775 the Warton estate, by Act of Parliament, was finally disbanded and sold. The Beverley property was bought by Charles Anderson Pelham (the great nephew of Elizabeth Warton and Charles Pelham whose only son had died without issue) who in 1763 had taken on the name of Pelham; in 1794 he became Lord Yarborough. Soon after he inherited the property he demolished the house in Beverley Parks – all that remains of that property today are two gateposts, a walled garden and part of the house - and the Warton house at North Bar Within; in place of the North Bar house he built, a handsome three-storey terrace, Nos. 55-63 North Bar Within, with steps leading up, iron hand rails and Adam style door cases.

By 1770 Sir James Pennyman was heavily in debt, partly as a result of extensive building programmes at his house in Beverley and at Ormesby Hall, and in 1772 he sold much of his land around Lairgate Hall. In 1780 he built Nos. 6 and 8 Newbegin (built by William Middleton) - No. 8 Newbegin has since had an extra storey added - and in 1781 he auctioned off much of the luxurious contents of Lairgate Hall. In 1782 he was once again mayor and in the parliamentary elections of 1784 was opposed by Sir Christopher Sykes who, after great expense, gained the majority of the votes; however, as Beverley was permitted to return two MPs to Parliament, Sir James, having won the second largest number of votes, was also returned. In 1789 Sir James was again in financial difficulties and was forced to sell the contents of Ormesby Hall. In the 1790 elections he was returned but with a much reduced majority. He died in Cleveland in 1808 and, spending to the end, was given a lavish funeral costing £501 15s. His only son, William, became the 7th baronet. Sir William had married Charlotte, daughter of Bethell Robinson of Catwick; they had no children. Until his death in 1852 he lived for much of the year at 76 Lairgate.

The third family to leave the record books of the town was the Gee family which had been associated with the town for almost 200 years. James Gee (1636-1751) - recorded as James Gee of Beverley - was the younger brother of Thomas Gee who lived at High Hall Bishop Burton. In 1727 he had married Constance, daughter of John Moyser, in St Mary's church. During the second quarter of the 18th century a large house was built for him in Bishop Burton, known as Low Hall (now demolished). When in Beverley he lived in the house he had built for himself, No. 10 Newbegin. After the death of Thomas Gee in 1749 the

A View of North Bar Within in 1780 and below a modern view.

A Bow Fronted Shop in Saturday Market from the mid 18th century

estate passed to his grandson, Roger Gee who was mayor of Beverley 1778. He was married to the 8th daughter and co-heiress of Sir Warton Pennyman. However the estate was already in financial difficulty and was sold after the death of Roger Gee in Bath in 1779.

David Hick's 1811 plan of Beverley, which is the back endpaper of this book, shows it to be a town with broad streets and wide open spaces. The layout of the town had hardly changed since the middle ages, although there was some development to the north of North Bar. It was a town with a number of large houses set in extensive grounds, while other housing was mostly along the main streets with orchards and open spaces between. With its clean air and its range of entertainments no wonder that visitors like to come to Beverley; many of them chose to settle there.

CHAPTER 11

1800 - 1900 THE INDUSTRIAL INCLINE

Historians estimate population figures of previous centuries from studying hearth tax or poll tax returns or parish documents. In 1801 came the first national census giving accurate figures.

National Census Population Figures			
	England	Hull	Beverley
1801	9,000,000	27,609	5,401
1901	36,000,000	240,259	13,183

The figures above show that while the population of England quadrupled during the 19th century and the population of Hull increased by almost nine times the original figure, the population of Beverley went up by almost two and a half times. The rise in the population of Beverley was steep but not nearly as steep as in other towns.

Throughout the 19th century the town needed to expand to accommodate the increase in population but it was to remain, essentially, a market town. To improve the movement of the increased traffic of people, carts, stage-coaches and ships to and from the town certain changes were made. In 1790 the 15th century brick gateway into Newbegin was demolished and in 1808 Keldgate Bar was taken down. In 1802 lock gates were fitted where the Beck ran into the river Hull so that falling tides did not restrict the passage of boats laden with grain and travelling along rivers to the developing industrial towns in the West Riding of Yorkshire.

At the beginning of the century members of the country gentry still resided in the town but over the years more and more houses were built for wealthy traders, professional people and a developing middle class. Ostensibly the town gave an appearance of wealth with handsome houses fronting onto the main streets but behind these houses poorer people were cramped into yards and closes with poor sanitation.

The Provision of Free and Fee-Paying Education

By the beginning of the century there was a growing interest in a need for education. A reduction of infant mortality meant that there were more children who needed to be trained for employment. At a time when government took little interest in the provision of education many educational religious bodies felt that schools would not only enable poorer children to read and write but would also give them the opportunity to peruse the scriptures. At first Sunday schools were the only form of education available for the children of the poor and in Beverley children were encouraged to attend with the opportunity of outings to the seaside and picnics on the Westwood. Elementary schools were later set up, provided by members of the churches of the town. The Church of England set up schools through the National Society for Promoting the Education of the Poor in the Principles of the Established Church. Such schools would be run on the monitorial system and would consist of one large room with a master in charge who would instruct monitors (pupils aged 10-11 years) who would then teach the other children in groups of 10-20 pupils. The first National School in England was in 1812. In June of that year, as a result of a meeting of clergy and gentry in Beverley, the East Riding District Society, affiliated to the National Society, was set up with Revd J Coltman, curate of the Minster, as secretary. The first National School was opened in 1813 next to the workhouse in Minster Moorgate; (later this site housed the Minster Infants' School – now it is a private house).

Revd James Graves, a curate at the Minster who died in 1807, left money for the teaching of poor children of St Martin's parish. At first income from the charity was given to existing dame schools but in 1810 two schools were set up as a result of

Schools Established to Provide Elementary Education in 19th Century Beverley		
Year founded	**School name**	**Location**
1810	Graves Boys School	In Saturday Market. 1814 moved to Register Square, 1826 changed premises with National school in Minster Moorgate. 1840 moved to Holme Church Lane 1846 converted to National School.
1810	Graves Girls School	In Wilkinson's Yard, Toll Gavel. 1814 moved to Register Square. In 1825 moved to room in Minster Yard North.
1838	St Mary's Infants School	Lairgate. In 1842 housed in new building.
1838	British School	Established in Minster Moorgate.
1838	Wesleyan School	Schoolroom at rear of Walkergate chapel 1844 moved to new building in School Lane.
1840	St Mary's Girls School	Quaker Meeting House, Wood Lane. In 1875 moved to Norwood
1845	Minster Infants School	Established in former school in Minster Moorgate, replaced by new building there in 1838 (building still remains).
1848	Minster National School	Lurk Lane
1849	St Mary's National School	Cross Street
1852	Minster Infants School	Flemingate
1860	St John's Roman Catholic School	
1875	St Mary's Girls School	Norwood
1880	St Nicholas School	Holme Church Lane
1885	Minster Girls School	Minster Yard North

the Graves' bequest: one for boys (in a room near the fish shambles in Saturday Market) and one for girls (in a room in Wilkinson's Yard, Toll Gavel). Both schools became National Society schools. Joseph Hind (a future councillor of Beverley) born 1816, first attended the National School at the age of six; by the age of thirteen he was head monitor and was often in charge of all 200 boys when, according to him, the master was too drunk to attend!

The Blue Coat School, a boarding school for poor children, opened in 1710, continued during the 19th century. In 1826 the school stipulated that students should be aged between nine and fourteen and be the sons of poor men of good reputation residing in Beverley. Children were provided with a uniform: a blue coat of medium length with a yellow collar, flat gilt buttons, a blue sleeved waistcoat, corduroy knee breeches with brass buttons and blue worsted stockings. They wore buckled shoes, a white neckerchief with linen bands and a soft blue cloth billycock cap. Discipline was strict. Pupils were permitted to visit their parents on Saturdays, and on Sundays after attending a service at the Minster where they were expected to sing in the choir. Holidays consisted of a week at Christmas, two days each at Easter and Whitsun, a day on the monarch's birthday and on each of the four great fairs in Beverley. They also had a half-day at the mayor's swearing-in ceremony when there was much merrymaking in the town. The boys were expected to take part in funeral processions through the streets, singing psalms and hymns along the route. When they left the school they would be apprenticed to a Beverley master who was supplied by the Charity with an apprentice fee of £3 in annual instalments of £1.

A typical pupil at the school was Andrew Gledhill who was born in 1800. Ten years later his father, a flax dresser, died. Andrew then attended the Blue Coat School where he remained until 1813. From 1816-1819 his brother David was also at the school. His mother managed to obtained poor relief to provide clothing for her children but in 1818 she and three younger children went into the workhouse in Minster Moorgate where she died. After leaving school Andrew was apprenticed to a shoemaker. When qualified he moved to Kilham where he died in 1889.

The 1851 census showed that 1,054 children (657 boys and 397 girls) were on the rolls of the public elementary schools and 471 children (176 boys and 295 girls) were on the rolls of private schools – this was a higher percentage of children on school rolls than in other towns. However, statistics as ever are misleading for being placed on the rolls did not necessarily mean attendance at school. By 1865 the elementary schools in Beverley were said to provide an excellent education for children of the labouring classes and for those of the class immediately above.

In 1814 the Grammar School building in the Minster churchyard, in use since 1609, was demolished and the school moved to a new building adjoining the schoolmaster's house in Keldgate. At this time the school was still 'in considerable repute'. The Municipal Corporations Act of 1832 meant that the corporation was no longer empowered to support the Grammar School. There was debate in the Council as to whether financial support should continue. In a meeting of the Borough Council in 1842 Joseph Hind was reported in the Beverley Guardian as saying that he 'now understood why councillors were so 'virulent' against the master of the Grammar School; 'for they themselves had not attended the school and he felt that they should devote their undoubted abilities to the cultivation of their mother tongue rather than emitting venom and rancour against all whose opinions might differ from their own'. In 1842 financial support was withdrawn and the Grammar School had to rely for its existence on tuition fees. By 1860 the fees were £6 6s a year for 'free' scholars and a minimum of £10 10s for other pupils. By1865 the Grammar School had only fifteen day pupils and the education provided was considered to be little more than an inferior elementary school with a 'lifeless and disheartening aspect'.

The Foundation School, was opened in Beverley in 1861, funded and endowed with the income of Archer's Charity money, a Chancery Scheme of 1854. The school buildings were those which are now used by the Health Centre in Albert Terrace. This school, which provided education for thirty-six boys, was for the sons of prosperous traders, farmers, doctors and solicitors. The fees were £2 a year for day boys – considerably less than fees at the Grammar School.

In 1822 Miss Elizabeth Stephenson opened her boarding school for girls in Highgate. Later she and the school moved to Eastgate, then to Hengate, then to Newbegin House in Newbegin, and lastly to Holland House in Register Square. The school closed in 1926.

Entertainments and Leisure Pursuits

In 1804 land was donated in Lairgate (at the junction of Lairgate and Champney Road) and the following year a new theatre was opened on the site, with galleries and seating for 600 people.

Members of the Butler family performed in Beverley until the death of Samuel Butler in 1812. Samuel Butler was instrumental in the building of theatres in Richmond (the Georgian theatre there still remains), Harrogate, Kendal, Northallerton, Ulverston, Whitby and Ripon. Every year his company of players would spend several weeks at each theatre. The plays they performed often introduce political themes of the day, such as the abolition of slavery. Samuel Butler died while in Beverley and his memorial is in the south transept of St Mary's church with the apt Shakespearian quotation: 'A poor player that struts and frets his hour upon the stage and then is heard no more'. After his death Beverley ceased to be part of the theatrical circuit for the Butler company.

In 1844 the theatre in Lairgate was demolished and the cream coloured bricks from the theatre were used to build a house in Station Square which in 2002 was converted into flats. Part of the grey brick wall of the theatre in Lairgate, with a blocked window, is still visible.

The Assembly Rooms were in use for the first part of the century. On 18th January 1804 John Courtney, now an old man, records in his diary:

The Ballroom at the Assembly Rooms

Queen's Birthday (Queen Anne 1702 – 1714) kept and my son and my daughter, Dolly, were at the Assembly. There was a great deal of company and very full room. There were brides and bridegrooms there. Mr Acklam was there, he looked pretty well, I thought, and seemed in good spirits. Sometime towards the latter part of the evening he came up to me and said 'I think it is about time I leave this bad air and this hot room', but he spoke cheerfully; he, however stayed some time after. I did not come away till 10 o'clock in the evening.

In 1840 the Assembly Rooms were extended and the building was re-named the Beverley and East Riding Public Rooms. Travelling players performed here, concerts were heard, society dinners held and lectures given on such learned subjects as that reported in the Beverley Guardian in July 1842 by Mrs Clara Lucas Balfour (authoress) 'The Moral and Intellectual Influence of Women in Society'.

There were several market gardens in Beverley where people could walk much as we do today at garden centres. The census for 1851 records seventy-five gardeners and nurserymen. William Tindall ran a thirty acre nursery garden which at one time employed fifty people. It was situated to the north-east of the Minster and covered the area of the Trinities, once the site of the preceptory of the Knights Hospitallers. However by 1830 the company was bankrupt. Another nursery was in the west end of Well Lane (now known as Champney Road.)

The publishing of Acts of Parliament increased a thirst for knowledge. Two newspapers came into circulation in Beverley during the 1850s. The Beverley Recorder (1855-1921), was a Liberal paper, printed and published by John Green at his premises in Saturday Market and in 1856 the Beverley Guardian, still available today, a Conservative paper, came into circulation. Other papers such as the Beverley Echo, the Independent, the East Riding Telegraph either did not last or were incorporated with other local papers. Talks and other social events, as well as news, were advertised in the papers.

In 1850 the Mechanics Institute, a place where the 'working man' could receive an education, was opened on the site of the present East Riding of Yorkshire County offices in Cross Street. The Hull historian JJ Sheahan was a frequent lecturer. Other speakers included Mr John Richardson of Hull (a surgeon dentist) whose subject was 'Oracles and Necromancy of the Ancients Contrasted with the Fortune Telling, Clairvoyance etc. of the Modern'. The Mutual Improvement Society also provided lectures on such subjects as 'The Moral Philosophy of the Human Form'. Churches and chapels ran clubs and societies providing educational opportunities. By mid-century there was a subscription library and Green's Public library which provided reading rooms.

Church goers, particularly the Methodists, regarded social work and care of the poor as part of their mission. The

The Beverley Arms Hotel

Temperance Movement, begun in the 1870s, aimed to offer an alternative to drunkenness and excessive expenditure on drink which members of the movement believed to be one of the major evils of society. In the Temperance Hall in Well Lane (demolished in 2000) lectures and musical entertainment in a non-alcoholic environment were provided; in order to encourage singing it had its own piano.

In 1822 there were thirty-six public houses in Beverley, many of them dating back several centuries. By 1893 the number of pubs and inns in the town had risen to fifty-six; over thirty of them remain today. In 1840 the principal coaching inns were the King's Head and the Green Dragon in Saturday Market from where coaches such as 'the Highflier', 'the Mail' and 'the Pilot' left regularly for Hull. In North Bar Within, the Tiger, the Beverley Arms and the King's Arms (the bracket for its sign still remains in the building next to Combes Yard in North Bar Within), saw the departure of the 'Mail, the 'Wellington', the 'Old Mail', the 'Beverlac' and the 'Queen Adelaide' for Hull while 'the Trafalgar', the 'Express' and the 'Scarborough' left for York. Other pubs in regular use were the Globe Inn (top of

Saturday Market – demolished in the 1960s), the Cross Keys (Lairgate), the Dog and Duck (Ladygate), the Holderness Hotel (No. 16 - 18 Toll Gavel; now converted into shops), the Pack Horse (next to the King's Head), the Wheatsheaf, The Lion and Lamb, the Valiant Soldier (now the Corner House in Norwood) and the White Horse (Hengate). In 1888 Francis Collinson became the tenant of the White Horse and he, his wife and their children – William, Frank, Arthur, Tim, John, David, Thomas, Lily, Nellie, Dorothy, Edith, Annie and Ada were to be the licensees for almost ninety years.

Peace Celebrated

For the first fifteen years of the century war continued with France. On 31st March 1814, Paris was captured and Napoleon was forced to abdicate. Louis XVIII was recognised by European countries as king of France.

The capture of Napoleon was met with general relief. In his history of Beverley (published 1829), Poulson gives an eye-witness account of the celebrations which took place in Beverley.

'On Tuesday, 28th June 1814 peace was declared to the accompaniment of the ringing of church bells and general rejoicing. The following day a procession started from the Guildhall which consisted of twenty-four constables with banners, a band of music, the mayor, aldermen, capital burgesses, the principal inhabitants of the town and neighbourhood, the tradesmen and other inhabitants, brethren of the Constitutional Lodge of Free-Masons, and members of the Benefit Societies.

'At midday this procession made its first stand at the cross (an obelisk, erected in 1723; removed 1881) in Wednesday Market, where the proclamation was formally made amidst the reiterated cheering of the people; it then moved forward to the Saturday Market-place, where it was received with a royal salute from eight guns, and peace was again proclaimed at the cross. After proceeding through the North-Bar to the extremity of the town, the assembly returned to the Saturday Market-place, and sung the national anthem of God Save the King in full chorus; separating until the hour of dinner with loud acclamations. The day concluded with a superb illumination, the most striking feature of which was the Market Cross. The columns were adorned with spiral wreaths of brilliant lamps, interspersed with laurel, olive, and evergreens, the emblems of victory and permanent peace, and the urns were decorated with elegant festoons of small lamps tinted with every variety of colour.'

However, the celebrations were too early. In March 1815 Napoleon escaped from the island of Elba, the place of his imprisonment, and landed in France where he was received with enthusiasm by the army. He was finally defeated at the Battle of Waterloo in June 1815. Hc was exiled to St Helena where he died in 1821.

As soldiers returned from war, seeking employment, there was a real fear of social unrest, inflamed by political ideas of liberty, equality and fraternity spreading from France and North America. In previous centuries the chief purpose of national government had been to raise taxes in order to defend the realm. In the 19th century Parliament more and more took on the role of suggesting means of relieving poverty in order to preserve law and order, and, when these reforms were not implemented, imposing rules and regulations on local governments to do so.

The Administration of the Law

Beverley Petty Sessions continued to be held in the Council Chamber (also known as the Court Room) of the Guildhall several times a week. Here trials were held for breaches of the peace, being drunk and disorderly, prostitution, thieving, quarrels between neighbours and speeding horses through the town. The right to have a town gaol had been established by the Elizabethan Charter of 1573 but by 1792 the town prison was in a poor condition. The prison was the late 14th century chantry chapel (described by Poulson as 'an antique dwelling of stone') which had been built as a result of the will of John de Ake, in Toll Gavel near Cross bridge. When the House of Correction was built in New Walk the old prison was demolished and the gaol behind the Guildhall was re-built as the town prison.

Beverley also continued to be the centre of justice in the East Riding. The government encouraged the building of sessions houses for meetings of Quarter Sessions. The Council Chamber, and the old prison attached to the Guildhall, was found to be inadequate for the administration of justice in the East Riding and a Sessions House was built in New Walk in 1810 (designed by Watson and Pritchett of York in 1804). With its large portico of Ionic columns and a pediment containing the royal coat of arms it gives the appearance of a stately home, quite in keeping with other houses in North Bar Without (housing did not reach New Walk until the late 19th century). On the pediment stands the full length coad-stone figure of justice (with eyes open, as in the plaster figure in the Council Chamber in the Guildhall). A frieze of manacles is the decoration on the portico ceiling – a grim reminder of what went on inside the building. The court rooms are panelled with oak. Meetings of the Quarter Sessions, trying cases of larceny, house breaking, assault etc, were held here in January, April, July and October. Trials for murder were held at York.

With an increase in lawlessness the severity of sentences increased:

Christmas 1817 - George Walls of Pocklington, labourer: for unlawfully entering into the wood at Pocklington and having in his possession a gun with the intent to kill and destroy game – hard labour, one year in the House of Correction. (At the same time William Carr the younger of Pocklington, was accused of a similar offence and ordered to be transported for seven years)

Beverley Sessions House from an early 19th Century print

Michaelmas 1819 – James Mowthorpe, late of Bishop Burton, labourer: for a violent assault upon one Jane Bulmer with an intent to commit a rape – to be confined to the House of Correction for two years.

Easter 1823 - Abraham Overfield of Cherry Burton, labourer: for stealing three gowns and two shawls the property of Hannah Ellerker – convicted to the House of Correction to hard labour for six months.

Behind the Sessions House was the East Riding House of Correction, opened in 1810. Early in the century houses of correction were set up throughout England which were expected to fulfil three conditions: they were to be secure, healthy and large enough to provide for the separation of prisoners so that those who had fallen foul of the law might have time to reflect on their crimes and thus, it was felt, become better citizens.

The House of Correction at Beverley was designed round the Turnkey's House, an eight sided three-storey building from which the turnkey (who held the keys to the prison) could view the whole complex of exercise yards. The two-acre site was surrounded by a high wall. In 1810 the prison had twenty-two cells and in 1812 four more cells were added plus workshops. By 1820 prisoners were divided into fourteen classes according to sex and severity of crime and thirty-three more cells were added. The prison still remained overcrowded and after the introduction of the silent system in 1835 day rooms were converted into cells giving a total of 126 cells.

On entering the House of Correction all prisoners would have a bath and a hair cut. They were then supplied with regulation prison dress and each week with linen. They were expected to attend the chapel which had screens which separated the sexes, although complaints were made by those in charge that the screens were too low. Most prisoners were allowed visitors once a week. As part of the process of reform, prisoners were expected to work at such tasks as pulling rushes for wicks of rush lights, washing, cooking and mending.

In 1835 it was decided that life in Houses of Correction was insufficiently harsh to bring about the reform of prisoners. In response to a national demand, tread-wheels were installed in several Houses of Correction. At Beverley prisoners would be sentenced to tread the wheel for twenty minutes, have a ten minute break and then back to the wheel until they had completed the stipulated 'labour of ascent'. The wheel was similar to the wheel of a paddle steamer, with small airless compartments to prevent prisoners communicating with each other, and a rail to hold on to. The back of the wheel was exposed so that prisoners could be watched as they worked the wheel to grind whiting or pulverise chalk stone. Clothes soon became soaked with sweat and did not have time to dry out before the next session. Both men and women would be condemned to work on the tread-wheel – the length of time depended on their sentence.

The Silent System was also introduced which forbade communication between prisoners. In 1839 a prominent political prisoner, Robert Peddie, was sentenced to three years in the House of Correction in Beverley. In 1840 he made a petition to the House of Commons complaining about the harsh treatment he was enduring. He referred to the 'black-hole', a small cell used for solitary confinement, which was without light or furniture so that the person confined in it must either stand or sit on the floor. Here he had been confined all day without food, water or light. The following morning he had been provided with a half-pound loaf and a quart of water for the twenty-four hour supply. When he was released from the House of Correction he left a permanent record of prison life in Beverley in a booklet entitled 'The Dungeon Harp' which was published in 1844 and gave much publicity about the conditions in the House of Correction at Beverley. However, the book showed that the system at Beverley was no harsher than that in other houses of correction.

Diet Table for Prisoners at the House of Correction at Beverley

Breakfast and supper The same throughout the week	One quart of oatmeal or pottage, 1/2lb bread
Dinner: Sunday and Tuesday.	One quart of stew heads, bones with 1lb of potatoes
Monday, Wednesday and Saturday.	One quart of oatmeal Porridge with 1lb bread
Thursday.	5oz of beef without bone with 1lb of potatoes
Friday.	One quart of beef broth from Thursday with leeks or onions and ¼ oz of oatmeal and 1lb bread.

In 1878 Houses of Correction ceased to be used and in Beverley buildings concerned with the prison, the house with the tread-wheel, the Turnkey's House and the cell block, set in the centre of the prison yards, were altered to became private residences; part of the prison yard remains as the grass lawn behind the wall in Norfolk Street. In 1884 the Sisters of Mercy of Anlaby Road, Hull, opened a branch of their convent in the former house of the governor. In 1888 the building was converted into a boarding and day school. In 1889 the convent was enlarged.

Anglican Church Restorations and Burial Grounds

The Rev. Joseph Coltman

'In memory of the Revd Joseph Coltman, MA, Principal Curate of this Minster (1814 – 1836) where for the space of 24 years he preach'd the Gospel to the poor with a truth and piety almost apostolical'

254

So reads the memorial in the north aisle of Beverley Minster to this one time incumbent.

Coltman, born in 1776 and of independent means, was a man of wide scholarship and sturdy principles. His memorial states that he was:

> Gifted with a peculiar felicity in communicating knowledge. He devoted much of his time and talents to education, training up children in the way they should go, forming the young in Christian principles and persuading men by the authority of doctrine and by the silent influence of virtuous example.

In 1810, because of his educational and charitable work, he was granted the freedom of the borough. He was a trustee of the Graves Charity and opened a girls' school for St Martin's parish in a room in Wilkinson's Yard, Toll Gavel. He was chaplain at the House of Correction where, until his death, he regularly held services and provided education for the younger prisoners. He cared for the children in the Blue Coat School and was said to have read Latin and Greek to the boys at the Grammar School before breakfast.

After Coltman moved into the Vicarage in Minster Yard the doors were widened to accommodate his great size. He weighed 37 stone 8 lb and moved around with the help of a velocipede (a bicycle without pedals). To enter the pulpit the churchwardens stood behind this machine and pushed with great force to enable him to go up the ramp into the pulpit. He died, at the age of sixty, from suffocation as he tried to turn over in bed. He is buried in the graveyard of the Minster in a lead lined coffin measuring 7ft in length, 3ft 2in. in breadth (2ft 2in. at the head and 1ft 8in at the feet).

His funeral took place on 24th June 1837. A measure of the affection and esteem in which he was held in the town comes across in a report of the event.

'Mr Coltman's funeral took place yesterday morning, about eleven o'clock. All the shops and almost every house had their windows closed till the conclusion of the ceremony. The corpse was preceded to the grave by Dr Alderson, and Thomas Sandwith, Esq. surgeon. It was followed by Sir Thomas Coltman, as chief mourner, by the domestics of the deceased, by the neighbouring Clergy, and all the respectability of the town.'

During Coltman's time at the Minster much restoration work was carried out under the direction of the master mason, William Comins, who also worked at St Mary's church. Coltman wrote a history of the Minster in which he expressed his dislike of the Georgian intrusions feeling that they were unworthy of such a magnificent Gothic building. Between 1824 and 1826 several of these items were removed – the onion dome placed by Hawkesmoor on the central tower of the Minster, the galleries standing on Doric columns in the nave which were referred to as 'unsightly encumbrances', the Corinthian reredos (29 feet long and 11 feet high), declared 'a deformity', and the Georgian wooden galleries. Some of these items were sold and used in other buildings in the town.

Once the Corinthian pillar, so hated by Daniel Defoe, had been removed it was found that the west face of the 14th century reredos had been badly damaged. Comins investigated the well which is to the southwest of the reredos and found that pieces of the medieval structure had been deposited there. When rebuilding the reredos he was able to base the design of the new reredos on that used in the original structure.

However, these improvements did nothing to increase the temperature of the Minster. A correspondent to the Hull Advertiser in November 1828 complained that the cold was 'almost intolerable' and that 'during the latter part of the service here, it is truly distressing to witness the pallid countenances, the shrunk forms and the shivering limbs of the congregation'. The first heating system was installed in the choir in 1841.

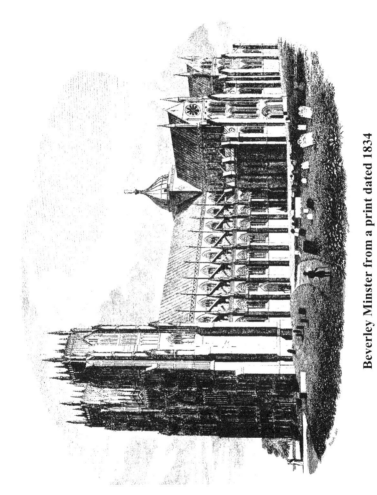

Beverley Minster from a print dated 1834

From 1826 until 1870 services were held in the eastern end of the church rather than the nave. Pews and galleries were crammed into the choir aisles and the east transepts with the result that moving around in the choir was difficult; panelling at the back of the 16th century choir stalls was taken away so that the congregation sitting in the aisles could see what was happening in the choir. The joiner/architect, William Fowler, provided a new pulpit which is in use in the nave today. The entrance to the choir was altered when the wrought iron gates, which had been placed at the entrance to the chancel, were moved to their present position in the north choir aisle and the two 18th century lead figures of St John of Beverley and King Athelstan were placed on plinths and moved to the south doorway.

In 1840 a Chapel of Ease of St John the Evangelist (now the Memorial Hall in Lairgate) was designed by H F Lockwood, an architect from Hull, and built on land donated by Mrs Jane Walker; the design of the windows of the chapel was based on the designs of the 13th century windows at the east end of the Minster. For the next fifty years this chapel was the fashionable place of worship for Anglicans.

By the 1860s Beverley Minster's role as the main church in the East Riding became recognized.

In 1863 the first Minster harvest festival was held. This quickly became a popular annual event sometimes attracting 1,500 people; crowds gathered outside the church an hour before the doors were opened only to find when they entered that all seats had been allocated to the favoured few and many had to be content with sitting in the nave imagining the scene in the choir. The service, attended by the mayor, aldermen and councillors in full regalia, began at seven o'clock in the evening with a processional hymn during which the clergy and choir, augmented by sopranos from the Choral Society and young ladies from Miss Stephenson's School, walked through the candle-lit nave before disappearing through the gates into the choir.

On these occasions no expense was spared in decorating the choir. The Beverley Guardian in 1865 describing the scene reported that there were floral decorations on choir stalls and on the organ case; the choir was lit by candles suspended from the vaulting over the crossing in front of the choir gates and by candelabra beside the altar, while strings of coloured chinese lanterns were suspended across the reredos. Sheaves of corn, evergreens and flowers surrounded the pulpit, the reading desk, the lectern, the gas-standards and the choir stalls while the altar had dishes of fruit and posies of flowers. Tropical greenhouse plants, borrowed from local nurseries, were arranged in masses on the altar steps and on the floor around the pulpit. The service lasted about two hours and finished with a special arrangement of the Hallelujah Chorus for the organ by G.J. Lambert, the Minster organist.

Church attendance was popular. The Beverley Guardian in 1867 reported that, 'Sunday after Sunday, men, women and children were sitting on the steps of the altar' and 'rows of the female sex were perched up above the reredos'; St Catherine's Chapel had benches full of school-boys and girls were seated in the opposite transept.

During the 19th century there was much restoration work at St Mary's. First under the guidance of the Minster's master mason, William Comins, who from 1829 – 30 removed the galleries installed in St Mary's in the 18th century. In 1844 AWN Pugin, an architect with a national reputation, who became known for his designs of the House of Commons in London, was appointed architect and continued restoration work until his death in 1852. He added buttresses to the exterior of the south transept; his final design, a weathervane on the south-west turret of the church, was sketched on the back of an envelope on the night he was taken to a private asylum in Kensington. He died shortly afterwards and his son carried on the work of rebuilding the turrets on the west front - one of the old turrets stands in the grounds of the East Riding of Yorkshire Council offices in Champney Road, the other was acquired by the antiquarian Gillyat Sumner. In 1861 – 2 the transept roofs were restored by Cuthbert Brodrick, an architect from Hull. By 1864 George Gilbert Scott - had begun a general restoration of the building and re-fitted the nave and the chancel. In 1881 Mr Oldrid Scott, son of

Sir Gilbert, designed the reredos which was carved by James Elwell, a local woodcarver.

By mid-19th century the churchyards of the two churches had become full. Burials in the Minster ceased in 1858 and in the churchyard in 1862. In 1860 two new burial grounds were consecrated for the parishes of St John's and St Martin's: half an acre of ground in Queensgate was apportioned to St John's parish for graves of residents of Beverley Parks, Molescroft, Thearne and Woodmansey and three acres in Cartwright Lane for St Martin's parish. Another portion of St Martin's ground was consecrated in 1873.

In 1829 a house, together with its grounds, which adjoined the late 18th century terrace on the west side of North Bar Within, was acquired. The house was demolished and a new burial ground was consecrated for burial of members of St Mary's parish on the site of the home and its garden. At the rear was the private burial ground for members of the Ellison family, owners of St Mary's Manor. The gateway and railings were supplied by Crosskill's Ironworks in Beverley. Burials in St Mary's church ceased in 1858 and in the churchyard in 1859. In 1864 Rachel Myers gave five acres of land on Molescroft Road to the church and after her death three years later a temporary licence was issued for her burial. In 1869 three acres of ground were consecrated and a mortuary chapel was built.

Non-Conformists and Roman Catholics

Non-conformist communities remained strong in the majority of northern 19th century towns, perhaps especially so in Beverley as a result of the preaching of John Wesley in the previous century. Many chapels built at the beginning of the century were replaced by larger chapels at the end. The Society of Friends moved from their meeting house in Lairgate. George Poulson, writing in 1829, describes the Beverley Quaker Meeting House as 'a plain and neat building in Wood Lane and of recent erection'. However, Quakerism was not strong in Beverley at this time for by 1830 the meeting house had fallen into disuse and

The Baptist Chapel, Well Lane. On the left is 11 Cross Street

from 1840 was used as a girls' school.

Methodism flourished in the 19th century. Early in the century the Methodist chapel in Wood Lane was found to be inadequate and in 1805 the Methodists built a larger chapel fronting onto Walkergate from where they intended to carry out missionary work in the industrial area of the Beck. In 1829 the chapel was enlarged and in 1868 an organ was installed at a cost of £300. The minister's house lay behind the chapel, nearer to Toll Gavel. By 1824 the Beverley circuit had broken away from Hull Methodists and had set up on its own. By 1825 a chapel for a breakaway group called the Primitive Methodists was built in Wednesday Market. The following year a Chapel in Landress Lane provided for another breakaway sect which had its origins in Beverley, the Church Methodists.

After the Reformation Roman Catholics were present in Beverley but they were never large in number. In a town where nonconformity was so strong there was violent anti-catholic feeling. The Catholic Emancipation Bill, which aimed to extend civic rights to Roman Catholics, was strongly opposed by many people in Beverley and leading opponents called for a meeting to be held in the Guildhall on 25th February 1829 to discuss the Bill. Feelings ran high, opinions were voiced that this was 'the most ruinous measure which has ever been proposed' and would be a death-blow to the British Constitution. The Reverend Coltman appeared at the meeting and said that vociferous extremists present 'did not necessarily represent the views of Beverley generally' and that a decision should be left to the good sense of Parliament. Hustings were erected outside the Corn Exchange in Saturday Market and a further meeting was held. Leading Protestants gave passionate speeches in which they pointed out a great fear of civil disorder if the Bill were past. Parliament received two petitions from Beverley, one signed by about 2,000 people opposing reform and another signed by 4 – 500 people in favour. The Bill was passed and the feared disorders never happened.

In 1846 Catholics in Beverley bought a house in North Bar Without for use as a chapel, and a resident priest was appointed. In 1851 the average congregation at services varied between sixty and ninety members. Numbers grew and an outbuilding was converted into a chapel which provided seating for 120. In 1898 a new church in the Gothic Revival style, just outside North Bar, was built dedicated to St John of Beverley.

In 1850 the Catholic hierarchy, having been suppressed since the Reformation, was restored. As Beverley was an ancient religious centre its name was chosen when a new Catholic bishop was created in the north. Later the diocesan boundaries were changed and the bishopric became Middlesbrough, rather than Beverley.

New Houses in the Classical Style

A glance at David Hick's map of 1811 (*back endpaper*) shows Beverley as a town with houses along its main streets behind which were large gardens, some belonging to countrified houses, and closes. During the 19th century many of those open spaces were to be built on to provide housing for the increasing population.

List of non-conformist chapels built in Beverley during the 19th Century

1800	Independent chapel in Lairgate rebuilt
1805	Methodist chapel opened in Walkergate, on the site of the present Sunday School building; 200 members in 1829.
1808	Scotch Baptist chapel built in Swaby's Yard, off Dyer Lane (now a restaurant). 70 members in 1829
1825	Primitive Methodist Chapel in Wednesday Market (where Boyes store now is). 70 members 1829.
1825	Wesleyan Methodist Chapel, Blucher Lane, Beckside
1826	Church Methodists built in Landress Lane (now demolished)
1834	Baptist chapel built in Well Lane (now demolished)
1856	Wesleyan Reform chapel opened in Trinity Lane (now Masonic Hall).
1868	Primitive Methodist chapel in Wednesday Market re-built
1882	Wesleyan chapel, Flemingate, opened 1886 Salvation Army citadel opened in Wilbert Lane
1887	Congregational chapel, formerly Independent, rebuilt in Lairgate
1888	Scotch Baptist chapel opened in Wilbert Lane (now the St John Ambulance Hall)
1892	Wesleyan Methodist chapel, Toll Gavel, opened (still in use) Old chapel in Walkergate became schoolroom.

St Mary's Manor

At the beginning of the 19th century there was an interest in Classical architecture and buildings were constructed in a style known as the 'Greek Revival'. The use of stucco also became popular. In Beverley pillared entrances with classical columns were added to Georgian buildings – the King's Head in Saturday Market, Newbegin Bar House, the Elms in North Bar Without. James Gee's house, No. 11 Newbegin, had a pillared entrance built on the west side (the two pillars came from one of the galleries removed from the Minster).

In 1794 Henry Ellison, who had married Mary Pennyman Berry, grand-daughter of Warton Pennyman Warton, bought the late 17th century house, built by James Moyser, in North Bar Within. Soon after acquiring the property Mr Ellison demolished the house. An early 18th century coach house and stabling to the north of the house remained and a wing of the previous building was kept and incorporated into the new house, set well back from the street. At the front of the property a banked garden was laid against a high wall built along the street front. No doubt this was intended to obscure any sight of North Bar Within which, with its medieval bricked entry into the town and its coaching inns must have been one of the busiest streets in the town. The four-acre formal garden behind the house was re-fashioned into a more landscaped 'villa' garden with sweeping lawns and trees. After the death of Mrs Ellison in 1826 the house, St Mary's Manor, was put up for sale; a detailed plan shows the layout of the ground and first floors of the house. The house did not sell and so Ellison decided to stay. In the late 1820s he added the Doric porch on the west front, enlarged the entrance hall and put in a grand staircase with an Ionic colonnaded landing to the first floor. The new staircase incorporated wrought iron altar rails from Beverley Minster.

Henry Ellison died on 2nd July 1836, aged 74, and he and his wife are buried in the retro-choir of Beverley Minster. His daughter, Caroline, and her husband, Captain Thomas Marten, moved into the house. The 1861 census showed that the houschold consisted of Thomas and Caroline Marten, a housekeeper/cook, a ladysmaid, a housemaid, an under housemaid, a kitchen maid, a butler and a footman. Thomas Marten, now General Marten, died in 1868 and was buried in the Ellison family private burial ground at the rear of St Mary's cemetery opposite the family home. His wife continued to live in the house until her death in 1882.

Before the 19th century there were no roads stretching from west to east across the town (apart from the ancient route way which led from the Westwood, through Wood Lane, crossed North Bar Within, continued along Hengate, across to Norwood and so out to Holderness); movement from one parallel street to another was generally through ginnels or rackets. In the early 1830s it was decided to extend Cross Street to join with Well Lane and Edward Page's design for a street lined with Greek Classical villa style buildings, with stucco Greek style pillars at the entrance, to go alongside the street, were accepted.

Edward Page lived in No. 11 Cross Street, with its cast-iron balcony; the pillars of the entrance to his house came from the Minster. Other houses in the street were the Particular Baptists Chapel in Well Lane, facing into Cross Street, the single storey

The Guildhall

Gentleman's Club with billiard table and reading room (opposite No. 11. Since 1939 this building has been part of East Riding of Yorkshire council offices), the Temperance Institute in Well Lane (demolished 2000) and the Mechanic's Institute (built 1850 and demolished 1893). On the north side of Register Square was the Guildhall; on the west side two houses were built, one of these was to become the medical dispensary.

In 1782 the corporation had agreed to subscribe £10 10s a year to a medical dispensary. In 1823, after the death of William Wilson who left the residue of his estate to the corporation for charitable use, a building in Lairgate was leased and the corporation agreed to subscribe £27 6s a year from the Wilson Charity to a new dispensary. The building was constructed in 1828 and during its first year 517 patients were treated.

The classical influence can be seen in other houses in the town such as the former Savings Bank (with its pilastered columns and Ionic capitals) in Lairgate (1843-4).

Town Management

Between 1824 and 1832 the Guildhall, the seat of local government in Beverley, underwent a refurbishment programme, costing £1,309. In 1827 a screen with Doric columns and a public gallery, (using materials acquired after the dismantling of galleries in the Minster) was inserted at the east end of the council chamber. On the screen was placed a reminder of the origins of the town – the town's badge showing a beaver set above blue and white lines depicting water. In 1830 a new chamber was built upstairs at the front of the building, known as the Mayor's Parlour, cleverly designed with light coming from the ceiling rather than through windows. In this room the members of the corporation would meet on the first Monday in every month to discuss the administration of the town.

The entrance to the building was changed. An old stone doorway, showing the Episcopal arms of the archbishop of York, placed as an entrance to the Guildhall in 1501 was removed and bought by Gillyat Sumner, a member of the Council. The new entrance has a large Greek Doric portico, designed by Charles Mountain, the columns of which, according to Pevsner and Neave, are 'of the type of the temple of Apollo on Delos'.

Gillyat Sumner (1793-1875) was an antiquarian who was to save many of Beverley's antiquities from destruction. In 1825 he bought an 18th century house in Woodmansey which he then proceeded to alter. At the side of the house he installed the old stone gateway from the Guildhall. In 1823 he acquired the font from the medieval church of St Nicholas (which had been used as a boundary stone on the Westwood). After his death the font was given to the newly built St Nicholas Church. In 1851 he bought one of the turrets removed from St Mary's church and installed it in his garden.

Until 1835 the local government of the town continued under the direction of the mayor, twelve aldermen and thirteen capital burgesses. The capital burgesses were elected by the freemen from a list of twenty-six names of those nominated for election by the mayor and aldermen.

The tasks of the corporation were various. In 1809 a sycamore tree was planted in front of the Sessions House and in 1822 chestnut trees were planted in North Bar Without and New Walk. Most of these trees still remain today. In an effort to limit crime street lighting was introduced. At the beginning of the century 200 oil lamps were ordered by the corporation to be placed in the streets and provide lighting from 5th October until 5th April. In 1824 a privately-owned company, the Beverley Gas Works, was founded by John Malam in Figham Road, near the Beck (the stone classical styled entrance still remains) and gas became available. At first gas lamps were provided by Thorncliffe Ironworks in Chapeltown, Sheffield, but in 1825 William Crosskill's iron foundry had moved from Butcher Row to Mill Lane and from then on provided gas lamps. Although now converted to electricity many of these lamps can still be seen today.

The first fire engine had been given to the town in the early 18th century by a Mr Fotherby and the two MPs of the town provided money for the buying of buckets. Later the corporation contributed towards the upkeep of two engines, one for each parish, which were kept in the Minster and St Mary's church. When fire broke out the church bells would be rung to alert the town. In 1861 a management committee was formed consisting of a churchwarden from St Mary's, a representative of the corporation and representatives of the fire insurance companies. The committee suggested that a fire brigade should be formed. They decided to lease an engine house, appoint an engineer and engage twenty-three paid firemen and also to give rewards to anyone who might assist in putting out fires. Part of the payment of these expenses was to come from those who had been helped; firemarks identified houses whose owners had taken out an insurance. By 1868 five engines were housed throughout the town. By 1885 the town had twelve fire engines and a volunteer fire brigade.

Bull baiting had been forbidden by the corporation in 1786. Early in the new century one of the town's MPs, John Wharton, was encouraged by 'by a certain class of his constituents'

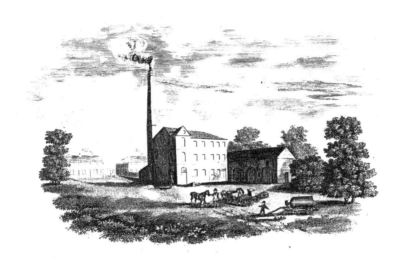

William Crosskill's Iron Foundry in Mill Lane

to renew this cruel sport. The magistrates banned the sport within the town but it continued in Newbegin Pits on the Westwood. In 1820 George Lane Fox, a wealthy landowner who was elected as one of the MPs for Beverley, said that the sport of bull-baiting 'is both cruel and barbarous and by abolishing it the burgesses of Beverley would not only do credit to themselves, but also to the borough and town at large'. An Act of Parliament against the cruel treatment of cattle was passed in 1822 enabling the corporation to ban the sport two years later. In Newbegin Pits, on the Westwood, a bull ring remains and the treading of the earth by the cattle at the extremity of the rope is still clearly visible.

1835 The Municipal Corporations Act

In 1833 Parliament appointed a commission to investigate the constitution of local borough councils. The commission reported that members of the corporations of most towns filled their own vacancies, appointed freemen of the town (often after money had changed hands) and conducted their proceedings in private. It accused corporations of mainly existing for the good of their own members and considered that, as a result, the population had lost all confidence in local government.

The result of this report was the passing of the Municipal Corporations Act in 1835 in which members were voted onto the borough council by the electorate which included householders as well as freemen. Towns were divided into wards, with people from each ward electing one or more members to represent them in the council. Whereas previous councils in Beverley had contained members of the gentry the new elected council was mainly composed of traders and business men. Beverley Corporation was given jurisdiction over the borough of Beverley and the six Water Towns of Beverley namely: Molescroft, Tickton-cum-Hull Bridge, Stork-cum-Sandholm, Weel, Woodmansey-cum-Beverley Parks and Thearne. In 1836 this was reduced to the three parishes of St Martin, St Mary and St Nicholas.

After the passing of the Act, responsibility for properties belonging to the Minster and St Mary's reverted to the churches. The advowson, the right to appoint the vicar of the Minster, was bought (for £3,300) by the Simeon Trust (established by the evangelical Anglican, Charles Simeon) with whom it remains. Responsibility for the Grammar School remained with the corporation for the time being.

Members of the newly elected Borough Council in Beverley decided to dispense with some of the more self-indulgent items of their predecessors and sold off the corporation's fine collection of pewter plates, silver and an excellent cellar of wine. One exception was the early 18th century silver snuff box which had been given by the former macebearer and chamber clerk, John Jackson. On the mayor's instructions this was filled with snuff and passed round at council meetings. The town's collection of pewter plates (dating from 1700 and marked with the beaver) was bought by Gillyat Sumner and later presented to the council. The silver waits chains (originating from 1423) were also sold. Two were returned by CF Hotham in 1883 and were worn by the mayor in the late 19th century and later by the mayoress; a third was bought back by the corporation in 1910 and was later worn by the deputy mayor. The mayor's chain was subscribed for in 1862 and an enamelled pendant bearing the same quartered coat of arms as the waits' badges was added in 1891. All these items are on display in the Guildhall.

Bribery at Parliamentary Elections

The system of electing two parliamentary representatives to the House of Commons continued with elections offering opportunities for bribery, corruption and income for the voters.

Elections were often colourful occasions. John Wharton, an active Whig with strong political views, was first elected to Parliament in 1790 (when he received 908 votes from 1,069 voters) and for the next forty years he was to dominate the political scene in Beverley. He came from a family whose home was at Skelton Castle (North Yorkshire) and inherited money from his aunt. In Beverley he represented the 'Bar Interest' and his patron was CA Pelham (who after 1794 became Lord Yarborough); perhaps the reason why he changed his name from Hall to Wharton was because so many members of the Warton family had been candidates for the 'Bar Interest'. Wharton was a strong supporter of the anti-slavery movement, favoured relief for Roman Catholics and constitutional and parliamentary reform. He had a popular following in Beverley. In the bye-election of 1799 he arrived four days before election-day to be greeted by a large crowd who removed the horses from his carriage and pulled him through the town. Each day he canvassed, accompanied by many followers with flambeaus, drums and callers. He was said to be a terror to any inhabitant of the town who was not on his side. However, despite an uproar at the polls, he was defeated by JBS Morrit. Wharton claimed that he had been beaten by bribery and corruption. In the general election of 1802 he, in turn, defeated Morrit who then declared that he had lost because there had been a third contender and because of bribery and corruption. After the

271

election in 1804 NC Burton of Cottingham, fought a bloodless duel with Wharton. In 1807 Wharton came second to Richard Vyse, son of General Richard Vyse, commander of the Yorkshire military district who since 1804 had lived in Beverley. Vyse received 1010 votes. 932 of his supporters had been paid at a rate of £3 8s for a single vote and £1 14s for a split vote. The expense of elections had been high and by now Wharton was in financial difficulties. To stand for election was a costly business – in the early 19th century the average cost for each candidate was £3,000. Wharton was successful in 1812, 1818 and 1820 but after being defeated in 1826 he retired and spent the last fifteen years of his life in financial hardship because of the money he had spent on his constituents.

The Reform Act of 1832 gave the vote for parliamentary elections to householders who paid a rent of £10 and leaseholders for twenty-one years of property over the value of £50. In 1831, 1,204 freemen had voted, out of a population of 7,432. After 1831 only 833 freemen retained the vote in addition to 138 newly enfranchised £10 householders. Compared with other towns this was a high percentage of voters which indicates the relative prosperity of the town. The 1867 Reform Act considerably increased the franchise. This threatened the Tory stranglehold over elections. In 1868 it was believed that out of 1,100 voters, 800 consistently supported one party or the other, the rest could be bought. A bribe of 2s 6d, or even 10s per vote, was tempting to a skilled worker who earned about £1 a week.

Four candidates stood for election to Parliament in 1868 one of whom was the author Anthony Trollope (a Liberal), another Sir Henry Edwards (a Tory). After coming bottom of the polls Anthony Trollope was instrumental in obtaining a royal commission to investigate the extent of corruption in elections in Beverley. A court was held in the town to hear the petition, under Judge Sir Henry Martin, in March 1869 and proceedings were, for six weeks, reported in the Times, which also published five leading articles on the subject. The judge found that the two Tory MPs who had the most votes were not fairly elected and he listed 104 people who had given or received bribes during the course of the election. Further investigation revealed that corruption was evident in all areas of the town and that since 1857 600 people had given or received bribes – names included Alfred Crosskill, Sir Henry Edwards, JE Elwell, Joseph Hind, Christopher Sykes and Sir James Walker, Bt. Bribery was evident in municipal elections, parliamentary elections, and even in the election of Pasture Masters in 1863 when twelve Tories had been voted in. Men applying to become freemen of

Anthony Trollope

Beverley would have their fee of £2 10s paid if they would agree to vote Tory. Bribes for the Tories were paid for by Sir Henry Edwards (a wealthy landowner) and organised by his agent, a Beverley draper named William S Wreghitt who had more or less controlled borough and parliamentary elections since 1857 when the election of Sir Henry Edwards broke the hold of the Liberals in the town. Landowners threatened to withdraw patronage of any traders who opposed them; at the Beverley Iron and Waggon Company Richard Norfolk, the manager, (who had been introduced from outside the town) was also the manager of the local Tory vote – remarkably three out of four employees at the foundry voted Tory. In a by-election of 1860 Tory followers had rounded up Liberal supporters who were intoxicated, took them to a room in Vicar Lane and 'sobered' them up with tea. The teapot contained tea, laudanum and rum.

The Liberals were not blameless either for in the 1865 election 80% of the Liberal voters had been bribed at a cost of over £1,000. Voters would be ushered into the Liberal headquarters in Toll Gavel (in the house once lived in by Ann Routh), paid, and ushered out by the back door. Polls at this time were open those paying bribes could check which way people voted.

The judge's verdict was that 'the place was a mass of corruption from beginning to end' and that Beverley was 'a town which is unfit to send members to Parliament'. As a result an Act of Parliament 1868 decreed that Beverley was to be disenfranchised. Maybe as a result of these investigations the Secret Ballot Act was passed in 1872 which stated that elections were no longer to be open.

Anthony Trollope claimed to have found Beverley an uncongenial town although his Liberal agents complained that he was not active in canvassing and preferred to go hunting. Trollope's book, 'Ralph the Heir', has a description of corruption in a parliamentary election which is believed to be based on his experiences at Beverley.

A local comment was that people born in Beverley drunk in bribery with their mother's milk.

Policing the Town

Until the 19th century the town was policed by constables appointed for each of the twelve wards who, after 1815, worked under the direction of a high constable and the serjeants who served the mayor and the courts. In 1812 the corporation agreed to meet the expenses of the twelve constables who had been appointed by the magistrates to keep a watch three nights of the week. In 1821 the night watch was increased to every night. Coats, lanterns, rattles to summon help, handcuffs and staves were provided by subscription, and given out from the guardhouse at the Guildhall.

The County and Borough Police Act of 1856 agreed to pay boroughs in England one quarter of the cost of the pay and clothing of a police force if the force was considered efficient in numbers and discipline; chief constables were required to report each year to the Home Secretary on the state of crime in the area.

This Act, deemed to be an interference in local government, was unpopular in many boroughs. In Beverley a meeting was held in the Guildhall to consider the Bill. When the meeting opened the mayor said that the Bill was simply an attempt of government to take control of the police; he asked 'What could the gentlemen in Whitehall know about Beverley?' A resolution that the bill would interfere with the liberties of the subject was carried unanimously and a petition was sent to parliament. However, the Act was passed and became law. In 1857 a government inspector visited Beverley and found that the force was not 'of the character contemplated by the 1835 Act' and that the town would therefore receive no grant. Looking for someone to blame, the Watch Committee sacked the superintendent of police, Inspector Holden, despite his popularity with many townsmen, and appointed Inspector Dove in his place. The force was re-structured and by 1859 consisted of a superintendent, a sergeant, two day police and six watchmen. Night watchmen would begin their duties at dusk when they would light the gas lamps – an activity which took one and a half hours. They then went off duty until eleven o'clock when they would extinguish the lamps after which they would walk their beats until dawn. When they came off duty they were replaced by two day policemen. The gaoler, who was also a police officer, had further duties which included attending the mayor and officiating at corporation meetings.

In January 1861 the Beverley police force was still found by the Inspector of Police to be inadequate and 'totally inefficient'. Despite disagreeing with the report the corporation dismissed Inspector Dove and appointed William Pattison. Once again the force was restructured with a sergeant and three constables for day duty, a sergeant and four constables for night duty and one constable held in reserve. Beverley thus received government approval, and a grant, so long as lamp lighting should cease to be police responsibility. In 1863 the corporation decided that the superintendent of police should also be the town gaoler and live in the house adjacent to the Guildhall. The gaol contained fourteen cells and three airing yards and here drunks would be sobered up and prisoners kept until taken before the petty sessions or quarter sessions. Thus the building attached to the Guildhall became the borough police station.

Water Supply, Sanitation and Drainage

Beverley had always had an adequate supply of water from the streams flowing through the town and from wells in individual houses. Streams were also used to carry sewerage and in the first half of the 19th century there was little drainage apart from open cesspits. During the century some streams were covered over. Some households had relatively clean water from shallow wells but in the latter part of the century much of the population relied on the 900 water pumps, some provided by the corporation (one of which remains in North Bar Within), some privately owned, which were placed around the town. The wealthier people had water pumped into their houses where it was stored in tanks and cisterns in the roof. The poor often had to share a pump with several other households in the streets or back-yards.

The increase in the size of urban populations, together with a new understanding of the connection between disease and impure water, caused a national concern about the poor state of drainage and water supply in towns. This led to the Public Health Act of 1848. An outbreak of cholera (first outbreak in England in 1832) in Hull the same year, in which many died, and ten deaths from the same disease in the Workhouse in Minster Moorgate in August 1849, led the people of Beverley to petition for an investigation under the Act into the water and drainage system in the town.

As a result of this petition George T Clark, a General Board of Health inspector, came to Beverley the following year to investigate the sanitary conditions of the town. His report was not encouraging. He found that in 1841 the death rate for the town was 23.6 per thousand, and in 1847 30.5 per thousand. Deaths in 1848 (many from typhoid) were 32% higher than in 1847. He noted that the town's surface drainage system emptying into the Beck was in a poor state and many of the poorer people lived in unsanitary conditions. He recommended that a complete new system of dealing with sewage and house drainage be provided and a water supply be laid into each house or court. The Borough Council, claiming that this was interference from London with the right of the Borough to make its own decisions, refused to comply. Three years later it created its own board of health and in 1854 imposed a rate of 5d in £1 to improve the system and raised money which was then spent on highways and pumps. No further efforts to improve drainage or the water supply was to be made for another thirty years.

Some efforts were made to clean up the town. In some cases householders had been given permission to build small arches over the sewers. In 1867 Bar Dyke 'a source of stench outside North Bar' was filled in.

Roads were generally in a poor state and still cobbled; street-sweeping was the responsibility of the householders. Owners of more prosperous houses in Hengate had raised the level of the road in order that they should not step from their houses into the mud and filth of the streets. This accounts for a house on the opposite side of the street being below street level. In 1862 sweeping streets, emptying cesspools and watering the main streets from New Walk to Beckside was contracted out for £5 a year. However, this was not found to be satisfactory and responsibility soon reverted to the householder.

Attempts to ensure that new housing showed concern for public health were made by acts of parliament. In 1862 the local board of health appointed a borough surveyor and from 1868 parliament passed a series of acts which were intended to improve public health and housing; bylaws included the provision that plans of new buildings should be submitted for inspection.

The Westwood Pasture

Between 1381 and the early 19th century Westwood Pasture and all of the Hurn had been cleared of trees with the exception of woods on the west side of the Westwood adjacent to the road to Bishop Burton – probably untouched because Archbishop Neville

Westwood Gatehouse on York Road

had stipulated, almost 500 years previously, when granting the pasture to the townsmen of Beverley, that his tenants at his manor at Bishop Burton should have the right to feed their pigs in these woods. This ancient woodland, known as Burton Bushes, still has ancient oak trees, gnarled and twisted with time and is preserved as a Site of Special Scientific Interest.

The pastures remained under the control of the corporation until 1835. However, the Municipal Corporations Act of 1835 cast doubts upon the corporation's rights to the pastures for the new electoral system included householders as well as freemen. In1836 the Beverley Pasture Act was passed by parliament which tried to solve this problem by granting ownership of the pastures (i.e. the soil) to the corporation but the right of running the pastures to twelve pasture masters who were elected by the freemen. Election Day was to be, and still is, held on the first Monday in March when elections take place in the Guildhall under the supervision of the mayor. The doors are open from 10am – 4pm but if no elector appears for a period of twenty minutes the mayor has the right to close the proceedings. To be a freeman you have to be born within the borough of Beverley, be the son of a freeman or have completed an apprenticeship within the town. Freemen have the right to own a 'gate' on the pasture which entitles them to graze their cattle. By 1890, although the population of the town had greatly increased, there were only 600 freemen.

The pasture masters were to have all the assets of the pasture – grazing, rent from the racecourse and, later, from the golf club, sale of trees (provided that they consulted the corporation before trees were felled), chalk and windmills. They were empowered to make bye-laws for the management of the commons and to appoint officers, including the neatherds, who carried out the day to day running of the pastures. The neatherds lived rent free in the six gatehouses, built in 1856 in gothic style at the edge of the pastures. Two gatehouses remain – at the top of Westwood Road and at the town end of York Road. Byc-laws defined the length of the grazing season and the 'gates' which could be claimed.

Freemen, or freemen's widows, who did not want to pasture stock could let their 'gates' and would be reimbursed by the council – this continues today. In 1842 there were 621 stockers who placed animals on the pastures as follows:

200 people put 407 animals in Figham
124   "   " 397   "   " Swinemoor
295   "   " 759   "   " Westwood and Hurn

A watering pond on the Westwood had been dug in 1784 and in 19th century new ponds and reservoirs were made – one can still be seen on the Hurn and one on the Westwood near the Newbald Road.

The limekilns had been in use in the 'archbishop's pits' since late 14th century. The last kiln was demolished in 1818.

The Westwood was a favourite place for outdoor activities. Horse racing continued on the Hurn. In March 1828 the Holderness Hunt began to meet on the race course but ten years later had moved to Burton Constable. In 1848 there were two-day race meetings in June and twenty years later a spring meeting in April. Race meetings, which were popular events for both rich and poor, were sponsored by the gentry whose ladies would sit in the grandstand well away from members of the 'lower orders'. Meetings were well attended and in 1851 between five and six thousand people came from Hull on trains laid on especially for the meeting. The Beverley Guardian reports in 1856 a string of thirty-nine horses being lead through the main streets of Beverley on their way to the race course.

Black Mill on the Westwood

In the 1860s archery became popular amongst the upper and middle classes and the East Yorkshire Archers held its meetings in a field off Norwood. Contests lasted all day and in the evening the company moved to the Assembly Rooms where prizes were given out, after which they danced to the Militia band. Pony races, foot races and picnics held on the Westwood were considered almost as good as a trip to the seaside.

The ordnance survey map of 1852 shows five corn windmills on or adjoining Westwood Pasture. The Westwood being the highest area of land around Beverley had been the site of windmills for centuries and it must have been a proud sight to watch the sails turning in a strong breeze.

Westwood Hither Mill (also known as Low Mill, Crathorne's mill or Wilson's Mill – the names of several owners) stood halfway between Black Mill and the south-west corner of Newbegin Pits. A mill on this site is first mentioned in mid-17th century. It would have been a post mill, constructed of wood with a central post surmounted with a cap so that the upper part rotated according to the force of the wind. In 1742 it was re-built after being damaged by the wind and thirty years later was again re-built, but with bricks rather than wood; it had five sails. After 1835 it became the property of Joseph Crathorne. By 1850, having become ruinous, it was demolished by the Pasture Masters. There remains an ancient track from the top of Westwood Road over the pasture which leads towards where the mill once stood.

The brick tower of Westwood Far Mill or Baitson's Mill (now known as Black Mill) is situated at the highest point of the Westwood. A mill on this site is mentioned in 1654. In 1802 Joseph Baitson was granted a lease of sixty-five years on condition that he built a new mill consisting of a brick tower and four sails. After being damaged by a fire and the collapse of the sails the timber part was dismantled by the Pasture Masters in 1868 but the tower remained. The miller's house was built near the mill together with other buildings. On the Sunday before races a football match was played from the area of the mill with the goal posts in the town. However, the matches were stopped in 1825 as they were found to be too dangerous. An annual game of cricket was played near the mill and often the miller provided refreshments while a brass band played.

The remains of Union Mill stand at the south-west corner of the Westwood immediately south of Walkington road. It had a tall brick tower and five sails. In 1804 it was leased to the Union Mill Society, a co-operative mill. In the 1890s it fell into disuse, the upper section was dismantled and the tower was converted into the clubhouse of the newly formed golf course.

Fishwick Mill (or Butt Close Mill) was a post mill which stood on the eastern boundary of the Westwood, adjoining St Giles Croft. In 1761 John Maud was granted a lease of 99 years at an annual rent of £1 to build a corn windmill on the site. He was allowed to 'dig and lead chalk in Westwood Pits for raising the ground to an agreeable height whereon to erect his said mill'. In 1801 the mill was leased to a miller named Fishwick for a period of sixty years. When the lease was up the corporation dismantled the mill and attempted to reclaim the land, known as Butts Close, on which the mill had stood. The freemen of Beverley felt that the claiming of the land by the corporation was an infringement of their rights over the Westwood. The Beverley Guardian of Monday 2nd September 1861 reports that John Steel, with Sergeant Dunn, a borough constable, and James Pearson were ordered by the corporation to go to Fishwick's Mill at six o'clock in the evening, to take possession of the premises and let no one into the enclosure which surrounded the site of the mill. By seven o'clock a small group of watchers had grown into a large crowd of over one hundred people assembled on the Westwood on the west side of the premises. John Duffill, the town crier, came to the south gate of the enclosure and demanded admittance. This was refused. Urged on by the crowd, with shouting and cheering, John Duffill insisted and he and two others threw down the gate walked into the enclosure followed by the crowd claiming their rights as freemen to enter this part of the Westwood. When John Steel began to take the names of the demonstrators, William Bielby came up and ordered him off the ground as he was not a freeman and threatened violence if he did not obey. Intimidated, John Steel left the grounds. The crowd at this time was quite orderly, and men sat on the mound where the windmill had been smoking their pipes. By 8.30pm the crowd had set the mill house alight and the fire raged until two o'clock in the morning. Some of the rioters were brought before the magistrates and ordered to attend the Quarter Sessions. However, they were acquitted and the corporation was denied the right to fence off Butts Close. The hump on which Fishwick's Mill stood came to be known as Duffill's mound.

Westwood Mill (also known as Lowson's Mill) was in a close, adjoining but not actually part of the Westwood, in an area near to the present Grammar School. First mention of the mill was in 1802 when George Jakeman was permitted to have a cart-road from the Walkington road to the windmill he had erected in his close. The mill was a brick tower mill with five sails. Ownership eventually passed to the Wilson-Lowson family. It was dismantled in 1891 and today only the lower part of the tower remains.

Beverley Poor Law Union Workhouse

In 1802 the three parishes in Beverley (St Mary's, St Nicholas and St Martin) gave 'relief' to 157 paupers, thirty-six of whom were in the workhouse; by 1833 the number receiving relief had risen to 450, fifty-seven of whom were in the workhouse in Minster Moorgate. In a time when sickness or unemployment could result in destitution, Beverley was fortunate in having a number of almshouses, charitable institutions and charitable trusts which provided for the poor in addition to money provided on the rates.

The Poor Law Amendment Act of 1834 aimed to reduce the burden on parishes of looking after the poor by taking all paupers into a centrally situated workhouse where, to discourage malingerers, conditions were to be worse than if the poor had received out-relief in their own homes. Parishes were grouped into poor law unions with boards of guardians employing paid officials. Out-relief was given only to the sick and people over the age of sixty. Beverley became the centre of a Poor Law Union and was expected to take paupers from thirty-six parishes in the area. The existing workhouse in Minster Moorgate was adapted and a perimeter wall, nine feet high, was built with iron bars fitted to windows. However, an inspection in 1858 found that the

The 18th Century Workhouse in Minster Moorgate

workhouse was inadequate; this led to a proposal to build a new one. Despite opposition the project went ahead. One opponent was Daniel Boyes, manager of the Angel Hotel in Toll Gavel, who worried about the cost and the fact that inspectors always felt the need to recommend 'something new and absurd'.

In 1860 a field, belonging to the Quakers was bought and a new building, designed by JB and W Atkinson of York, was built in a Tudor style overlooking the Westwood. It stood at the top of what previously had been Wood Lane; when the workhouse was built the western part of this lane became Union Road (later changing to Woodlands). When land was bought so that vegetables might be grown to put in the paupers' soup, Daniel Boyes claimed that the garden only served to 'demoralise the paupers' because when they were allowed onto it they tended to 'escape' into the town. Children (many of whom were orphans), single mothers, the mentally ill, men (mostly former labourers), the old (those over the age of sixty) and vagrants (who were permitted one night's shelter - in 1866 there were an average of fifteen vagrants each night) were all placed in this institution. The sexes were segregated.

The guardians provided clothing and blankets for all entering the workhouse. Inmates were expected to attend church or chapel and the children, wearing their workhouse uniforms, went out daily to schools in the town. Food was monotonous and limited and seems to have been deficient in green vegetables and fruit. Women were expected to do domestic duties such as preparing food, cooking, sewing and washing while the able-bodied men worked outside the workhouse breaking up cobbles for the road, picking oakum (unravelling tarry ropes for caulking ships) and in 1861 acting as street sweepers. Sick paupers were looked after by other inmates in separate wards. The old were permitted to sit on seats overlooking the Westwood and to walk into town. Coffins for inmates who died were made on the premises. As the guardians believed that the workhouse should be run at the lowest cost to the ratepayer conditions inside were harsh with few toys for children and no comforts for adults.

However, on one day of the year, as the result of a subscription raised in the town, the inmates of the workhouse were supplied with a good dinner and various treats. In 1869 the Beverley Guardian reported that the Union Workhouse fare on Christmas Day consisted of:

'Roast beef, legs of mutton, plum pudding, and beer, which the inmates did justice to, and enjoyed most thoroughly. In the afternoon the children were supplied with raisins, nuts, oranges, and treacle cake; the women with four ounces of tea and a two-pound cake each; and the men with a quarter of a pound of tobacco each. On Christmas Eve the inmates were regaled with a plentiful supply of frumenty'.

Out-relief still continued to be issued depending on good behaviour. In May 1857 Ellen Knowles's out-relief was discontinued when she was found to be 'keeping a bad house' whilst neglecting her children, who were said to be filthy and diseased. They were all taken into the workhouse.

Improved Communications

A postmaster of Beverley was first mentioned in 1682; from 1766 a post office is recorded as being in Toll Gavel but in 1852 it was moved to a house on south side of Cross Street. Later this building was described as 'no better than a hovel, hardly fit for a cow house'. After the arrival of the railways post would be delivered from Hull and London at eight o'clock in the morning and carriers would go out immediately to deliver throughout the town and surrounding villages, unless the mail was to be collected at the post office window. Another delivery would arrive at five o'clock in the evening and mail for the town would be immediately dispatched. On Valentine's Day 1865 nearly 3,000 letters passed through the Beverley Post Office.

From 1864 a telegraph service was organised from an office in Register Square which in 1872 was taken over by the Post Office.

The proposal for a railway line linking Hull, Cottingham, Beverley, Driffield and Bridlington aroused controversy. Turnpike Trustees and innkeepers feared a decline in the coach trade and landowners and farmers feared farms would be divided, drainage channels interrupted, estates lose privacy and hunting affected. At a public meeting in the Guildhall anxieties were voiced that taxes would be raised, retail trade destroyed and property depreciate. Councillor Robinson feared accidents would occur where the line crossed Flemingate and insisted that a pedestrian bridge must be provided. Others suggested that the railway would create a demand for more labour and more houses and would increase investment in the town and even lower the rates. The corporation, despite the fact that the coming of the railway might cause a decline in revenues from the Beck, supported the idea and in February 1846 a decision was made that the railway should be built. The idea of a station at the end of St John's Street was mooted but the site eventually chosen was on fields to the east of the town known as the Trinities which

Beverley Railway Station

belonged to the corporation and which had previously been let to Tindalls', the market gardeners.

Once the decision had been taken, enthusiasm for the project gradually gained ground, although when in June trucks were already trundling up and down the line there was a complaint that 'the quiet folks of Beverley are almost frightened out of their propriety by the shrill whistles and rumbling of truck wagons'. The station was designed by GT Andrews. The official opening of the Hull to Bridlington line took place on 2nd October 1846. Over 1000 people in East Yorkshire took part in the celebrations at individual stations along the line. Representatives of the corporations of Hull, Beverley and York joined representatives of Trinity House, Hull, the Dock Company and the Commercial Chamber in Hull in order to board the train. At 10.52am, three engines and sixty-six carriages began the two hour journey from Hull to Bridlington. Undeterred by torrential rain, people flooded onto the platforms at Beverley, Driffield and Bridlington and bands played while the crowds waited for the arrival of the train. At Bridlington a 'sumptuous' lunch was provided for 900 people and there were numerous toasts and speeches – one by the mayor of Beverley included a sentence in which he said that the coming of the railway would mean that the people of Hull would now be able to enjoy the 'more salubrious' air of Beverley. In Beverley there were celebrations throughout the day, shops were closed, bands played and there was a public dinner in the afternoon, followed by a ball in the evening.

Travel by train seems to have been an immediate success and carriages quickly became crowded. The mayor of Beverley's statement at the opening of the line proved to be true and commuters from Hull were now able to work in Beverley. By 1847 George Hudson, the railway king, before his business collapsed, had taken the railway from York as far as Market Weighton. It was to be another 20 years before the line linking Beverley with Market Weighton was to be built.

Until the coming of the railway the only exits from Wednesday Market were Butcher Row to the north and Eastgate and Highgate to the south. In 1849 two land-agents, Edward and Gregory Page, laid down a new road (Albert Street, later Railway Street) over existing fields which led from Wednesday Market to the railway station. On either side of the street three-storey terraces were built.

Inevitably the railway caused a reduction of the coach trade. Soon after the coming of the railways the Tiger Inn, in North Bar Within, was unable to compete with other inns and was closed. The building remains, now divided into shops.

The Agricultural Economy

By the beginning of the century fairs declined in importance but market days, as always, attracted people from the surrounding area.

From the early 1820s William Cobbett, essayist and radical politician, carried out a series of tours of England on horseback.

He wrote a journal about his travels which was published, in instalments, in the Weekly Political Register. These instalments were collected together and published as Rural Rides. In 1830 William Cobbett wrote about his visit to Beverley. He began by commenting on the antiquity of Beverley with its great 'college' at the Minster, St Mary's, its three famous hospitals and two friaries. He went on to say:

'It is still a very pretty town; the market large; the land all round the country good; and it is particularly famous for horses; those for speed being shown off here on the market-days at this time of year. The farmers and gentlemen assemble in a very wide street, on the outside of the western gate of the town; and at a certain time of the day, the grooms come from their different stables to show off their beautiful horses; blood horses, coach horses, hunter, and cart horses; sometimes, they tell me, forty or fifty in number. The day that I was there (being late in the season), there were only seven or eight, or ten, at the most. When I was asked at the inn to go and see 'the horses', I had no curiosity, thinking it was such a parcel of horses as we see at a market in the south; but I found it a sight worth going to see; for besides the beauty of the horses, there were the adroitness, the agility, and the boldness of the grooms, each running alongside of his horse, with others trotting at the rate of ten or twelve miles an hour, and then swinging him round, and showing him off to the best advantage. In short, I was exceedingly gratified by the trip to Beverley. The day was fair and mild; we went by one road and came back by another, and I have very seldom passed a pleasanter day in my life.'

In 1808 on alternate Wednesdays cattle markets were held in Norwood, where the street was wide. By 1863 there were complaints that the market had become too crowded and that cattle went onto the footpaths; additional pens were provided. To

North Bar News, a well-preserved 19th century shopfront

ease pressure in 1864 a new market was provided on a two acre site between Norwood and Morton Lane

A larger population meant an increased trade in corn. In the mid-19th century many market towns built corn exchanges which consisted of spacious halls in which dealers could set up their stands. This was felt to be an improvement to selling outside in inn yards or the market-place. It was felt that a well-equipped market hall would attract buyers and sellers. However, in Beverley, farmers preferred to conduct trade as they had always done in the inns and inn yards. In 1886 Samuel Musgrave of Hull designed the red brick Corn Exchange in Saturday Market which we have today with Public Baths behind.

The Industrial Economy

The 1851 census reveals that while Beverley was not an agricultural town, most of its industries were linked to agriculture. Almost all the fifty-two wheelwrights, fifty-two blacksmiths, twenty-two millwrights, forty-four engine and machine workers were industrial workers employed in Crosskill's Iron Works. Other industry continued, mostly on a small scale, with thirty-eight tanners and twenty-eight iron manufacturers.

Crosskill's Iron Works was the largest employer in mid-19th century Beverley. William Crosskill was born in 1799 in Butcher Row. He grew up a strong Methodist and in 1845 was to become mayor of Beverley. After the death of his father in 1811, he worked with his mother in the family tinsmith business which was so successful that in 1825 a foundry was set up on a seven-acre site in Mill Lane. Here agricultural machinery – ploughs, drills, wagons, threshing machines – was manufactured. Transportation of goods became easier after the coming of the railway in 1846. Crosskill's clod-crusher, which was exported all over the world, was exhibited at the Great Exhibition in London in 1851. During the Crimean War (1854 - 1856) the works produced over 3,000 army carts and wagons. In order to expand the business, Crosskill borrowed from the East Riding Bank, which in 1855, when trade became depressed in Hull as a result of the war in the Crimea, demanded re-payment. Unable to pay, Crosskill was forced to resign and the bank took over the business, which was then managed by his two sons. Later the business was sold to Sir Henry Edwards, the Conservative MP for Beverley who claimed to have bought the 'Old Foundry' as an act of charity in order to save the employees from destitution (and thereby gain their votes at the next election). Its name was changed to the Beverley Iron and Waggon Company.

By 1864 Crosskill's sons, Alfred and Edmund, had set up a rival firm – William Crosskill and Sons, on a site in Eastgate where they continued to make railway wagons and farm carts until 1904.

Tanning had been carried on in Beverley throughout the medieval period. During the 19th century the largest firm of tanners was Hodgsons in Flemingate. When William Hodgson arrived in Beverley from Durham in 1812 there were five tanneries in Beverley: three in Flemingate, one in Keldgate and one on the Hull Road. William was forced to retire early, crippled with rheumatism, and in 1841 was succeeded as managing director by his twenty-one year old son, Richard; the company became known as Richard Hodgson and Son Ltd.

Hodgson's site in Flemingate gave easy access to the Beck. This facilitated importation of hides from Spain, Holland, Germany, Russia, Argentina and South Africa and for carrying coal to feed the steam engine which the company had acquired in 1822. The company seems to have gone from strength to strength and the tannery was enlarged in 1829 and 1834; in 1851 seventy men were employed. The 1851 census shows that the majority of tannery workers lived in the Flemingate area where there was another tannery owned by George Catterson. In 1834 George Cussons acquired a tannery in Keldgate which was worked by members of his family. In 1851 Cussons employed thirty-nine men.

Grain milling had been established in the town for many centuries, indeed Domesday Book records three mills in Beverley. Mention of windmills on the Westwood has already been made; in 1834 there were nine millers including five on or near the Westwood, two at Grovehill and one, a water mill, operating in Hull Road; by the end of the century all but one was out of business. Josiah and Robert Crathorne bought a windmill at Grovehill and, when in 1850 they added steam power to the existing wind power and enlarged the mill, the business flourished. The mill burnt down in 1907 but was not replaced – perhaps it was not economic for grain to be brought eight miles up the river from Hull to be ground at Grovehill.

The processing of agricultural products and making of goods for agricultural use continued along the water's edge. Seed crushing and fertilizer manufacture continued at Hull Bridge and at Beckside. Tiger and Company operating at Grovehill concentrated on the making of fertilisers. From 1834 chalk was quarried at Beckside and also at Beverley Parks.

Mid – Century Social Statistics

The 1861 census showed that Beverley had a population of 9,654. Professor William Speck of the University of Leeds fed the census data into a computer and came up with some interesting discoveries. He found that in 1861 only about half the population of Beverley had been born in the town – this shows a higher percentage of immigrants than in other towns; newcomers came from elsewhere in the East Riding, from Yorkshire and, the majority, from elsewhere in England, with a few from Scotland and Ireland including ten out of forty-eight prisoners in the House of Correction who came from Ireland.

The majority of people married in their early twenties. While there were some exceptionally large families with thirteen or fourteen children, the average family size was 4.2 persons. In 1861 about 27% of the population of Beverley was under the age of ten. However, early mortality meant that many did not reach maturity and hearses with tiny coffins must have been a familiar sight in Victorian Beverley. A letter in the Beverley Guardian on 19th December 1868, a day on which eight deaths in Beverley were recorded, gives the ages of the deceased as 68, 19, 9, 6, 3, 2, 18months and one month. Almost every family suffered the death of at least one child. A correspondent in a letter to the editor of the Beverley Guardian in 1868 noted:

'It is well known, I believe, that smallpox and scarlatina have been raging among young children in the town for some time past, and that there has been great mortality among young children in consequence'.

An advertisement claimed that

'coughs, asthma and incipient consumption are effectively cured by Keating's cough lozenges. What diseases are more fatal in their consequences than neglected coughs, colds, sore throats or lungular affections?'

Medical science was still crude and many women died in childbirth. This contributed to the 8.6 % of all families with children up to the age of fifteen being headed by single parents under the age of sixty-five (both widows and widowers). In fact,

Professor Speck, writing in 1986, says that there was a higher proportion of single parent families in Victorian Beverley than there are in England today. The availability of domestic servants would help those single-parent families who had an adequate income. In Beckside 92.3% of households had no living-in servants and the remaining 7.7% had only one. However, North Bar Without was a different story; of the 77 households, 43 had servants (44%). Some of these servants were very young, aged only 10, 11 or 12. Most servants seem to have moved from one employer to another. The Turner Charity was set up to encourage servants to stay with a particular household. It gave £10 10s to each of those domestic servants who had been the longest in service in the district; the minimum length of service to qualify was five years.

Life expectancy in 19th century Beverley was considerably lower than it is today and there seem to have been relatively few households in which members of three generations lived together. The census returns showed that in 833 households in the parish of St Mary's there were only 459 people over the age of 55 (11.8% of the population). Many 'old' (i.e. fifty-five and over) were in institutional care: thirty-two widows in Ann Routh's Hospital; twenty-three people, the oldest being aged ninety, in Warton Hospital; twenty-nine people, only nine under the age of sixty, in Le Maison de Dieu; and ninety-three paupers of all ages, sixty-seven under sixty, in the Union Workhouse.

Builders and Architects

Between 1871 and 1901 the population of Beverley was to increase from 10,218 to 13,183. There was a continual demand for new housing and available land was soon built on. After the building of the new workhouse in 1861 the old workhouse on the south side of Minster Moorgate was demolished and replaced with new houses.

By the beginning of the 19th century Keldgate Manor, the Hall, Lairgate, Norwood House, St Mary's Manor, and 56 North Bar Without all had large gardens laid out as small parks.

Willow Grove

New houses would be built with extensive gardens behind; in 1854 Richard Hodgson moved from his house near the tannery in Flemingate to Westwood Hall, newly built in Westwood Road with a large garden stretching up to the Westwood; and in 1845 Edward Hutton, from a wealthy family in Lincolnshire, and his wife Marianne, whose family lived in a house in Walkergate (now the Grosvenor Club) bought 1.5 acres of 'orchard or garden ground' in New Walk and built Hurn House set in its own parkland. Newbegin House and Walkergate House had smaller gardens laid out in villa style with shaped beds and flowing paths.

In other areas closes and parts of gardens were sold so that houses could be built for tradesmen and professional people.

The northern end of Beverley was the fashionable side of town - North Bar Without, New Walk, which developed towards the end of the century, and to the west of the town land adjacent to the Westwood. A lane at the top of Newbegin, previously known as Newbegin Lane, was in 1800 listed as Westwood Road. Here, as the town expanded outside the surrounding medieval ditch, (at this point at the top of Newbegin) residential houses were built, those on the south side mostly developed 1830 – 50 and those on the north side 1870 – 80. These houses are not directly on the street front, as was customary in medieval and Georgian times, but built behind small gardens. Houses overlooking the Westwood, Westwood View, were built 1880s and 1890s. St Giles Croft was developed from the 1870s.

Several builders and architects were working in the town during the latter part of the 19th century and each was to add his own distinctive style. Marmaduke Whitton was a builder who was often helped by his brother, James, an architect from Lincoln. His houses can be easily recognised for he preferred to work with grey rather than red brick He developed a terrace of houses along the edge of the Westwood on a site where once willow trees grew. These houses in Willow Grove were first advertised for sale in 1853. Seven years later more of his houses, again in grey brick, were built on York Road on land which had been part of the property of the Elms in North Bar Without (in 1880 the red brick houses nearer the town were built on land which had been the walled garden of the Elms. Again in grey brick, Whitton built Park Terrace in North Bar Without; he lived at No. 6 and it is said that the bay window over the archway was built so that his daughter, on the morning of her wedding, could stand there in her wedding dress and be seen by the crowd outside.

William Hawe (1822-97), at first a landscape gardener, moved on to architecture with no formal training. In 1842 he settled in Beverley and his Italianate, French and German Renaissance style can be seen in his commercial buildings. He designed No. 52 and 53 in Saturday Market (the latter for Charles Hobson). In 1861, the same year that Cuthbert Brodrick (a Hull architect who in 1852 had won national recognition as a result of his design for Leeds Town Hall) was building No. 37 North Bar Within (Pizza Express), William Howe designed No. 4 Saturday Market (National Westminster Bank). Again his distinguished style is apparent in his designs for 2 – 10 New Walk (1870). Ten years later he added a new Italianate style frontage to No. 15 North Bar Within (opposite the west end of Hengate). In 1886 he was responsible for the alteration of Bar House giving it a stucco façade and parapet with urns and balustrades and an Italianate tower which provided an observation platform (on which it is said that the owner of the house stood in order to watch his horse on the race course).

He also built a new brewery for Robert Stephenson in Toll Gavel. In 1769 Robert Stephenson had acquired a lease for one year of a messuage on the east side of Toll Gavel and by 1797 Stephenson, a brewer, had become a freeman of Beverley. The business expanded during the 19th century and was able to buy up several other inns nearby – the Half Moon at Market Weighton, the Blue Bell and the Duke of York in Cottingham. It owned the Black Swan in Highgate and the Ship Inn in the Market Place Beverley. The brewery was re-built by William Hawe in 1866 behind the Golden Ball, a public house in Toll Gavel. The malt kiln was in Mill Lane. By 1881 Robert Ranby Stephenson employed eight men and lived in Oak House, North Bar Without.

By 1875 Frederick Stead Brodrick, a Hull architect, (1847-1927) (nephew and former assistant of Cuthbert Brodrick) was in partnership with Richard George Smith (1837-1901). In 1878 they designed 9 – 11 New Walk (Brodrick lived in No. 11) and in 1885 the redbrick Minster Girls' School (now the Parish Hall), but their largest and grandest design was to be the new East Riding County Offices in Cross Street built in 1893. Some would say that their style is often more suited to a building in a city rather than a market town.

A craftsman who left his mark on late 19th century and early 20th century Beverley was James Elwell (1836-1926). His family moved to Beverley when his father, Samuel Elwell, was employed on the Hull to Bridlington railway. He later worked as a clerk for a firm of wood merchants. Samuel, who died in 1855, and his wife had eight children. Aged fourteen, James was apprenticed to a Beverley cabinet maker, Robert May. He then moved to London but returned to Beverley in the 1860s and became foreman for another cabinet maker, Richard Jameson; eventually he succeeded to the business which at one time employed seventy craftsmen. In 1863 James Elwell became a

Elwell's Mock Tudor House outside North Bar

freeman of Beverley. Much of his late 19th century woodwork can be seen in the town; the reredos for St Mary's Church, the organ screen in the Minster, No. 43 Oak House 1880 (designed by Smith and Brodrick) with much interior woodwork by Elwell, including the staircase, and No. 45 1894 (designed by Elwell himself, for himself) with a carved panel over the door depicting a scene from 'The Cloister and the Hearth'. In 1892 Elwell remodelled two late 18th century buildings outside North Bar into a mock-Tudor style which makes an arresting entry to the town from the York Road. The roof is a series of wood pinnacles and pointed gables with the carved figures of St John of Beverley and St William of York, beneath, until recently, was a figure of St Bede; a red imp nestles against a round tower. An elaborately decorated cove lies under the eaves while over the door are two panels of cartoons relating to the battle for political power between Disraeli and Gladstone.

The 1870 Education Act

Towards the end of the century the government became aware of the importance of a literate workforce and the Education Act of 1870 brought about a whole re-thinking of the provision of elementary education. Church schools received government funding and district Board of Education schools were established to provide elementary schools for children aged between five and ten (by the end of the century the age was raised to 12). Soon after the 1870 Act attendance at school became compulsory and education became free. No Board Schools needed to be built in Beverley although schools were built in Norwood, Holme Church Lane and Minster Yard.

The Grammar school was closed in 1878 and the school building in Keldgate demolished, although School House remained. In 1890 the Blue Coat School and the Foundation School were closed. The Grammar School was re-opened in that year in the buildings of the Foundation School in Albert Terrace. Pupils from the old Grammar School and the Foundation School were helped by grants from the country council and endowments from both schools were passed to the Grammar School. In 1902 the school was moved to its present purpose built buildings in Queensgate. The former master's house, now no. 54 Keldgate, was used for boarders from 1913.

Social Activities and Societies

By the end of the century Beverley provided a highly active social life. In 1880 the Holderness Hunt Ball was held in the Assembly Rooms in Norwood. It was organised by the Wilsons of Tranby Croft (a wealthy shipping family from Hull). It was attended by 400 people, including the Prince of Wales who was staying at Tranby Croft. The day after the ball carriages were arranged to take people to the races on the Hurn. Clive Wilson, a younger son of the Wilsons, lived at St Mary's House in Hengate.

299

During the second half of the century a number of societies were formed, some of which remain today:

1859 The Natural History Society
1860 The Chess Club
1865 The Minster Choral Society
1874 The Musical Society
1875 The Gymastic Society
1881 The Beverley and East Riding Tennis Club
1886 The Cycling and Athletic Club
       The long established lodge of Freemasons acquired the former dispensary in Register Square.
1889 The Golf Club on the Westwood
       The Swimming Club
1893 The Photographic Society
1896 The Choral Society

A Piped Water Supply and Improved Sewage System

By the early 1870s most large cities and many smaller towns had a piped water supply but in Beverley the majority of the inhabitants still depended on wells and pumps. In 1872 the local board of health was wound up and the corporation took over the role of an urban sanitary authority, appointing its own medical officer of health. In November 1873 a private company offered to set up a piped water supply for the town and some nearby villages. It was suggested that a deep well be sunk near the southern edge of the Westwood, near the newly opened East Riding lunatic asylum between Beverley and Walkington. From that point water could be pumped into the town and supplied to subscribers. This required an Act of Parliament and so the Beverley Water Bill was proposed. Many members of the council, led by Daniel Boyes, were bitterly opposed to the whole idea thinking that it would involve the council in unnecessary expense and give large profits to the water company rather than the Borough Council. A parliamentary enquiry was held before a Select Committee of the House of Lords in which both viewpoints were expressed. The Committee agreed to refuse the

300

scheme on the condition that the Borough Council would provide some kind of water supply. This was agreed but not done.

Support for the scheme came mainly from Tories, such as JR Pease of the Quaker banking family, and Joseph Beaumont, the borough surveyor and co-designer of the scheme while Liberals, led by Joseph Hind, (whose electioneering cry was 'No waterworks, no half-crown rate') continued with a somewhat laissez-faire attitude which had mostly disappeared from other parts of the country.

In 1881 another company applied to Parliament for a private Act which would give it powers to provide Beverley with a piped water supply. Opposition from the council was even stronger than before; stories went round that the water company would cause pumps to go dry in order to force people to buy water; there was a fear of contamination from the tanks supplying the water. Once again the Borough opposed the Bill, employing barristers to speak on its behalf before the Parliamentary Select Committee. However, despite spending £3,000 on their defence, the Bill was passed and the Beverley Water Act came into being. Building of the waterworks began in October 1881.

Available funds for the new waterworks were limited. In 1882 – 1883 Borough receipts totalled £3,746 - £1,166 tolls and dues, £832 rents and £491in government grants towards the police force – while expenditure totalled £3,359 - £888 went on the police, £492 on public works, £475 on salaries and £644 towards repayment of loans.

In 1884 there was an outbreak of typhoid fever in several hundred houses in Beverley – fifty of those houses had been connected with the new water supply - and eighteen people died including HE Silvester, a former mayor and a director of the water company. Liberals in the town said that the disease had been caused by piped water. Others thought it was the bad state of the drains. The source of the typhoid outbreak was traced to the lunatic asylum. Further outbreaks of typhoid in 1893 – 1895 and in 1904 resulted in the council purchasing the water company for £20,850 in 1907.

In 1884 the General Board of Health had been asked to investigate the problem of water supply and an inspector was sent to Beverley by the Board to look into the problem. He presented his report to the Council in February 1885 and condemned the 'irregular and for the most part antiquated system of sewerage'. He found that there had been no proper inspections or reports by the town's Medical Officer. After one third of the houses supplied by the water company had been attacked by fever, the Local Government Board asked the Town Council to provide an adequate system of sewage. Again there was opposition to this idea, lead by Hind and Crosskill but new blood on the council – which included JE Elwell and Richard Hodgson - after the elections of November 1884 caused a shift in stance. At last action was taken and 1886 the Council accepted a sewerage scheme prepared by BS Brundell, an engineer from Doncaster, who proposed a system of main drainage following the gradient of the town (there is a drop of eleven feet and six inches between North Bar Within and Beckside) with outfall works on the south side of Beverley beck. Work began in 1888.

A Cottage Hospital is Built

The dispensary had continued in Register Square but was found to be insufficient for the needs of this growing town. In 1878 a house in Norwood, used as a Cottage Hospital for members of the East Yorkshire Militia when billeted in Beverley, was leased for inpatients from the dispensary. In 1885 a new dispensary and hospital, designed by Smith and Brodrick of Hull, (the Cottage Hospital - demolished 1996) with fourteen beds was built on land in Morton Lane, previously part of Crosskill's Ironworks, and the building in Register Square was vacated.

St Nicholas Church

From 1873 – 1876 the Revd Edward Carr Glyn was the vicar of St Mary's and his responsibilities included the parish of St Nicholas. He was the fourth son of Baron Wolverton who died in

1873. In his will the Baron left £6,000 for the building of a church in memory of his sons. Carr Glyn managed to persuade the trustees of his father's will to direct the money as capital for the building of a new St Nicholas church, near Beckside, to serve the growing industrial and working-class community of Beverley. The land where the previous church had been was too wet and so the new church was built on nearby land which had been willed to St Mary's parish some years earlier. The first building contractor, who had somewhat grandiose schemes, went bankrupt. F.S Brodrick of Hull was appointed architect for the revised project, Simpson and Malone of Great Thornton Street, Hull were employed as builders and James Elwell was appointed to execute the woodwork. Lady Wolverton gave a further £1,000 to finance the building of the church tower. The building was designated a chapel of ease to St Mary's church and was consecrated by William Thomson, the Archbishop of York on 3rd August 1880. In 1886 the churchyard was consecrated for burials. St Nicholas' continued to be part of the parish of St Mary's until 1960 when it got its own vicar.

Two Successful Industries

By 1890 Hodgsons Tannery, having grown considerably from its early days, had a workforce of 450. When, in that year seventy-five employees went on strike, they were dismissed by Richard Hodgson who was an opponent of trade unionism. Members of the Docker's Union in Hull came out in sympathy and refused to handle material going to the tannery and seamen refused to carry Hodgson's products. Richard Hodgson made no concessions and the strike collapsed four months after it had begun; Beverley residents maintained that this was because the wives of the strikers drove their men folk back to work with brooms and brush handles!

Shipbuilding continued at Grovehill and alongside the Beck and once the lock had been installed a dry dock was made; a further dry dock was created in 1858. Towards the end of the century, as Hull trawlers changed from wind to steam propulsion

A launch at Cochrane's Boat Yard

and from wood to steel construction, there was plenty of re-building work. Henry and Joseph Scarr, who already had engineering works near the head of the beck, in 1882, launched two iron boats; in 1890s the company moved to a more spacious yard by the river in Weel. In 1882 Vulcan Iron Company of Hull established a shipyard on land owned by the corporation and in September of that year launched two ocean-going vessels of 1,500 tons. Two years later the company was wound up and let to Cochrane, Hamilton and Cooper who, between 1884 and 1901, built 245 vessels. The narrowness of the river meant that ships had to be launched sideways.

Extension of the Workhouse

In 1893 an infirmary was added to the workhouse. To prevent inmates strolling into town, high walls and a new arched entrance – over which was fixed a sculptured head with so fierce a face that it might well cause anyone entering through the archway to abandon all hope - were designed by Messrs Hawe and Foley. The doorway to the Master's house was decorated with the beaver badge of Beverley.

East Riding County Council is Formed

In 1889 the East Riding County Council was formed and in January held its first meeting at the Sessions House in New Walk. The following year the council decided to build a new chamber and offices in Cross Street. The Mechanics Institute was demolished and building began. The offices, designed by Smith and Brodrick were opened in 1893.

The Borough Council continued to meet in the Guildhall.

Canon Nolloth, Vicar of Beverley Minster

By 1870 weekly congregations at the Minster averaged 600 – 700 and after a gap of nearly fifty years services were once again held in the nave.

During the 1870s a restoration scheme took place in the Minster under the guidance of George Gilbert Scott, designer of the Albert Memorial in London and known after 1872 as Sir Gilbert Scott. The whole of the interior, which had accumulated the dirt of centuries, was cleaned and the Purbeck marble shafts repolished; the roof was redecorated. The Hawksmoor choir screen was removed and replaced by an oak organ screen carved by James Elwell. The Revd Birtwhistle died in 1879 and a brass lectern was made in memory of his time as vicar of Beverley Minster.

Music in the Minster declined between 1856 – 1874 when the organist, G J Lambert, become increasingly deaf and infirm. Lambert's successor was AH Mann and it was he who began the Minster custom of singing from the towers on Easter morning – a custom which still continues. Less than a year after his appointment he become organist of King's College, Cambridge and in July 1876, John Camidge, with no qualifications apart from coming from a family of York Minster organists, was appointed as Organist and Choirmaster of Beverley Minster.

Three months after his appointment he began the regular Thursday Choral Evensong with its emphasis on music. He remained as organist until 1933.

The Revd Henry Edward Nolloth (1846-1929), from 1896 a canon of York Minster, was instituted as vicar of Beverley Minster on 16th May 1880. He was to remain at the Minster for forty-one years. Canon Nolloth was the son of a navel officer and was educated at Worcester College, Oxford. A year after arriving in Beverley he married Marian, daughter of Thomas Crust, town clerk, a prominent solicitor and clerk of the Minster Old and New Funds. The Nolloths had no children and devoted most of their lives and considerable private fortune to Beverley Minster.

Nolloth was a strong protestant with a dislike of ceremonial and ritual and had many disagreements with his churchwarden Lt Col. George Cussons, owner of the tannery in Keldgate, who was an Anglo-Catholic. Soon after his arrival in Beverley Nolloth gathered round him a team of helpers. To aid his administration of the large Minster parish he secured posts for two permanent assistant curates and two stipendiary curates who worked with a band of voluntary and paid lay workers. He took no stipend for himself and from his own pocket paid the stipends of those he employed. The curates were mostly graduates from Oxford and Cambridge and some had had evangelical training. In 1887 he bought part of the old Friary for the Minster as a clergy house for unmarried curates. One particular curate was the Revd Reginald Pyne (1899 – 1910) whose open air services at the Beckside were attended by 600 – 700 people.

By 1884 the average congregation was between 950 and 1000 and Easter Day communicants had risen to 514 by 1911.

Nolloth sought to take the church into the community. He believed in the education of the young and was concerned about the secularisation of learning after the passing of the Education Acts of 1870 and 1902. In 1883 he used the Wesleyan Mission room at the west end of Keldgate for a Sunday School and also as a meeting place for a working men's club, Mothers' Union meetings, sewing classes and evening Sunday services. In 1885 he built a new girls' school on the north side of the Minster which was enlarged in 1899. In 1902 a large classroom was added to the boys' school south of the Minster. By 1894 there were sixty-two Sunday School teachers in the Minster parishes.

On Sundays there would be three or four services at the Minster and up to eleven services elsewhere in the parish. In 1896 the mission room at Molescroft was replaced by a chapel-of-ease, St Leonard's. In 1896 the church at Tickton was restored and two years later the service at Woodmansey were transferred from the

Robert Smith

National School to the new church of St Peter's.

In 1882 The Old Fund and New Fund of the Minster were amalgamated and a new administration formed, named The Old Fund, consisting of the mayor of Beverley, the vicar of the Minster, the archdeacon of the East Riding and eight others. At this time Minster property consisted of fifty-six acres of ground, ninety houses in Beverley and a piece of land at Etton plus a rent charge of £5 and £827 stock. The Old Fund is still in operation today; nearly all the Minster property in Beverley has been sold.

In January 1897 Nolloth called together a conference at the Guildhall at which he launched the idea of placing statues in the niches of the West Towers of the Minster. He met with much local support and many offered to subscribe to the scheme, although inevitably there were some who opposed the idea. On 22nd June 1897 3,300 people attended a service in celebration of the Golden Jubilee of Queen Victoria. After the service the crowd gathered round the north side of the West Tower and the first statue, which was a statue of the Queen carved by Robert Smith and paid for by the women of Beverley, was unveiled. Also in celebration of the Golden Jubilee a commemorative avenue of trees was planted along roads crossing the Westwood.

One of those attending the Golden Jubilee service would no doubt have been Admiral Walker. During the 19th century the Hall in Lairgate, with its lands stretching up to the Westwood, was lived in by members of the Walker family. James Walker was a merchant in Hull who in 1802 bought 'Pennyman House' in Lairgate. His grandson, later to become Admiral Walker, left home at the age of thirteen to join the navy as a mid-shipman; he served in the Black Sea during the Crimean War. By the age of twenty-eight he was a commander rising to rear-admiral by the time he left the navy in 1873. Admiral Walker's father, Sir James Walker, had received a baronetcy, and vacated the house in Beverley when he moved to an estate at Sands Hutton. After retiring from the navy, Admiral Walker moved into the Hall, Lairgate. He devoted himself to worthy causes and became a benefactor of the town; he was a JP, gave money to the Conservatives and the Church of England, gave money for a mission hall and reading rooms being built under the guidance of Canon Nolloth in Flemingate and Keldgate, a fountain at Beckside, and donated money to the Cottage Hospital in Morton Lane and various organisations for young people such as the Scouts, Guides and Cadets. In 1889 the press reported that as a result of his kindness sixty poor families had been receiving excellent soup every other day during the previous and presents weeks.

A New Wesleyan Church

By the end of the century the Wesleyan Chapel in Walkergate was found to be too small and a new one was built behind nearer to Toll Gavel, on the site of the minister's house. On 10th February 1892 extra trains were provided to bring Methodists to Beverley to take part in the opening ceremony when 1,000 people packed into the church. During the service of

Toll Gavel Church

dedication they were told that the aim of the church was to attract
people who had no place of worship. After the dedication tea was
served to 480 people who were served in three sittings. The crush
to get into the hall was so great that when one of the inner doors
was opened the people behind pushed those in front with such
force that they were jammed against the door posts and one old
lady fainted and had to be carried out.

Philip Brown Sums up 19th Century Beverley

Philip Brown, in 1963 Deputy Librarian at Beverley Library
and later until his death in 1987 Reference Librarian, had an
immense knowledge of the history of the town. In 1983 he
produced his book 'Old Beverley' which contains pictures and

drawings of houses in Beverley which give us a glimpse of how the town must have looked in previous centuries. In his introduction to the book he quotes from comments made by visitors to the town during the 19th century and his own words are a summing up of the town at that time:

'With its somewhat withdrawn geographical position, with a strong element of inward-looking middle-classes among its population, and (apart from one or two notable exceptions) its lack of involvement in much of the Industrial Revolution, we can well understand how this town was for so long so little affected by the pressures of the great Victorian Age of Improvement. The resulting Beverlonian atmosphere certainly made a vivid impression upon such eloquent observers as Edwin Waugh ('the Lancastrian Burns'), or the popular novelist Mary Elizabeth Braddon. For them Beverley must have been primarily an anachronism – charming, antique, quaint, and ever-so-slightly ludicrous. Edwin Waugh came here in April 1868: he writes of a feeling 'as if I were leaving the 19th century behind', of 'a somnolent pool of quaint-featured life, left gleaming upon the shore of the past by the receding tide of modern change.......a spell-bound spot'. He was deeply impressed by 'the general appearance of slow-grown comfort.... And the tranquil charm that enfolded all'. He noted the typical Beverlonian burgesses: 'they hardly seem to know that there is any world outside of their own garden-girdled town; or, if they do, they seem as if they didn't care about having anything to do with it'.....

In the 20th century that feeling of remoteness was to begin to change.

CHAPTER 12

1900 – 2003. CHANGES IN THE LANDSCAPE

The creation of the East Riding County Council in 1889 did little to alter the government of Beverley and the Borough Council continued to control the development of the town. This two tier system of government continued until the formation of the County of Humberside in 1974. As the century progressed the County authorities took over the responsibility for education, planning, police and libraries; central government demanded reports and the imposition of laws on various aspects of the life of the town. Beverley, inevitably, became caught up in national concerns.

Throughout the century Beverley was forced to change in order to accommodate an increasing population and the motor car. In 1901 the population of the Borough of Beverley was 13,183, by 1951 it was 15,504 and in 2001 it was approximately 25,000. Consequently, there was a continual call for more houses and the replacement of derelict property. At first developments were slow but were to gather momentum after the First World War and accelerate after 1980.

Industry

At the start of the 20th century Beverley's main sources of employment were with shipbuilding, tanning, ironworks and the processing of agricultural produce.

The industrial success of 20th century Beverley was often dependant on the commercial state of Hull. By 1900 Hull trawler owners were fully employed and demanding larger vessels. Cochrane, Hamilton and Cooper were unable to deliver these

311

because of the narrowness caused by the silting up of the river Hull. In 1901 the firm was taken over by Cook, Welton and Gemmell. They provided engines and dredging gear which cleared the river of mud and contained the erosion of the banks with the result that larger ships could be built at Beverley and go down the river to the Humber. Throughout the first half of the century the firm went from strength to strength. During the 1930s, generally a time of industrial depression, the firm survived and continued to build trawlers and other small ships required by Hull. In 1954 it launched fifteen new vessels and employed 650 people. The success of the firm was partly as a result of its manager, Harold Sheardown, who was also vice-chairman of Kingston Steam Trawler Company in Hull which bought many ships from the dockyard at Beverley.

At the beginning of the twentieth century, Hodgsons continued to do well with fifteen powered barges taking goods from the tannery along the river to Hull. In 1911 Colonel Hodgson died at the age of 91. All Colonel Hodgson's sons, with the exception of William who became a solicitor, followed him into the business. The success of Hodgsons was increased by new ventures begun by Phillip and Richard Hodgson: by 1892 Phillip had started the manufacture of glue and gelatine. After the death of his father he became managing director while Richard started a new plant within the tannery precincts for the manufacture of Vegetable Tanning Extracts. In 1915 Hodgsons bought its oldest rival in Beverley, Cussons tannery in Keldgate, which had been worked by members of the Cussons family since 1854. During the First World War Hodgsons expanded to provide leather for HM forces and by 1920 was one of the largest and best equipped leather producing units in the country. However, after the end of the war the firm stagnated and in 1920 was taken over by Barrow Hepburn and Gale which meant that it was no longer run as an individual company but as part of a group. In 1920 George Odey, who had been an under secretary of the Group, came to the north to continue his apprenticeship at Richard Hodgson and Sons; having worked his way through every department of the firm in 1923 he became its General Manager and by 1931 had been promoted to Managing Director. In 1933 he was appointed Managing Director of Barrow Hepburn and Gale and in 1938 became its chairman. Through his guidance the Group grew into the largest leather producing group in Europe and the firm of Hodgsons became one of the largest employers of labour in Beverley. The firm at Beverley produced both heavy and light leathers and at one stage was processing 250,000 cattle hides a year. A report from the company at this time states that:

'Last year the boilers consumed 20,972 tons of coal producing thereby 312,660,000lbs of steam and 5,900,00 K.E. hours of electricity. This quantity of steam and electricity together with nearly 600 million gallons of water from wells inside the factory were used to manufacture 10 million pounds weight of leather, over 1,600 tons of glue and gelatine and more than 24,000 tons of tanning extracts.'

After the deaths of Alfred and Edmund Crosskill, William Crosskill and Sons was, in 1904, taken over by East Yorkshire Cart and Wagon Company. In 1914 this company, renamed the East Yorkshire and Crosskills Cart and Wagon Company, went into liquidation. Five years later it revived as the Beverley Waggon Works but finally closed in 1927.

In 1919 one of the old established industries in Beverley ceased. During the late 19th century the cheapening of the price of tea combined with other activities, including the Temperance Movement, contributed towards a decline in beer drinking; larger brewery concerns using mechanisation also resulted in many small brewers going out of business. After the death of Robert Ranby Stephenson (aged 81) in 1919 the Golden Ball brewery in Toll Gavel was sold to the Hull Brewery Company Limited.

Tigar Manure Company, which manufactured fertilizers had begun in 1848 but was closed in 1923. In 1925 the site at Grovehill was bought by Charles Deans of Hull Ltd who made musical instruments. The firm expanded after it turned to producing motor vehicles and furniture components. After the closure of Tigar's Manure Company the seed crushing business at

Armstrongs Engineering Works 1960

Hull Bridge closed.

A new and successful firm was begun in 1907 when Gordon Armstrong, from Cumberland, an engineer and entrepreneur, opened a garage and workshop in the one remaining timber-framed house on the west side of North Bar Within. By 1909 Armstrong had built his first car and continued to manufacture cars until the First World War when he changed to the manufacture of munitions and a newly developed piece of farming equipment – the tractor. The firm continued to grow and in 1917 his works moved to the site in Eastgate previously occupied by William Crosskill and Sons. From 1919 the main product of the firm was shock absorbers and by 1926 Armstrong's Factory was producing 200 shock absorbers a week. The business was increased when, in 1926, it received an order from Ford cars and two years later an order from Morris. This meant that the firm was enlarged tenfold and by 1928 there were

314

new and larger works on the Eastgate site. By the following year Armstrong Patents Limited produced 4,000 shock absorbers a day and employed 450 workers. Armstrong's premises at the 15th century building at North Bar Within continued as a garage but was sold and in 1982 the 15th century entrance with the premises behind was converted into Beverley's only shopping precinct, St Mary's Arcade.

In 1910 air flight was only just beginning. In that year Gordon Armstrong, tested the 'Bleriot' on the Westwood. A large crowd gathered to watch the flight of one of the first aeroplanes, to marvel that it left the ground at all but to be disappointed that it was airborne for only a few feet.

Between 1931 and 1933 there was a trade depression throughout the country. In January of 1931 unemployment in Beverley was 498, in 1932 it was 547 and in 1933 it was 981. In 1934 recovery was beginning and unemployment figures dropped. In order to attract customers to the town and industries a Carnival and Shopping Week was arranged. This included the Crowning of the Carnival Queen, a Grand Carnival Ball, a Shop Dressing Competition, a Carnival Parade and a Gymnastic display. Carnival Week proved to be so successful that it was held for the following four years.

Beverley Library and Art Gallery

There had been a subscription library in the town for many years, but in the first decade of the 20th century two inhabitants of Beverley worked together to create a free library.

John Champney was born in Newbegin in Beverley in 1846 and went on to become a prosperous textile manufacturer in Halifax. William Spencer was born in Rawcliffe, near Selby in 1826. He came to Beverley at the age of twenty-two when he was appointed headmaster of the Wesleyan Day School. When he arrived the school consisted of one main room and one smaller room with fifty-seven pupils. In 1863 a school inspector's report stated that:

'The school is well filled with children and fully deserves to be so. Nothing short of steadfast zeal and great ability devoted to the school through several years could have produced so satisfactory results.'

From 1866 Latin was included in the curriculum. During his headship the school was enlarged three times and by the time he left it had 283 students and was the only mixed school in Beverley. After his retirement in 1887 William Spencer was elected to the Council, in 1895 became an alderman and in 1904 mayor.

While Spencer was mayor Champney, who had no children to inherit his fortune, decided to provide money to create a free library in Beverley. The site chosen was in Well Lane but had a mortgage owing of £520 4s. When he became mayor Spencer, a staunch Methodist, felt that instead of paying money on ostentatious entertaining he should pay off the debt owing on the site so that the library could be built. This was done and the library was built. At an elaborate opening ceremony on 8th August 1906 Alderman James Elwell, Chairman of the Library Committee, presented Champney with a 'gold key of very artistic design' to open the new building and then to keep as a momento. In 1906 both Champney and Spencer were created honorary freemen of the town.

The need for an art gallery and a museum soon arose. In 1908 the corporation bought 220 views of Beverley and its neighbourhood. William Spencer died in 1910 and in his will left £5,000 to the Library and museum. In 1928 Champney paid for an extension to the original library in order to provide a Reference Library and Art Gallery. The new Art Gallery soon received donations of paintings and artefacts of Beverley. John Champney died a year after the opening of the Gallery and in his will bequeathed twenty paintings and water colours. His executer, Mr E Evelyn Barron, added to the bequest a large collection of art objects, drawings and prints. Colonel JR Pease (a Hull banker who lived in Westwood House) gave sixty prints of local interest. Today the Art Gallery has a collection of many prints and paintings of Beverley's past including fifty-five works of Fred Elwell, the majority of which were bequeathed by the artist. One painting is a portrait of John E Champney and is titled 'Benefactor and Wool Merchant'.

Champney's will left £5,000 to establish a trust fund for the Reference Library, £1,600 to create the Champney Gardens Endowment Fund and his own collection of 5,000 books. He also donated £1,250 for laying out the gardens to the rear and side of the building.

The names of Champney and Spencer are still remembered in the town. In 1927 the street in which the library and art gallery was built was renamed Champney Road. In 1905 the school in which Spencer taught was renamed Spencer County Primary School in recognition of 'his long and honourable career'. In his will Spencer left £100 to the Council in order to provide each child at the school with a yearly gift of an orange (a luxury at that time). After the £100 had run out the Israeli Citrus Board continued the tradition by providing oranges for every child at Swinemoor Junior School (which succeeded the Spencer school after the demolition of the old school in 1958). Today, on the schoolday nearest to the birthday of William Spencer, the Mayor of Beverley visits the Swinemoor Junior School and presents an orange to each of the 232 pupils.

Frederick Elwell

Fred Elwell was born in 1870, the second son of James Elwell the Beverley woodcarver. He left home at the age of fifteen to study art in Lincoln, Antwerp and Paris. After working in London and Paris he returned to Beverley where he set up his studio in Trinity Lane. He worked regular hours, taking a break for lunch when he would often be seen with friends in the Beverley Arms. He was a familiar figure in Beverley, walking through the town with his black velour hat and patterned scarf round his neck. Every year, from 1911 until his death, he exhibited pictures in the Royal Academy. From 1914 he and his wife, Mary, lived in North Bar House in North Bar Within ('the loveliest street in England' according to Elwell) where they employed five indoor staff and two gardeners. Elwell's aim in painting was to make a beautiful picture rather than to portray passion and his many scenes of Beverley, both outside and within its houses, achieves this. Many of his pictures are in the Beverley Art Gallery and also some commissioned works in the homes of Beverlonians. His wife, Mary Elwell, was also a gifted artist as was shown in an exhibition of her works in 2001. Her paintings are masterpieces of interior studies and landscapes of Beverley. Over a period of twenty-two years fifty-eight of her paintings were exhibited at the Royal Academy. After the death of Fred Elwell, in 1958, his house was sold for £2,400. It became an art gallery, offices and in 2001 reverted to being a private house.

First World War 1914 – 1918

At the outbreak of war in 1914 over 3,000 men from Beverley joined the armed forces and 400 Special Constables volunteered. To help the war effort about 150 people in the town, 80% of them being women or girls, went to work in the munitions factories. By the end of the war over 400 men from Beverley had been killed and 600 wounded, gassed or were missing.

In 1916 an airfield was opened on the west edge of the racecourse from where missions were flown to defend the country from Zeppelin attacks. Hangers and workshops were built on the south west corner of the site. Squadrons from here patrolled the Humber ports. Flying ceased after the war but part of the site remained with the Royal Air force for many years.

In 1917 St Mary's House in Hengate, on the east side of the church, was destroyed by fire and the family and maids in the house narrowly escaped death. After the fire Clive Wilson, the owner who was a younger son of the wealthy Hull trawler owners, decided not to re-build but gave the house and garden to the borough as a public park to be maintained by him in perpetuity. After the fire he and his family moved to Little Tranby (York Lodge), a large red-bricked house overlooking the Westwood which had recently been built by his brother.

On 19th July 1919, after the passing of the Treaty of Versailles, the town celebrated the coming of peace. There was a parade of decorated vehicles, children's sports, a gymkhana on the Norwood cricket ground, a presentation of medals to war heroes, cinema shows of silent movies and afternoon tea. The day ended with a Peace Ball in the Assembly Rooms.

In the south transept of Beverley Minster are several memorials to those who lost their lives in the First World War. In the niches of the cenotaph illuminated scrolls bear the names of officers and men of the East Yorkshire regiment who gave their lives in the Great War 1914 -1918. Other screens show the names of 7,500 men of the East Riding who were killed when serving with other regiments. A wooden cross had been erected on Henin Hill, Arras, France which was dedicated to the officers and men of the 64th Infantry Brigade who fell on April 9th 1917 in capturing part of the Hindenberg Line. In July 1931 this wooden cross was replaced by a stone cross and the original was placed in the north-east chapel in the south transept of Beverley Minster. The stained glass in the south window of the south transept was put in 1921 in memory of those who had died in the war and symbolises 'the Age-Long Conflict between Good and Evil'.

In St Mary's Church a wooden triptych lists the names of the 112 men of the parish who died in the war; a brass memorial list the names of twenty members of the East Yorkshire Constabulary who had joined various regiments and who had died in battle.

After the end of the war a memorial was built in the centre of the garden behind St Mary's church dedicated to those men from Beverley who had died as a result of war. 420 names are listed. The memorial, designed by a local architect, Richard Whiteing, depicts four seated figures representing the armed forces and nursing.

Beverley Workhouse becomes the Westwood Hospital

By the beginning of the century new houses had been built along Union Road – the road leading to the workhouse. In 1905 the road was renamed Woodlands.

The Liberal Government of 1908-1911 looked into the whole question of poverty and took steps to relieve the plight of the poor. The National Insurance Act of 1911 and the implementation of various health and unemployment measures eventually made institutions such as the Poor Law Institutions, the new name for workhouses, redundant. The Local Government Act of 1929 officially abolished the term 'pauper', together with boards of guardians, and local authorities were encouraged to convert workhouses into infirmaries. In 1929 the Beverley Poor Law Institution was disbanded and ten years later became the Beverley Base Hospital (later the Westwood Hospital) run by the Council until 1948.

Clean Water; Good Health

In 1902 the Town Council appointed its first full-time Inspector of Nuisances, a Mr Thomas Mooney, who, over a period of ten years, carried out house-by-house inspections of drains in an effort to tackle the problems of poor sanitation and ill-health. He reported many cases of houses in poor conditions.

In 1905 there was a further outbreak of fever and diarrhoea. After investigation it was found that piped water was being contaminated by sewage. Consequently, in 1907 the corporation bought the waterworks at Beverley Parks and decided to find a new source of water. Their search was unsuccessful. In 1911 the corporation decided to use the existing works adding mechanical filters for purification. By 1912 mains water reached 50% of houses. By 1934 water closets were in about half the houses and twenty years later were in almost every house. In 1948, when the wells became polluted after flood water had drained into them, it was decided that the town's water would be provided by Hull Corporation.

In 1914 the minutes of the March meeting of the Health and Safety Committee showed that twelve people had died that month making the death rate for March 10.5% per 1,000 of the population; a third of the people who had died had been over the age of sixty-five. This death-rate was below the national average of 14%.

On 16th May 1914 the Beverley Guardian reported on a meeting of the Health and Safety Committee. Mr Wray, the chairman, pointed out that the death rate for the quarter ending March 31st was the lowest but one in the whole history of the town although certain houses in Lairgate and Beckside had been reported as being unfit for human habitation. Knowing what a prominent part smallpox, diphtheria and typhoid fever had played in the town in past years, he said that it was interesting to note that during the previous year there had been only one death from any notifiable disease which had come to the notice of the Medical Officer of Health, and that was from the infantile complaint – poliomyelitis. There were also only five deaths from zymotic disease during the year – one of whooping-cough and three of diarrhoea. There had been no case of enteric fever in the town during the whole year, only two cases of scarlet fever, twelve cases of diphtheria, none of which had proved fatal, and there had not been a single case of small-pox. The total number of infant deaths, children under one year of age, had been twenty, as compared with twenty-five in the previous year, and forty-three two years before. The mortality rate in England and Wales was 109 per 1,000 and the twenty deaths in Beverley worked out to sixty-six. He thought that this improvement was due to the fact that this town had at last secured an absolutely pure supply of water.

'Homes Fit for Heroes'

Between 1901 and 1914 the Medical Officer of Health for Beverley condemned an average of eight houses a year as being too small and unsuitable for human habitation. Little replacement of demolished houses took place during the First World War so that by 1918, as elsewhere in the country, there was a shortage of accommodation. At the end of the war the cry went out from the government for houses to be built which were 'fit for heroes'. The

Housing and Town Planning Act of 1919 made it a duty of every local council to prepare a housing plan which provided accommodation for the working classes. As an inducement government loans were offered to councils to buy land and build houses. In 1919 the Medical Officer of Health conducted a survey in Beverley in which he found that of the 2,923 working class houses in the town, thirty-nine were dilapidated (of which twenty-one were empty), 115 overcrowded and thirty-three had more than one family.

The Borough Council bought land on the north side of Grovehill Road and by 1923 eighty-six concrete houses had been built. New streets were named after past and present residents of Beverley – Neville, Warton, Routh Avenues. Three years later seventy-eight more houses had been built – including Schofield Avenue (Schofield's was a shop in Beverley) and Hotham Square.

There remained a shortage of building land within the borough. A solution to the problem emerged after the death of Admiral Walker in 1926. Admiral Walker had continued to live at the Hall, Lairgate and during the war had kept a herd of Highland cattle on his parkland. After his death he was buried in Beverley Minster (a special dispensation as burials within the church had ceased from 1859). His paternal grand parents, mother and two of his sons, one of whom had been killed in France during the first few weeks of the war, are also buried in the Minster and there is also a memorial to his father, who was buried at Sand Hutton. When the Hall and its land, which stretched as far as the Westwood, came up for sale it was bought by the Borough Council. Between 1926 and 1930, 119 houses were built on that part of the estate which lay between the Hall, Keldgate and the Leases. In 1930 the Hall itself was adapted for use as the Beverley Municipal Offices.

On the northern edge of the property was a lane which over the centuries had had various names. This lane, which ran from the west end of Champney Road to what is now the Leases, was recorded in 1202 as Gilegate (ie the lane next to St Giles' Hospital) or in 15th century St Giles Croft Lane. By 1828 it was called Captain Lane and in 1927 was renamed Champney Road. The Leases is built on the medieval town boundary ditch. In 1928 the ditch was filled in when the road was used for residential purposes.

By 1930, 285 council houses had been built, but after the Housing Act of 1930 had charged local authorities with the duty of identifying and replacing slum areas the pace of building quickened. Several new estates were developed on land to the east of the town: between 1931 and 1933 126 houses were built on Cherry Tree Lane and between 1936 and 1938 128 houses were built on Mill Lane.

Many of the houses from both these estates were occupied by people who had been living in slum property which had been demolished. Demolition of old property continued but this was not always met with approval and by 1933 some owners resented the destruction of their properties and won an appeal against demolition.

Changes in Church and Chapel

Canon Nolloth remained as vicar of Beverley Minster until his retirement in 1921. Under his guidance the embellishment of the Minster continued. Between 1897 and 1908 a further 105 statues were placed in the niches of the West Towers. Twenty-nine statues were placed on the interior of the West Window of the nave. Between 1911 and 1913 statues were placed in the niches over the choir stalls and in 1918 statuettes were placed on the pillars supporting the new organ loft which had been paid for by Nolloth. In 1905 Nolloth paid for railings, set on a low wall, to replace the brick wall 'of squalid ugliness' which surrounded the churchyard.

Nolloth was interested in campanology and became a principal benefactor of bells at both York and Beverley Minster. In Beverley he paid for the overhaul of the bells in 1896 and 1901. When the bells were re-hung in August 1901 there were four new bells, four recast bells and two, which had been recast in 1896, which were placed in the North West Tower. The two remaining bells, both of them medieval, were placed in the South West Tower, one to become the prayer bell, and the other, Great John, to ring out the hour while the ten bells in the North West Tower chime out the quarters to a tune devised by John Camidge, organist at Beverley Minster at the beginning of the 20th century.

After his resignation Canon Nolloth moved to Oxford but he retained his interest in the Minster until his death in 1929. After his death his widow continued to give financial and other support to the church. In her will Mrs Nolloth left £1,700 in trust towards the income of a senior curate, £300 for the upkeep of the bells and £100 for the care of the churchyard. During her lifetime Mrs Nolloth bought Hall Garth Field which lies immediately south of the Minster and which was where the medieval archbishops of York had their manor house. In a codicil to her will she left £800 to her nephew, Canon Rigg who followed Canon Nolloth as vicar of Beverley Minster, which was sufficient for him to buy Hall Garth from her estate. He later conveyed the field to the York Diocesan Board of Finance on condition that the churchwardens and the vicar of Beverley Minster were to be the trustees. Hence the field has been saved from any development.

After the First World War church attendance decreased. Indifference, the wireless and the pleasures of motoring all competed for attention on Sundays. In 1914 the numbers regularly taking communion at the Minster on Easter Sunday was 464, while in 1938 it was 345.

In 1936 the Friends of Beverley Minster was formed as a registered charity. It aims to unite in common fellowship all those who wish to be associated with the work and worship of the Minster and to ensure that any new furnishings are of the finest quality. At first 223 people enrolled as Friends and money raised was spent on paying the salary of an assistant curate. In the 1980s numbers rose to over 1,300 and money has been spent on preserving the fabric and furnishings of the Minster; most of the modern furnishings in the Minster have been provided by the Friends. Today the Friends is a world wide organisation with a membership of about 900.

Restoration work in the Minster continued after the war. It was financed by the Trustees of the Old Fund, the Friends of Beverley Minster, the Parochial Church Council and the generosity of many benefactors. In the 1950s a programme of cleaning the exterior of the Minster and repairing the roof and stonework began. In 1974 the cry went out once again for money for the restoration of the stonework of Beverley Minster. Weathering, wood-worm and years of decay had taken their toll and it was feared that if immediate action was not taken the damage might be irreparable. A committee was formed under the presidency of the Earl of Halifax, the chairmanship of Lord Middleton and the guidance of the secretary and treasurer, Tom Liddle. An appeal was launched to raise £500,000. Money was received from all over the country and within two years the target had been reached and work began. The Minster was to be shrouded in scaffolding for the next eleven years. Hodgsons supplied the red leather used to cover the seats of a new set of chairs in the nave.

Repair work also took place at St Mary's. The 15th century painted ceiling in the choir was cleaned in 1939. The panel portraying the legendary monarch Lochrine was replaced by a new panel giving details of the reigning monarch, King George VI.

In 1953 gravestones were moved to the edge of St Mary's churchyard in North Bar Within. The area was then transformed into gardens to commemorate the coronation of Queen Elizabeth II. The gates to the original cemetery which came from Crosskill's ironworks were retained.

In an effort to cut back on expenses the vicarages of the Minster and St Mary's were sold and new ones built. In 1963 the Old Minster Vicarage (built 1704) in Minster Yard North was sold after a new one had been built in the garden of the old Blue Coat School, No. 48 Highgate, which remains Minster property. St Mary's Vicarage, re-built in 1791 in Vicar Lane was sold and a new vicarage built on Molescroft Road on ground which had been given to the church.

For four centuries Beverley had been known for its strong protestant religion but in the 20th century several smaller sects, including the Scotch Baptists and United Methodists failed and their chapels were closed. By 1964 there were only fifty-seven members of the Primitive Methodist circuit, many of whom were elderly, and there were insufficient funds to keep the large chapel in Wednesday Market going; in 1958 it was demolished and Crystal Garage built in its place – providing for the new religion, the motor car. From then on the large Wesleyan church in Toll Gavel became the town's main Methodist church, smaller chapels serving other districts in the town.

In mid-century two new denominations had places of worship in Beverley. The Jehovah's Witnesses built Kingdom Hall in Arden Road and the Church of Latter Day Saints built a chapel in Manor Road. In 1961 the Society of Friends built a new meeting house in Quaker Lane.

Leisure Activities

Throughout the century leisure pursuits were encouraged for all levels of society. At the East Riding Lawn Tennis Club tournaments were held to which stars from Wimbledon were invited. During the Second World War the club was closed to members and only officers and gentlemen of the forces were permitted to play. Today it has a membership of over 300. In 1909 the Norwood Park Recreation Ground of six and a half acres of a twelve acre site was bought by JA Dunkerly and became a bowls club, cricket ground and tennis courts. In 1948 the site was enlarged and sold to Beverley Town Cricket and Recreational Club. Previously the only public swimming bath in the town was the small baths behind the Picture Playhouse. In 1973 new baths were opened in Mill Lane, on a site which had been part of Crosskill's works and then St Mary's Boys School. The old swimming baths in Ladygate became a store selling second-hand goods. The Leisure Centre in Flemingate was opened in 1990 and in 2003 money has been allocated towards the building of new swimming baths near the Leisure Centre.

Beverley Picture Playhouse

The first cinema show to which the public was invited was in January 1897 when the 'Royal Cinematescope' put on films in the Assembly Rooms. This new art form proved to be so popular that in 1911 the Corn Exchange in Saturday Market was converted and re-named the Beverley Picture Playhouse – the first of its kind in the country at which films were shown regularly. The Edwardian decorations of the Playhouse with draped silks, carved Grecian heads and muted lighting were typical of the time. The manager of the cinema, Ernest Symmons, made films of local events which were often shown with the main feature. He also organised 'live' events, such as musical talent competitions or 'bonny baby' competitions with prizes. In 1916 The Marble Arch Cinema (for years known locally as the Marble Itch!) was built in Butcher Row with a seating capacity of 1,000.

In the thirties Hollywood films were at the height of their popularity and a third cinema in the town was needed. In 1934 the Assembly Rooms were demolished and replaced by the Regal cinema with a typically 1930s style hoarding advertising the fact. The 19th century hall at the back was retained for dances.

A decline in the film industry began in the 1960's. In 1967 the Marble Arch in Butcher Row closed and in 1968 the Regal was transformed into a bingo hall. Discos were held here and it became a favourite place for the young people of the town. It was demolished in 2000 and a block of flats and shops built on the site.

In 1969 the Beverley Picture Playhouse ceased showing movies. There were fears that the Borough Council, landlords of the Playhouse, planned to use the cinema and the adjoining public swimming baths for an indoor market. In 1973 Thelma Symmons, widow of Ernest Symmons, established a Playhouse Film Society. Members of the society paid an annual subscription which enabled them to see some of the old films, which were unlikely to be shown on television, at monthly intervals at Beverley Picture Playhouse. As only short term leases for the building were given by the Council it was impractical, even if the money had been available, to refurbish the interior of the playhouse and so the decorations of 1911 remained.

Second World War – 1939-1945

Beverley was fortunate during the Second World War that it did not receive the intense bombing and devastation that was meted out to Hull. However, like every other town in England the people of Beverley felt the effects of shortages, restrictions, rationing, blackout and the need for war work. Military personnel from the RAF station at Leconfield and soldiers from the army barracks at Queensgate would have been a constant presence in the town. Strict black-out was imposed and if a chink of light was seen by one of the wardens patrolling the streets a penalty had to be paid. People found difficulty in walking through streets in pitch darkness, especially pipe smokers who suffered from having their pipes rammed down their throats when they bumped into people. A problem arose when East Yorkshire buses, with their roofs, specially shaped to pass through the Bar, tried to go through in total darkness. They were constantly bumping into the roof damaging both the bus and the Bar. A concession to lighting was made when a light was placed in the centre of the roof of North Bar with a beam shining down the walls rather than onto the road. There was no need for lighting when the city of Hull was bombed for the streets of Beverley would be lit up by the light of fires burning in Hull.

By 1942 twenty-six public air raid shelters had been built, one remains on York Road next to the neatherd's yard. Sirens were placed around the town and when the wailing of the sirens gave warning of an air attack, people would hasten to the shelters for safety. Here they would sit on hard wooden benches chatting amongst themselves but as the German bombers passed overhead there was complete silence. Once the all-clear was sounded they knew that danger had passed. On 27th October 1940 a German plane flew low over North Bar, opened fire and machine gunned several of the main streets in Beverley. People fled for shelter in shop doorways; luckily only two were injured but much damage was done to property. St Mary's church has a small hole in the back of one of the pews made by a bullet from this bomber.

As it was impossible to black-out St Mary's church evening services in the winter were held in the Playhouse Cinema. These services were so popular that often the cinema was full and people had to be turned away at the door.

In 1940 iron railings were requisitioned by the government. They were removed from around most buildings in the town but if a special case was put forward, proving that the building was of particular historic interest, they could be kept. Only in the last few years have some railings been replaced.

During the war there was a feeling of people pulling together in order to help the war effort. When the government encouraged people to 'dig for victory' and grow their own food there was an instant response. Flowerbeds, lawns, grass verges and even window boxes were converted to produce vegetables. Part of the Westwood was ploughed and corn was grown. Week long events would be organised to raise money for the war effort. The East Yorkshire band would play and concerts, dances or whist drives would be organised. £550 was raised within the town to remove the glass from the East Window of the Minster, the only medieval glass in the church, for safe storage in the Percy chapel.

In 1942 Ernest Symmons arranged a treat for 100 children whose fathers were prisoners of war. He invited them to the Playhouse Cinema to see Walt Disney's film 'Dumbo'. Afterwards tea was provided for them at the Rambla Café in Saturday Market and each child was given two shillings and sixpence. A similar event was organised for children in the town who were evacuees from the east end of Hull. About seventy evacuee children, including some who had been in Beverley for over five years, were entertained at the pictures and then for tea at the Rambla café where each child was given one shilling and a packet of sweets. The Cottage Hospital in Morton Lane organised a 'win a car' competition, despite the fact that there was petrol rationing and many people had to lay their cars up during the war. Gordon Armstrong donated a Morris Eight Saloon valued at £128 as first prize (or a cash alternative).

Gordon Armstrong proved to be quite a benefactor to the town. In 1937 he gave £1,000 to the Cottage Hospital and in 1938 a similar amount to Hull Royal Infirmary. In 1938, at a cost of £250 he presented the Boy Scouts with a clubroom. In 1935 Gordon Armstrong bought Longcroft Hall in Gallows Lane. During the war he moved into converted stables at the Hall and lent his home to the Ministry of Health as a temporary hospital – it had fifty beds. He established the Pale Moon Coffee Stall in Saturday Market which offered free coffee and tea to everyone in uniform. Mr Armstrong personally opened the stall at six each morning and kept it open until everyone had been served. It was reopened from six in the evening until midnight. By the end of the war it was estimated to have served 250,000 cups of tea or coffee.

In 1940 he presented Hurrican 'Vicy' to the nation with the proviso that it was to be stationed at a local aerodrome and be used to defend Beverley and the surrounding area. He also presented a lifeboat, costing £8,500, to a lifeboat station in Devon in memory of his wife who had died while on a cruise.

There were fears of German spies coming to England. People were warned not to talk to strangers and to report any unusual happenings. All signs on houses and streets which might identify a town were removed. Sometimes signs were never replaced. Until it was demolished in 2000 the sign over the Beverley school clinic in Champney Road read: 'The …….. School Clinic'.

Memorials to those who died in the Second World War were placed in both the major churches. In St Mary's church there is a door which was carved by Robert Thompson, the 'Mouse Man' of Kilburn whose firm uses the sign of a mouse on every piece of furniture carved by them, which lists the names of thirty-five men from the parish who lost their lives in the Second World War. In the Minster there is a chapel and cross, carved by Robert Thompson, in the South Transept dedicated to those who lost their lives in the war and an altar rail to commemorate those killed in Malaya. The East Yorkshire Regiment has its own chapel in the Minster to commemorate its long history.

In 1950 St John's Chapel in Lairgate became the Memorial Hall. At the beginning of the 20th century the chapel, which had been refurbished in 1893, was mostly frequented by middle class Anglicans who rented pews. In 1920 it was still attracting congregations of up to 200 but Canon Nolloth felt that it was not a mission church and had 'outlived its usefulness'. By 1939 attendance had fallen to about thirty and the chapel was closed. In 1950 the Borough Council bought the building and designated it a Memorial Hall in memory of those who had died in the Second World War. It was converted into a community centre for the use of the inhabitants of Beverley and became a venue for theatre groups, concerts, meetings and other forms of leisure-time pursuits. The Borough Council appointed sixteen trustees who had charge of the land and building.

In 1874 a ten acre site in Queensgate, in Beverley Parks, became the site of barracks and a depot for the East Yorkshire Regiment as well as housing the East Yorkshire Militia. Wooden huts extended these barracks during the Second World War and it was here that men were trained for the D-Day invasion of France. In 1958 the East Yorkshire Regiment, which had been formed in 1685, was amalgamated with the West Yorkshire Regiment to become the Prince of Wales' Own Regiment of Yorkshire. The barracks were vacated but remained until the 1980s when they were demolished and Morrisons superstore and other shops were built on the site.

Education According to Age, Aptitude and Ability

Two Local Education Authorities had been established under the 1902 Education Act – the County and the Beverley Borough Local Education Authorities. They were to assume overall responsibility for elementary and secondary education, teacher training, technical and adult education.

In 1902 the Grammar School, which had amalgamated with the Foundation School at the end of the previous century, moved from Albert Terrace to a purpose built school for boys in Queensgate. The school grew fast; in 1906 there were fifty-two pupils, in 1924 there were 164 and in 1941 340. After 1913 the school house, No. 54 Keldgate, was used for boarders. Various charities continued to provide an income and the school remained independent of the state.

There was still no provision of secondary education for girls. In 1908 the East Riding County Council put up buildings in the twelve acre grounds of Norwood House and opened a secondary school known as Beverley High School for Girls. Norwood House became a boarding house for teachers and pupils. 100 free places were offered at the school which, at first, included a mixed kindergarten and junior department. The school began with nineteen pupils in 1908 but eight year's later there were fifty-seven day pupils and sixteen boarders and so further temporary accommodation had to be provided; by 1924 there were 145 day pupils and twenty boarders. Both the Grammar School and the High School were fee paying schools but the corporation offered scholarships.

The Borough Council was essentially concerned with elementary education and by 1915 had built two new schools and modernized another. The County Council provided a teacher training centre at first in the Wesleyan Spencer School and from the 1920s in a building in Lord Roberts Road.

The Second World War drove home the lesson that a modern industrial nation needs an educated population. The Education Act of 1944 aimed to provide free secondary education for all children, according to their 'age, aptitude and ability'. The school leaving age was raised from fourteen to fifteen – later to sixteen. Primary, secondary and further education was to be provided (the secondary level often divided into Grammar, Secondary Modern and Technical).

As numbers at the Grammar School had increased, more huts were built to provide additional accommodation. A new building was opened in 1936 and extended in 1965. By 1941 there were 340 pupils. The school retained selection and at first held out against becoming comprehensive until 1974. In 2002 there were 758 pupils.

In 1944 the junior department of Beverley High School was phased out and admission to the school became wholly selective. More buildings were added and by 1961 it had 400 pupils. In 1973 it became comprehensive. In 2002 the number of pupils was 835. In 1979 the sixth forms of the High School and the Grammar School amalgamated.

After the passing of the 1944 Education Act there was continual pressure for more places at Beverley's secondary schools. In 1951 Longcroft County Secondary School, in Molescroft, was built to provide an education for less academic children in Beverley and the surrounding villages. It was the first of its kind in East Yorkshire and became a model for other schools. In 1973 a new building was opened increasing the accommodation from 1,350 to 1,700 when the school became comprehensive. In 2002 a Performing Arts Studio was built and the school was renamed Longcroft School and Performing Arts College. In that year it had 1,602 pupils.

In the 1960s and 1970s nearly all existing primary schoolswere replaced. Opening dates of new schools were:

Opening Dates	Name of School	Number of pupils in 2002
1962	St John of Beverley Roman Catholic School	125
1967	Swinemoor County Primary School	391
1972	Minster Primary School	674
1972	St Mary's Primary School	
1915	St Nicholas' Primary School	377

In 1913 St Mary's National School for boys moved to a new building in Mill Lane. After a fire in the building in 1946 the school moved to Longcroft Hall. The numbers at the school soon outgrew the building and in 1970 the school was amalgamated with the girls' school and became St Mary's Church of England Junior school.

Evening institutes had been popular in the previous century and in 1923 technical education had been provided in the evenings in the Minster Boys School. Under the 1902 Education Act the provision of technical education became the responsibility of the county council. Adult education was provided in a number of premises, mostly elementary schools, until finding a permanent site at Longcroft Secondary School where, in 1950, 1,200 students enrolled. In 1936 it was known as the Evening Institute but in 1950 was renamed Beverley Technical Institute. In 1960 it moved to new buildings adjoining Longcroft Hall. In 1971 the Institute moved into Longcroft Hall and was re-named the Beverley College of Further Education – now East Yorkshire College.

Remodelling the Town

At the end of the Second World War there remained the double problem in Beverley of people living in sub-standard dwellings and an overall shortage of housing. A deliberate policy of slum clearance and rebuilding began which was to continue at an ever increasing rate. In 1952 the Medical Officer of Health identified 511 houses which needed to be demolished immediately and 719 houses which would need to be demolished at a later date. During the 50s houses were demolished at a rate of twenty to forty a year; many were in side streets and yards off the main streets in the centre of town. Once old houses had been demolished new ones were built. In 1959 five and six-storey blocks of flats, totally out of keeping with other buildings in Beverley, were built in Wilbert Lane.

By 1961 the population in Beverley had risen to 16,031 – an increase of almost 3,000 from the beginning of the century. Extensive housing schemes took place to the north of the town, and Molescroft, which was outside the borough, became a suburb of Beverley. In 1968 permission was granted for a three-storey extension to the Beverley Arms, which continues to be a blot on the skyline of the town when viewed from the Westwood. In the town centre demolition of old property continued and in 1958 one of the few remaining timber framed houses was pulled down on the west side of Highgate and was later replaced by a terrace of houses.

The motor car came to Beverley early in the century. The Beverley Guardian of 24th January 1914 reported that on the previous Sunday afternoon PC Gibson had been standing on Kemp's Corner when a motor car, travelling along Toll Gavel at 'a suicidal and murderous speed' of eighteen miles per hour, attracted his attention. The driver, Miss Mary Murdock, was apprehended and brought before the justices and accused of exceeding the speed limit of five miles per hour.

Beverley Market Place in 1955

The coming of the motorcar meant that the old road system was inadequate. In order to provide a southern route into the centre of Beverley, avoiding Butcher Row and the central spine of the town, Lord Roberts Road (named after Lord Frederick Roberts (1832-1914) a hero of the South African War) was built in 1909. It joined Wednesday Market with Well Lane and Cross Street. For the road to be built certain buildings had to be adapted or demolished; part of No. 1 Wednesday Market was demolished as was the whole of the classical style Particular Baptist chapel in Well Lane, built 1834. It was replaced by the chapel we see today; built in a free Gothic style next to the new road.

During the war a scarcity of petrol meant that motoring had declined but by the 50s there had been a revival and traffic congestion in streets became a problem. Plans were put forward to demolish houses east of Saturday Market in a road widening scheme. Happily, these plans were turned down.

Houses at street corners houses were demolished, or partly demolished in order to increase visibility for drivers. Kemp's printing house at the bottom of North Bar Within was demolished in 1955 and replaced by a new building, now an opticians with HSCB bank behind, set further back. The house at the northern end of Eastgate, where the street enters Wednesday Market, was pulled down. Another house to go was at the junction of Newbegin and St Mary's Terrace.

Within the town, larger Georgian and Victorian houses had stabling which could be converted into garages but 20th century inhabitants of old terraced houses had to be content with street parking. Additional parking spaces and an efficient road system in the town were desperately needed. In 1958 Wylie's Road was developed from what had previously been a narrow lane variously called Wylie's Racket, Elwell's Racket or Ticklebelly Alley. To widen the lane it was necessary to demolish the Georgian House, lived in by Robert Wylie until his death in 1894, which stood next to the timber fronted houses outside North Bar. In 1969 Manor Road, which at one time led to the manor of Pighill, was widened, though houses had already been built along this road since it was re-named in 1929.

The same pattern of development was being carried out in all parts of the country. Gradually, as in other towns, local people became concerned at the way in which historic buildings were being destroyed and altered. The talk of Beverley town officials that the needs of traffic must take precedence over history and that 'history cannot rate very high in the list of priorities' was challenged. The Beverley and District Civic Society was formed in 1961. It was a body through which the voice of the residents of Beverley could be heard. Two of the leading campaigners for the Civic Society were Councillor George Odey, Managing Director of Hodgsons, who lived in Keldgate Manor and was MP for the town, and Gordon Armstrong, Manager Director of Armstrong Patents Limited. In 1967 the government responded to the wishes of conservationists throughout the country and the Civic Amenities Act was passed. This act required local authorities to list areas which were of special architectural or historic interest, 'the character or appearance of which it is desirable to preserve or enhance'. In Beverley that part of the town from the Sessions House in New Walk to the Minster at the bottom of Highgate in 1968 became a Conservation Area. The Town and Country Amenities Act of 1974 made it possible for the local authority to prevent the demolition of all buildings in a Conservation Area unless consent had been obtained.

An inner road relief system was also developed. In 1967 a short road was planned linking Sow Hill at the top of Saturday Market with Walkergate. There was strong opposition to this proposal which included the demolition of old properties including the Globe Inn. However, the scheme was approved by the Council in 1967 and the road completed the following year. In 1969 the county council's plans to demolish houses and widen Lairgate were rejected by the town council. There was a public inquiry when plans were put forward to destroy many old properties in order to build a new road leading from Walkergate to the Railway Station. These plans were rejected by the Department of the Environment in 1972. A new scheme was put forward, and accepted after a further public enquiry, with the result that New Walkergate, travelling along the east side of the town, was opened in 1980. This meant that Toll Gavel and Butcher Row could become a pedestrian zone; this was done, the streets repaved and iron lamps manufactured by the Thorncliffe and Crosskill iron works in 1824 were placed in position.

A way of reducing traffic in the centre of the town was to prevent it from entering. In 1971 – 1972 three bypasses were planned. First was the eastern bypass, opened in March 1973, which began with a road and bridge over the Beck to link Hull and Swinemoor Lane and so north to join roads leading to Hornsea, Bridlington, Driffield and Malton. The southern bypass was opened in 1981 linking Hull with the York road – it passed through Beverley Parkland. The third bypass, the northern bypass, was opened in the 1990s and linked the Driffield road with the Hornsea road. Housing was then developed to the limits of the bypasses.

The Friary

By the mid-20th century the Friary, which in the 19th century it had been divided into three separate dwellings, was completely swamped by the ever expanding Armstrong's factory and was in a poor state of repair. Seeking for further expansion the factory bought the friary from the owners, Richard Whiteing who owned one part and the Minster which owned two. The building was left to deteriorate into such a poor state that by 1960 almost its entire roof had gone. Armstrong's then put in an application to demolish it. At first this was agreed to by both the County Council and the Borough Council. However, several citizens in the town strongly objected to this treatment of one of the town's most historic buildings. They argued that Beverley's Dominican friary was almost unique because, as friaries had been built in town centres, over the years almost all of them had been demolished and new housing built where they had once been. Beverley Friary was one of the few remaining friaries. After persuasion the Council laid a Building Preservation Order on the friary which prevented demolition for the time being. A public inquiry was held after which the Ministry of Housing and Local Government confirmed

The Refurbished Friary with its 20th century extension on the right

the preservation order. The Friary, now in the ownership of the Borough Council was leased to the Beverley Friary Preservation Trust. The Borough Council gave £3,000 towards the cost of restoration and the Historic Buildings Council promised half of the then estimated restoration cost of £65,000 if the rest were found from other sources. After much determined hard work and extensive fund raising efforts by members of the Beverley Friary Preservation Trust restoration work began in 1974 and ten years later this ancient building opened as a Youth Hostel. The Friary, as it did in medieval times, once again offers hospitality to the traveller. Open in the summer for visitors and throughout the winter months for private functions and public meetings or events the building survives but only with the continued financial support of the Trust.

The Beverley and District Civic Society was responsible for two acts of preservation concerning the Friary. Soon after the Society was formed members removed the post-Reformation 16th century gateway to the west of the Friary to the wall on the west side of Eastgate in order to ensure its permanent preservation.

The society also re-built an ancient gateway. For some years a pile of ancient carved stones, which had been in the grounds of a house at Woodmansey once owned by Gillyat Sumner, had lain in a builder's yard at Woodmansey. In 1990 these stones were given to the Civic Society. On investigation it was confirmed that they were the stones belonging to the medieval gateway which had once been the entry into the Guildhall in Beverley, placed there when the building had been bought by the corporation in 1501. When a new front was built onto the Guildhall in 1834 the old gateway had been removed and bought by Gillyatt Sumner. After some discussion amongst members of the Civic Society as to where this gateway might be re-erected, the gateway was rebuilt in the grounds of the Friary.

Another protest campaign was mounted in 1966, following the Beeching Report. British Railways gave official notification of its intention to withdraw passenger services on the line between Hull and Scarborough. There was much opposition to this suggestion and a major campaign was mounted to save the line. After a public enquiry a decision was made to retain the line. However, the line from Beverley to York, via Market Weighton, was closed.

The Guildhall Gateway

The White Horse Inn

The White Horse Inn is still known locally as 'Nellie's' after Miss Nellie Collinson who, with her two sisters, was the last licensee of the Collinson family. Miss Nellie kept strict control over what went on in the pub; ladies were limited to certain rooms and any drinkers who over indulged were quickly shown the door. In 1975, after the retirement of Miss Nellie and her two sisters, the White Horse was bought by Samuel Smith's Old Brewery at Tadcaster. Folk music can be heard here on Monday nights and Wednesday nights is a popular time for lovers of New Orleans Jazz. Still lit by gaslight, with stone floors and 19th century furniture, it is little changed in 100 years.

Boom and Bust

Most of the old staple industries in Beverley recovered after the war and for a time unemployment was low. In 1952 Barkers and Lee Smith at Beckside changed from seed crushing to the production of animal feedstuffs. Deans and Son at Grovehill enlarged their factory. Armstrong's shock absorbers continued to sell well. By 1954 the firm was working at full pressure and by 1964 had 2,000 employees. In 1970 the firm was still working to capacity and had a branch in Canada. In 1964 Richard Hodgson and Sons diversified into the tanning and the dressing of leather for shoe uppers and for the clothing industry – one of the first companies in the world to recognise the importance of leather in the fashion world. In 1971 the company announced record profits and bought new firms. At Grovehill, Cook, Welton and Gemmell launched fifteen vessels, including three minesweepers, four trawlers and a tug in 1954. An oil tanker was launched in 1957 and at that time the firm employed 650 men.

After 1945 the livestock market increased and the cattle market at Beverley, re-built by the corporation, in 1966 became one of the largest pig markets in the country.

By 1963 4,300 people were employed in the twenty factories in the town, seven of those factories having been established since 1941. The Council, realizing the need to look to the future in 1964 created a new ten acre industrial estate in Swinemoor to attract the setting up of a variety of light industries. By 1971 six firms were making caravans in Beverley.

The years 1970 to 1974 were to be considered boom time. However, these good times were not to last and between 1974 and 1978 many of the industries of the town were to collapse. In 1973 unemployment in Beverley was below 200, by August 1974 it had risen to 248; a year later it was 741 and by July 1978 was 1,026 (which included school leavers).

The collapse of the fishing industry in Hull meant that new trawlers were no longer needed. At Grovehill difficulties had already been encountered at the shipyard and by 1963 Cook, Welton and Gemmell was affected; the firm was taken over by CD Holmes and Company who then sold it to the Drypool Group in 1973. Two years later Drypool called in the receivers. In 1976 Phoenix Shipbuilders took over the yard but when difficulties arose the government refused to give financial help and the firm was finally closed in 1977 with the loss of 180 jobs. Hodgsons tannery was threatened by competition from imports and from the introduction of synthetic materials. In 1978 the parent company, Barrow, Hepburn and Gale closed most of its departments in Beverley with 750 redundancies. All that remained was the chemical works which had been started as a separate company in 1956, under the name of Bevaloid, and which is still in operation in 2003. The oil crisis of 1973 hit the car and caravan industry and by 1984 only four caravan companies were left. Competition from large companies was another concern. Storry, Witty and Company had been making whiting in Beverley Parks since 1895 and paints and colours since the Second World War but it was taken over in 1970 by Expandite, a subsidiary of Burmah Industrial Products, and closed down.

The cattle market became unprofitable and in 1978 the corporation, having lost £36,000 in the previous four years, handed over its management to a consortium of local auctioneers.

The corporation, being the ground landlords of the shipyard developed the site for small industries and it became the Acorn

New Houses in Eastgate

Industrial Estate. Hodgson's premises in Flemingate were sold for other purposes – one of which was to house the Museum of Army Transport which was opened in April 1984 by Sir Patrick Wall, one time parliamentary representative for Beverley.

The Museum of Army Transport became one of the main attractions for tourists. In this vast building were housed trucks, motorcycles and a car used by one of the top German generals in the Second World War. Recently a rocket launcher, used during the Falkland's war, was brought to the Museum. In 1985 2nd Viscount Montgomery came to Beverley to open the Montgomery centre, a meeting hall which is attached to the museum. However, in August 2003 it was announced that the museum was to close.

The continuing decline in the British car industry caused Armstrong Patents to close its works in Eastgate in 1981 with 300 redundancies. After the demolition of the buildings the site became available for housing. The conditions on which permission for building was granted was that the development should follow the street line, should be in a style sympathetic to the Friary and the Minster and should be of high quality materials. This was done and the developers received several awards for the style and detail of these modern town houses.

In the 1980s there were further industrial setbacks. In 1986 the last tanners, Melrose Tanners in Keldgate (which had formerly belonged to the Cusson family) was closed. By 1982 much of Humberside, including Beverley, had been classified as a development area and was receiving government money to encourage new industrial growth. By 1986 unemployment had reached 10% of the population.

Humberside County Council and Beverley Borough Council

In 1972 the whole system of local government in England and Wales was under review. The result was that smaller authorities were united with others in order to make larger administrative units. Part of the old East Riding, a little of the West Riding and parts of Lincolnshire were grouped together to form the County of Humberside. The headquarters of the County Council was based at Beverley, the central point of the new county and long recognised as a county town, and the East Riding County Council building in Cross Street was taken over by Humberside County Council. Under this authority Beverley Borough Council (which had functioned from 1573 – 1974) was joined with Beverley Rural District Council (1894 – 1974) and Haltemprice Urban District Council (1935 - 1974) and amalgamated into one new second-tier authority, the Beverley District Council – renamed the East Yorkshire Borough of Beverley Council in 1981.

The District Council took over three of the buildings which had previously belonged to the old Borough Council. The Guildhall in Register Square, the Hall in Lairgate and the 18th century house known as the Gables, also in Lairgate. The Guildhall was used for ceremonial and other purposes. In 1979 the Gables was sold to the County Council and extensions were made to the Hall in Lairgate.

The new District Council abandoned plans for car parking in the area east of Saturday Market and instead permitted the re-

345

1930's Shop in Saturday Market

building of the area with houses and shops in lanes and courtyard in a style sympathetic to the older buildings. The Council limited the encroachment of supermarkets within the town, the only large one being Safeways, on the site of the Marble Arch Cinema – built in a style sadly out-of-keeping with other retailers in the street. High rent on retailers' properties meant that many of the small shops could not compete when the multiple stores moved into the town and were forced to close.

In 1982 development plans to build a large estate of houses on land immediately south of the Minster stretching along Queensgate were strongly opposed, particularly by three residents of Beverley who took the case to the High Courts. However, the objection was overruled and building took place.

In 1983 the fire station, now the responsibility of Humberside County Council, moved to a purpose built site in New Walkergate. A professional fire brigade of nine men had been formed in 1924. A new engine was bought and stationed in unused cells at the Guildhall. In 1941 the brigade became part of the National Fire Services and the fire engine was moved from the Guildhall to the municipal offices in Lairgate. By 1947 an East Riding County Brigade was formed to serve Beverley and nineteen parishes. The drill hall in Albert Terrace was converted into a fire station in 1950 and used until the removal to New Walkergate. The drill hall became a health centre.

In 1983 the Borough divisional police force building adjoining the Guildhall was found to be structurally unsafe and the town police were moved to the Sessions House. In 1928 the Borough police force had merged with the East Riding Constabulary whose headquarters were at the Sessions House in New Walk. In 1959 the Convent behind the Sessions House had been adapted as further police accommodation. The Borough divisional force had been based at the police station which adjoined the Guildhall.

Consolidated Charities

Charities left to the town over the previous centuries continue to benefit the less fortunate members of society but some charities were of such small amounts that they were difficult to administer. In 1911 forty-four charities were amalgamated into the Beverley Consolidated Charities which was divided into two branches; one to deal with almshouses the other to deal with pensions. The income from these charities in 1914 amounted to £1,649.

The Beverley Consolidated Charities became wealthy as a result of the new housing development in Queensgate. Caroline Walker, who lived in Lairgate House, Beverley, died in 1957 and in her will bequeathed 48½ acres of land in Beverley Parks to the Consolidated Charities. For many years this land brought in a negligible income but once sold for development the charities greatly benefited. Consequently, the Ann Routh and Charles Warton hospitals were completely refurbished and altered into thirteen and twelve, respectively, self-contained flats. The

Consolidated Charities bought or built new houses with the result that the number of residents offered accommodation in houses owned by the Charities has risen from eighty in 1986 to 114 in 2003. To acquire accommodation people have to be over the age of sixty, have to have lived in the town for a period of ten years at some stage of their lives and have to demonstrate some sort of need – either financial or social. Each case is assessed individually.

Changes Within the Town

Large gardens and open spaces in the centre of Beverley have now, mostly, been built on. As you walk around the town glimpses of St Mary's or the Minster are now often obscured by new buildings. After the death of Caroline Walker, Lairgate House was sold and became the Lairgate Hotel. The walled-garden to the west of the house, which stretched as far as Albert Terrace, was sold for development. The wall fronting onto Grayburn Lane was demolished and houses built, set back from the road. Over the past thirty years many new houses have appeared alongside lanes leading west from North Bar Within, on land which in early medieval times would have been strips of farm land. Terraces of three-storey houses have been built in Waltham Lane with an estate of quality houses placed at the end; a modern terrace has been added to Victorian houses in Wood Lane. Previously Tiger Lane had been a private entrance into the stables of the 18th century coaching inn – the remains of gate hinges can still be seen at the entry into the lane. Now a complete new development has taken place and the 19th century St Mary's parish hall has been converted into a private house.

1996 – 2003

In 1996 there was a further change in local government. The County of Humberside was abolished and the area was divided into five unitary authorities and Beverley, together with most of the area of the old East Riding, is now controlled by the East

Riding of Yorkshire Council. Over half of the funding of the council comes from central government, a fifth from Council Tax paid by residents in the area. The council has sixty-seven elected members, six of whom represent the Beverley wards of St Mary's (and Molescroft) and Minster and Woodmansey. Since the new Council has been in control it has encouraged the building of new houses on any brownfill sites (sites which have been built on in the past). Large gardens have been divided and built on, empty spaces have been developed.

At the time of change there was no provision for a town council. A three year battle ensued, with strong opposition from certain members of the East Riding of Yorkshire Council, and in 1999 a Town Council, with a mayor of Beverley was created. The East Riding of Yorkshire Council controls the funding of the Town Council by allocating a proportion of the rates. The Town Council holds monthly meetings in the Guildhall. Its concerns are with local issues such as considering applications for development, tree felling, licensing, highways which could affect the parishes of Beverley, allotments, toilets, street lights, litter bins and notice boards.

When it came into being the East Riding of Yorkshire Council assumed control of buildings, furnishings and artefacts, such as collection in the Art Gallery, which had belonged to the Borough. Many of the buildings the Council inherited had been sadly neglected in previous years and were in desperate need of renovation. One of these was the Guildhall. In 1999 English Heritage provided £250,000 for the much needed restoration of the Guildhall – a building which still seems to lack an overall purpose and is only open to the public on one day of the week. Other property has been sold. When new extensions were planned at County Hall, including a large extension in Champney Road (completed in 2002), the Hall in Lairgate was no longer needed for local government purposes. In 1999 it was sold for £500,000 to Barnetts Office Developers with the agreement that the general public should have access to the Chinese Room in the Hall. £3,000,000 was spent on the building and it has now become prestigious offices. In 1999 Norwood House was no longer

The New Magistrates' Courts

required by Beverley High School. For many years this building had been allowed to deteriorate and is now in urgent need of a restoration programme. The Council has passed responsibility for the building to a newly formed group of trustees which is trying to raise money for the restoration programme. By 1999 the Sessions House was no longer used for magistrates meetings and has now been sold to a private owner. As it is a Grade II listed property there are heavy restrictions as to what can be altered in its oak panelled court rooms.

The lease of the Cattle Market off Norwood ran out in 1994. The Council announced its proposal to close the market and sell the site for £7,500,000 to Tesco's Super Store. This was strongly opposed by a great many of the residents of Beverley and several thousand people signed a petition against such a development. They feared that the superstore would take trade from the heart of the town and that increased traffic would cause congestion. Almost 400 people, including traders, conservationists, campaigners and householders, attended a public meeting in the Memorial Hall on 27th October 1998 but neither the supermarket chain nor members of the council were present as they said that as all the information about the proposals was already available the meeting served no useful purpose. The one councillor present agreed to pass the views of the meeting on to the spokesperson on planning. Because of the controversy the final decision on the building of the store was made by John Prescott, the Deputy Prime Minister. The scheme went ahead and the store opened in the autumn of 2002. One condition of the sale was that there should be free car parking behind the store so that once people had shopped in Tesco's they could walk into town.

In 2002 the Memorial Hall in Lairgate, as a result of lack of maintenance, was considered unsafe for public functions. Its future lies in the hands of the trustees who are hoping to raise £2,000,000 to refurbish it and turn it into a community centre. Early in 2003 the Beverley Picture Playhouse closed. Mostly, the showing of current films five nights a week had been poorly attended but live events on Thursday evenings had been successful. However, a new multi-screen cinema just five miles south of Beverley proved to be too great a competition for film goers seeking comfortable seats and first class projection. The building is owned by the Council but its future is under debate.

The Past Moves into the Present

While the population for St Marys/Molescroft and Minster/Woodmansey ward comes to a total of 30,351 it is difficult to estimate the population of the old borough of Beverley which before boundary changes in 1974 was 17,132. Large developments have been built to the north and south of the town outside the boundary of the old borough. Following government directives for more housing the number of houses in the town has increased but these are mostly two-three bedroom properties to suit an average household of 2.29 and 2.77 persons.

In August 1990 BBC Two produced a series of programmes entitled 'Town Portraits'. John Grundy, the presenter of the

2001 POPULATION CENSUS FIGURES FOR BEVERLEY
Released by HMSO for Beverley
These figures relate to the electoral wards of Beverley rather than
the borough of Beverley before the boundary changes of 1974.

	St Mary's & Molescroft ward	Minster & Woodmansey ward
Population 2001	15,566	14,785
People over the age of 60	3,764	3,029
Average size of household	2.29	2,77
Single occupancy		
Pensioner	1,046	935
Other	964	1,027

programme, talking about Beverley said:

'To move through this town is to move through a sequence
of fine spaces, each one wrapped round with good buildings
and then closed off at the end, hiding the view beyond and
tempting us to believe there is something equally good
behind.'

To walk through the main spine of the town is to prove this
point.

To the north of North Bar is a large space where the horse
market was once held. To enter the town it is necessary to pass
through the confined space of the Bar and so come into the widest
street in the town. In the early part of the 20th century shops in

352

North Bar Within supplied all the everyday needs of local residents.

During the last fifty years there have been a number of changes in the street: No. 61 North Bar Within, the first house in that late 18th century terrace, for a short while a fish shop, has long since returned to being a private house. Armstrong's garage has been transformed into St Mary's Court, a shopping precinct. St Mary's Manor is still a striking Regency building. Having been a private home until 1948 it was bought and occupied by the Ministry of Agriculture and Fisheries, which in 1984 moved to new premises in Crosskill House in Wilbert Lane. In 1996 it was sold to a private company and converted into luxury flats. The building was extended at the back over its gardens.

Alongside St Mary's church, set back in the graveyard, is the only 20th century building in the street – the Parish Hall, designed by the church's architect, Andrew Anderson. As the church receives no outside funding the £300,000 needed to build the hall was raised by the parishioners. One of the stipulations for the building was that it was to be set at the level of the church. This necessitated the digging out of the graveyard. Permission was needed from relatives in order to remove and re-bury the bones found. Once digging began, by hand as mechanical aids were banned, it was found that the graveyard was a double burial ground with one layer of graves above another. This accounts for the fact that the graveyard is higher than the base of the church. The Church Hall was dedicated by the Archbishop of York in October 1994 and since then has been a great benefit not only to the church but also to the town as it is one of the few places in the centre of Beverley which can seat 100 people, where lectures, meetings, classes and events can be held.

All restoration work that is carried out on the church is funded by the parishioners -a heavy burden on a few people in order to preserve one of the great treasures and a major tourist attraction of Beverley. In 2001 the Friends of St Mary's was formed but as yet numbers are small. Today there is a great deal of restoration work which needs to be done immediately if the building is to survive. St Mary's remains an active church with a strong sense of community amongst its parishioners – as was the case when it was built by the wealthy merchants of Beverley.

The Beverley Arms Hotel, with its re-vamped coffee area, is still a popular meeting place for the residents of Beverley and for visitors. Almost next to it is the gentlemen's outfitters, Murray Todd, one of a number of family businesses remaining in the town. Steep roofs indicate a pre-mid-18th century building that may have been thatched – one such shop is No. 9 North Bar within which, on the north side shows a timber frame structure.

As North Bar Within nears Saturday Market the road divides into Lairgate and the main market of the town.

A building at the top end of the market place, No. 2, Prescott's, has been a jewellers for over 100 years. The building is still in width the size of a medieval burgess house. Built in 1790 No. 13, the old Doll's House, is a reminder of a late Georgian shop. In the centre of Saturday Market is a group of 18th century buildings known as the Dings, or Butterdings, built where the archbishop's medieval stone house once stood. When this block of buildings was built as a speculation in the 1750s the corporation ordered that the buildings should be in a similar style. The sign of a swan hangs over Michael Phillip's shop indicating that there was once a pub here named 'The Swan', and almost next to it is a shop with a bow fronted window which for 182 years was run by several generations of the Akrill family, selling guns and sporting equipment. It ceased trading in 2001. The Push Inn (so named because the word 'push' was written on the door handle) was originally a chemist shop which also sold wines; gradually the wine selling took over.

In the main part of Saturday Market there is the opportunity to observe buildings from many centuries. No timber framed medieval buildings can be viewed from outside but first floor rooms in several shops on the east side of the market, and in Ladygate, which runs along the original line of the medieval market, reveal medieval timber framed roofs dating back to the 15th century. At the southern end of the market place are the only 20th century buildings - the 18th century building of the Yorkshire Bank, demolished in the early 1970s, was immediately re-built in almost the same style; on the corner of Toll Gavel, Hawkshead/Burton is in typical 1930's style building.

One of the best known shops in Saturday Market is Briggs and Powell Ltd. This site has seen a variety of changes over the years. 900 years ago it would have been a strip of land granted to a medieval burgess. The area would have consisted of a shop at the front, living quarters at the back and an area behind in which to keep pigs or grow vegetables Over the centuries the shop has extended over the whole allocation of land. The medieval building has long gone and new shops have been built. Briggs and Powell began trading in the 1880s and by 1920 the shop had become a limited company. Thomas Jarrett begun work here, as an apprentice, at the age of fifteen. Gradually he bought up more and more of the shares of the company so that by the time the previous managers, Messers Jones, Kitson and Appleton, had retired he was the principal share holder. He became manager in 1935. As always shops have to be updated to new styles. Thomas Jarrett took over a dark and gloomy shop, with counters stretching down the centre and merchandise hanging from the ceiling or piled high on the floor. The shop was gutted and the interior we see today was built. Like so many other traders Briggs and Powell has had to adapt to the needs of the day. It began as an ironmongers and became profitable during the Second World War when the wireless became popular and a Murphy Wireless could be rented from Briggs and Powell for 2s 6d a week. As an ironmonger trade was affected by the coming of the out-of-town do-it-yourself stores and in order to survive merchandise had to be changed. In Briggs and Powell more emphasis was put on electrical goods. Today the shop is managed by Mr Jarrett's daughter, Sue Cattle, and her husband, Graham, and customers are served by staff who have been with the shop for many years.

Over the past thirty years the majority of shops in Saturday Market have changed owners. The building next to the NatWest Bank was once the gentlemen's outfitters run by three generations of the Brown family. John Brown died in 1890 and his widow and son, Arthur, carried on the family tailoring business. After the death of Arthur Brown in 1937 the business was continued by his son, John who developed it into one of the highest quality gentlemen's outfitters in the East Riding. After his death in 1982 the business was sold to the Edinburgh Woollen Shop. Further down the street Greens Stationers, the original home of 19th century John Green, closed a year after a fire in 1975. It was bought by Fletcher's food store. The original Fletchers store closed 2000-2001 and was taken over by Mark's Bakery but traded as Fletcher's Foods until it closed in 2002. In March 2003 it became a food outlet for Marks and Spencer.

In the market square the names of several multiple stores appear – Vyella, Jaeger, Country Casuals, and Monsoon. Over the years multiple stores have moved into the centre of the town, taking over one or two shops, trying in their fascias to establish their corporate identity (forgetting the corporate identity of this market town). Most have gutted the shops of Georgian and Victorian staircases and other details in order to create the modern style of retailing store.

For over nine centuries there has been a market day in Saturday Market. Early each Saturday morning stalls are put up and produce laid out on trestle tables. Once trading begins people pour into the market place, the young and the old, toddlers and children in push chairs all wanting to know what is for sale. Popular are the brightly coloured stalls selling fruit and vegetables – for competition from supermarkets has meant that there are no greengrocers in Beverley today. Other stalls sell cakes, meat, cheese, dog food, china, carpets, bric-a-brac, shoes – much as market stalls have always sold. At the end of the day children are gathered up, stalls taken down and paper lying in the street collected. By six o'clock a silence descends over the market place before the square is once again disturbed, this time by evening, scantily clad, revellers moving from one pub to another across the square. The police are usually present to prevent disturbances. By midnight quiet once more descends and for a few hours there is a hush in the market place.

Throughout its history, Saturday Market has been a social centre for the town; here demonstrations have been staged, parades have been held, military bands have played. On

Remembrance Sundays the salute is taken on the Market Cross while members of the forces and local youth groups march past. The Christmas Market, with stallholders dressed in 19th century costume, attracts thousands of shoppers from Beverley and elsewhere. At weekends motorbikes, cyclists, or vintage cars assemble here before various activities get going. On 12th July 2002 Queen Elizabeth II and Prince Phillip, came to Beverley as part of the Golden Jubilee celebrations. After attending a Service of Thanksgiving for Rural life in Yorkshire in the Minster they did a walkabout in Saturday Market amongst the hundreds of people who had gathered. Afterwards they went to the Race Course for a lunch and another walk-about amongst the crowd.

As Saturday Market is left behind the Alta Via of the town narrows as it enters Toll Gavel. The original shape of the market places and the central streets remain the same and mostly the upper storeys of the shop fronts have changed little from when they were built in the 18th and 19th centuries. Medieval shop fronts, altered by Georgian traders (with their small paned, often bow fronted windows), have in turn been adapted by the Victorians into larger windows and in the 20th century plate-glass has become fashionable. In many cases two shops have been made into one. In Toll Gavel the same pattern of change is repeated but with the inclusion of some uninteresting 20th century building. On the west side the important 18th century Holderness Hotel (No. 16 – 18) became Hutchinson's furniture store with a handsome staircase and separate rooms selling merchandise of different sorts but the building was gutted of any interesting features when it was sold in the early nineties and divided into two multiple stores selling clothing. The Wesleyan Church still stands, set well back from the road and is unaltered since it was built in 1897 except for the enclosure of the entrance. In 1969 the Golden Ball Inn was sold and demolished by the new owners of the site, Woolworth's. Just before Toll Gavel widens into Cross Street is the 18th century shop front with two lead snakes twining round the pillars of the doorway - this shop was at one time a chemist (snakes represent Aesculapius, the god of medicine).

No. 65 Toll Gavel, where Ann Routh once lived, is now a

Old Chemist's Shop Front in Toll Gavel

teashop. On the corner where Walkergate joins Toll Gavel, one of the 900 pumps in the town once stood. At this point the Walkerbeck flowed through the street with Cross Bridge providing a dry crossing for shoppers. This area was one of the stopping places for performances of the medieval mystery plays. In the early 20th century, when the circus came to town, people stood here to watch as the clowns, trapeze artists, circus animals, and sometimes an elephant, paraded through the centre of the town.

Throughout the main shopping streets building societies and house agents have replaced single traders. In Butcher Row shop usage has changed with a number of charity shops and travel agents replacing individual traders. No. 11, the Antiques Centre, was for many years the regimental museum of the East Yorkshire Regiment.

At the end of Butcher Row is the Tourist Office providing information for Beverley's new industry – tourism. Opposite is Safeway supermarket built where Marble Arch Cinema once was.

Once again the space opens up as the walker enters Wednesday Market. The market ceased to operate in the mid 18th century but was re-started in 1997 with markets held here on Wednesdays and Saturdays. The only 20th century building in Wednesday Market is Boyes Store, a welcomed replacement for Crystal Garage. Wednesday market has several family owned shops: Peck's fish shop, Jack's grocer and the Mayfair toyshop give us a glimpse of the small intimate shops of the past.

From Wednesday Market the Alta Via narrows as it enters Highgate, a street of mostly 18th century private houses, which continues down to Beverley Minster, the church built round the tomb of St John of Beverley. Simon Jenkins, in his book 'England's Thousand Best Churches' writes:

'There are many candidates for 'best' non-cathedral church in England, but Beverley Minster most often takes the palm.'

On Advent Sunday, the Carol Service on Christmas Eve, Christmas Day, Easter Sunday and on other ceremonial occasions, the Minster is packed with people who come to take part in the religious celebrations. This church provides both traditional and evangelical services and each Sunday about 235 people, plus forty people under the age of sixteen, take part in the services. Flower festivals, Organ Recitals, Art Displays, an Exhibition of the Quaker Tapesteries in 2001 all draw large crowds through the doors of this great church. The musical tradition continues under the direction of Dr Alan Spedding the Master of the Choristers and Organist; 2002 was the first year that women were admitted to the choir because of the lack of choristers. The twice yearly choral works sung by members of the East Riding County Choir, organ recitals throughout the summer months and visiting choirs and orchestras fill the building with music.

It was the Revd Reginald Collwyn Hargreaves (vicar of Beverley Minster 1947 – 1958) who began the tradition of the St John of Beverley service. Each year, on the Sunday nearest to the 7th May, the day of the death, almost 1,300 years ago, of St John of Beverley, town and church join in the celebration of Beverley's saint when members of the civic authorities, dressed in their full regalia, go to Beverley Minster to attend the Civic Service of St John. During the service children from the village of Harpham, where St John is believed to have been born, place baskets of primroses on the tomb of this saint without whose influence the town might never have developed.

All the major churches in Beverley have regular Sunday congregations. It should be remembered that the parish of St Mary's is smaller than other parishes and that the area from which St John of Beverley draws its congregation includes Beverley and surrounding villages:

Average Sunday Attendance in Churches in Beverley in 2002	
The Minster	270
St Mary's	110
St Nicholas	100
St John of Beverley (RC)	450
The Society of Friends	35
Toll Gavel Methodist church	250

The Westwood and the Beck

Away from the centre of the town fewer changes have taken place. The Westwood is still a place of buttercups, bluebells, skylarks and grazing cattle. The summer of 2001 is the only year in recorded history when, because of the foot and mouth disease, cattle have not been present on the Westwood. Here leisure pursuits such as dog walking, golfing, sledging (although in recent years there has been less snow), horse riding, picnicking or flying model aeroplanes takes place. More buildings have been added to the Race Course on the Hurn. A new Grandstand was built in 1959 and further buildings have been added since then. Race meetings take place from April to October and racing at Beverley is now firmly on the national racing calendar.

The pastures, the Westwood and the Hurn, Swinemoor and Figham, continue to be run by twelve freemen elected from the 170 remaining freemen of the town. As the old apprenticeship schemes in Beverley have ceased and so the only way to become a freeman is to be the son of a freeman and born within the old boundary of the town. Efforts are still being made to make daughters of freemen eligible. The future of the freemen is uncertain for today, because of the removal of the maternity unit to Hull, only home births can provide future freemen of Beverley.

The Westwood Hospital, originally Beverley Based Hospital, developed over the years into an important amenity for the town. After the Second World War huts were built to provide extra wards and by 1983 there were 213 beds. In the 1990s Princess Diana opened a state of the art maternity unit. Now the huts have been demolished, the maternity hospital moved to Hull and the Westwood Hospital remains only as a community hospital. Fifty houses are to be built on the site where those huts once were.

At the beginning of the century ships using the Beck were a useful source of income to the town. Because of the amount of industry in the town and along the banks of the Beck, tonnage increased from 31,000 in 1898 to 101,540 in 1905. However, when shipping at Grovehill and the Beck ceased, road and rail became the major form of transport.

Work on repairing the Beck stopped during the First World War but in 1921 dredging work was renewed. The last brickworks, an industry which had been carried on at Grovehill and along the Beck for at least eight centuries closed in 1928. In 1958 the lock was re-constructed and the Beck was kept open for navigation by periodic dredging and repairs to piling and banks but the waterway was too little used to justify further work and commercial activity ceased in 1987. Three boatyards were kept.

Over the past eight years the East Riding of Yorkshire Council has encouraged the building of houses either side of the Beck and once again this area of the town, so important in the medieval period, is being revitalised. In August 2003 there are plans to start a regeneration programme of the waterway costing an estimated £2½ million. It is hoped that this area will become a leisure area with fishing, walking and cycling along the path to the shipyard and the lock gates at the end. One of Hodgsons powered barges, the Sylvan, has been restored and there are plans to set it up on the Beck as a museum.

The Continuing Story

Today about 70,000 tourists come to the town of Beverley each year. They do much the same as visitors to the town have always done. Having marvelled at the two great churches they wander round the markets, see what is for sale in the shops, enjoy the buildings and refresh themselves at one of the many cafes, restaurants or at one or two of the thirty-five pubs in the town. Medieval visitors came to take part in religious festivals while today's visitor may come to take part in one of the music festivals in a town which for hundreds of years has been known for its music - in May the Early Music Festival, in June the Folk Festival, in August the Jazz Festival and in September the Chamber Music Festival.

The main streets are now filled with shoppers – some say because of the arrival of Tesco's superstore, others because of the opening of Marks and Spencer's food store in Saturday Market. Previously the town was full mainly on Saturdays when the market is here, now it is every day. Inevitably more shoppers mean more traffic. New car parking fees, always a debatable point, are to be installed in October raising the cost of long term parking from £1.50 to £2 and of annual permits from £120 to £180.

In July came the news that the East Riding County Council had selected five bids from prospective buyers of the Beverley Picture Playhouse. Each of the hopeful candidates intended to refurbish the Playhouse and turn it into a pub/restaurant or coffee bar. Immediately the news was released in the press there was a strong outburst of feeling from many residents of Beverley who disliked the idea of one of the prime buildings in the town being turned into yet another pub. An action group was formed and an open meeting held in the Cross Keys Hotel, Lairgate, which was attended by 150 people. The result was that the council was asked not to lose control of the site by selling it and that a feasibility study should be carried out as to the viability of turning the Playhouse into a mini conference/entertainments centre for community use. This was agreed and an announcement is to be made in October.

Work on the regeneration of the Beck, costing £2½ million began in October and £2 million is being spent on restoring Wilbert Lane flats. In August 2003 the Museum of Army Transport, which for 20 years had been one of the principal tourist attractions to the town was closed. With £140,000 being needed to restore the roof and a fall in visitor numbers it was impractable for the Museum, occupying a large area of council held land, to continue.

Walkergate Infant School had closed in July 2002 but for the following year had been used by children from the reception class and year 1 of St Mary's School. In August 2003 the Council announced a £10 – 12 million scheme whereby Minster Towers, a residential home in Lord Roberts Road, was to be closed and a new home built on the site of Walkergate Infant School. The land in Lord Roberts Road would be used for high quality housing – the money from this development being used to rebuild the residential home and two other residential homes in Grovehill, the Lilacs and the Laurels, which would be rebuilt on the site of the swimming pool in Mill Lane, once the new pool was built near the Leisure Centre in Flemingate.

An announcement was made that the long promised work on building a new southern bypass would begin in 2006. Inevitably this will result in a massive building programme to the south of the town up to the limit of the bypass.

The Sealed Knot, sponsored by the Town Council, held a

two-day event at the Defence School of Transport at Leconfield. Here was re-enacted 'the Battle of Beverley' based on the Civil War of the 17th century. The £7,000 raised from this event will be used to pay for a feasibility study to assess the possibility of restoring the Memorial Hall as a community centre. An announcement was also made of a feasibility study to consider the future of Norwood House.

Beverley is a town on the move and Philip Brown's description of Beverley at the end of the 19th century as being a sleepy market town certainly no longer applies.

However, visitors continue to come to the town and some so enjoy what they find when they come to Beverley that, as has always been, they decide to stay, become part of the community and take part in the activities of the town. The responsibility for the town and the future of the Beverley now passes into the hands of those who live here today. What we do today will become, to future generations, part of that long, eventful and continuing saga - the history of Beverley.

BIBLIOGRAPHY

When researching material for this book several sources have been constant companions and have supplied information for most chapters. These are listed under General Secondary Sources at the beginning of this bibliography.

The three main sources have been:
The Victoria History of the County of York East Riding Vol. VI
     Beverley (VCH)
Beverley Minster: An Illustrated History (BM)
Beverley: An Archaeological and Architectural Study (RCHM)

General Secondary Sources

Allison, J (Ed) VCH Vol. VI Beverley. Oxford University Press
     (1989)
Brown, J. The English Market Town (1750 – 1914) Crowood
     Press (1986)
Clarke, R. St Nicholas Church. St Nicholas PCC (1989)
Crowther, J (Ed) Descriptions of East Yorkshire: De La Pryme to
     Head. East Yorkshire Local History Society (1992) –
     extracts from journals of John Wesley, Tate Wilkinson,
     Arthur Young, William Cobbett
Foreman, M. Beverley Friary. The History and Archaeology of an
     Urban Monastery. Humber Archaeology Partnersip
     (1998)
Friar, S. The Batsford Companion to Local History. Batsford
     Limited (1991)
Hall, I & E. Historic Beverley. The Beverley Bookshop in
     association with Beverley Borough Council. Printed by
     William SessionsLtd. The Ebor Press, York (1973, 1981)
Hart, AT. Ebor: A History of the Archbishops of York from
     Paulinus to Maclagan 627 – 1908. William Sessions Ltd,
     Ebor Press, York (1986)

Horrox, R (Ed). Beverley Minster: An Illustrated History. Friends of Beverley Minster (2002)

Markham, J (Ed). Philip Brown's Beverley. A Guide to its History. Humberside Heritage Publication No. 20. Humberside Libraries and Art (1989)

Miller, K: Robinson, J: English, B: Hall, I. Beverley: An Archaeological and Architectural Study. RCHM Supplementary Series: 4. HM Stationery Office

Mount, D (co-ordinator). Beverley Minster (St John and St Martin) Monumental Inscriptions. East Yorkshire Family History Society (1997)

Mount, D (co-ordinator). Beverley St Mary's (including Coronation Gardens) Monumental Inscriptions. East Yorkshire Family History Society (1998)

Neave, D & Woodward, E. Lost Houses of the East Riding. Georgian Society for East Yorkshire 1988

Norfolk, R. Militia, Yeomanry and Volunteer Forces of the East Riding 1689 – 1908. East Yorkshire Local History Society (1965)

Pevsner, N & Neave, D. The Buildings of England: Yorkshire: York and the East Riding. Penguin Books (1995)

Sheppard, J. The Draining of the Hull Valley. East Yorkshire Local History Society (1958).

Sherwood, D. Complete Streets of Beverley. East Riding of Yorkshire Council Library and Information Service in Association with the Local History Unit, Hull College (2003)

Smith, W. St Mary's Church, Beverley. An account of its building over 400 years from 1120 – 1524. Friends of St Mary's Church (2002)

Wilson, S. The Cult of St John of Beverley. Thesis submitted for degree of PhD in the University of Southampton, History Department with translations of various medieval documents concerning St John of Beverley. (2000)

CHAPTER 1. FROM NOMADS TO ROMANS

Secondary Sources

VCH, Medieval Beverley by RE Horrox
BM The Archaeological Origins of Beverley Minster by DH Evans
RCHM Historical Introduction by Barbara English
Beverley and District Civic Society (1969) Westwood Study
Halkon, P (Ed). New Light on the Parisi. Recent discoveries in
        Iron Age and Roman East Yorkshire. East Riding
        Archaeological Society and the University of Hull School
        of Adult and Continuing Education. (1989)
Hunter, J & Ralston, I. The Archaeology of Britain. Routledge
    (1999)
Norman, A. The Romans in East Yorkshire. East Yorkshire Local
    History Society (1960)

CHAPTER 2. ANGLO-SAXON SETTLEMENT

Printed Primary Sources

Bede. The Ecclesiastical History of the English People.
    Translated by Bertram Colgrave, edited with introduction
    and notes by Judith McClure and Roger Collins Oxford
    University Press (1994)

Secondary Sources

VCH Medieval Beverley by RE Horrox
BM The Early Medieval Minster by DM Palliser
RCHM Minster Urban Development
Bilson, J. Beverley Minster. Architectural Review Vol. III
Dugdale, W. Monasteries of St John. York Monasticon
    Anglicanum Vol. 11
Hopkins, P. St John of Beverley. Hallgarth Publishing (Beverley
    Minster) (1999)

Humberside Archaeology Unit. Sheffield Excavations Report I
(1991) 'Report on Excavations at Lurk Lane' 1979-1982, by
P Armstrong.
Johnson, M. Our English Church Heritage from the Beginning to
1662. Turnstone Venturies (1987)

CHAPTER 3. NEW ARRIVALS, THE VIKINGS AND THE NORMANS

VCH Medieval Beverley by R E Horrox

Binns, A. 'East Yorkshire in the Sagas.' East Yorkshire Local
History Society (1966)
Binns, A. 'The Viking Century in East Yorkshire.' East Yorkshire
Local History Society (1963)
Brooks, F 'Domesday Book and the East Riding.' East Yorkshire
Local History Society (1986)

CHAPTER 4. 1100 -1200 UPWARDS AND ONWARDS

Printed Primary Sources

Malmesbury, W. William of Malmesbury: A History of the
Norman Kings (1066 – 1125) Llanerch Publishers (1991)
A facsimile reprint of the Latin by Joseph Stevenson, first
published in the series The Church Historians of England,
by Seeleys of London

Secondary Sources

VCH Medieval Beverley by RE Horrox
BM Early Medieval Minster by D M Palliser
Barnwell, P. 'The Church of Beverly is fully repaired'. The roofs
of Beverley Minster. Transactions of the Ancient
Monuments Society Vol. 44 (2000)
Humber Archaeology Partnership. Report on Excavations at
Eastgate, Beverley by D Evans

CHAPTER 5. 1200 – 1300. THE STEADY CLIMB

Primary Printed Sources

The Sanctuary Act Book of the Collegiate Church of St John of
   Beverley (1478 – 1499) British Library
Mcdermid, RTW. Beverley Minster Fasti – being biographical
   notes on the provosts, prebendaries, officers and vicars in the
   church of Beverley prior to the dissolution. Yorkshire
   Archaeological Society. Record Series Vol. 149 (1993)
   Surtees Society. Sanctuarum Dunelmense et Sanctuarium
   Beverlacens. London 1837. Beverley Library

Secondary Sources

VCH Medieval Beverley by RE Horrox
BM The Later Medieval Minster by R Horrox
RCHM Medieval buildings
Bentley, J. A Calendar of Saints. Tiger Books International,
   London (1986)
Evans, DH. & Crooks, KH, A Further Assessment on the Site of
      the Knights Hospitallers, Beverley (1992).
Jennings, B. Yorkshire Monasteries: cloister, land and people.
   Smith Settle (1999)
Kirby, M. Sanctuary: Beverley a Town of Refuge. Beverley and
   District Civic Society (1986)

Morris, R. 'Beverley Minster before the early 13th century.'
   British Archaeological Association IX. Medieval Art and
   Architecture in East Riding of Yorkshire Ed. C Wilson
Neave, S & Stephen E (Ed). A Historical Atlas of East Yorkshire.
   University of Hull Press (1996)
Riley-Smith, J. Hospitallers: The History of the Order of St John.
   Hambledon Press (1999)
Watkins, J & Williams, R. An Excavation in Highgate, Beverley
   (1977). Extract from East Riding Archaeology No. 7. p. 71 –
   84.

Wilson, C. Early 13th century Architecture of Beverley Minster. 13th Century England. Bydell Press, Woodbridge

CHAPTER 6. 1300 – 1400 REACHING THE PEAK

Printed Primary Sources

Surtees Society Vol. 108/98 Chapter Act Book of the Collegiate College of St John the Evangelist at Beverley 1286 – 1347.

Secondary Sources

VCH Medieval Beverley by R Horrox
BM The Later Medieval Minster by R Horrox
BM Spedding. A. Music in the Minster.
Frost, P. Molescroft: Beverley's Northern Neighbour.
    Highgate Press (1995)
Dobson, R. Risings in :York, Beverley and Scarborough.
    Cambridge University Press (1984)
Hilton, R & Aston, T (Ed) The English Rising of 1381.
Lloyd, E. Poll Tax Returns for the East Riding of Yorkshire; 4
    Richard II (1381). Archaeological Journal 20 (1909)
Leach, A. A Clerical Strike at Beverley Minster in the 14th
    century. Archaeologia, Vol. 55 (1896)
Los, P & W. Brick and Tile Making in East Yorkshire. East
    Yorkshire Local History Society Journal No. 57 winter
    1997/8
McKisack, M. The 14th century. Oxford University Press (1991)
Neave, S. Feast of Fools. Article in Yorkshire and North
    Humberside Times, 27th December 1974.

CHAPTER 7. 1400 – 1500 DESCENT INTO THE VALLEY

Printed Primary Sources

Butler-Bowden, W. The Book of Margery Kempe 1436. Jonathan Cape, 30 Bedford Square, London (1936)

Report on the Manuscripts of the Corporation of Beverley (1900)
Records of the Borough of Beverley

Secondary Sources

Jameson, N. Organisation of Military Levies in Beverley 1400 –
1450. Article from Medieval Yorkshire No. 23 (1994)
St John Parker, M. The Wars of the Roses. Pitkin Guide

CHAPTER 8. 1500 – 1600 THE VALLEY OF CHANGE

Printed Primary Sources

East Riding Antiquarian Society Transaction Vol. 10.The trew
confession of William Stapulton of the attempts committed
and doon by hym against the kynges highness and the lawe.
Printed for the society by A Brown and Sons Ltd. The
Saville Press 1903.
Gee, Thomasina memorial – transcription by National
Association of Decorative and Fine Arts, St John of
Beverley Minster
Warton M (died 1688) Inventory of his goods (in archives of
University of Hull)

Secondary Sources

VCH Beverley in the 16th century by KJ Allison, GHR Kent
BM The Minster and the Reformation by DJ Lamburn
BM Jones, M. The Misericords
Borland, M and Dunning, J (Ed). Bishop Burton and its People; a
Village History. Highgate Publications Beverley Ltd. (1992)
Cross, C. The End of Medieval Monasticism in the East Riding of
Yorkshire. East Yorkshire Local History Society (1993)
English, B & Neave, V. Tudor Beverley. Beverley: Walkerkgate
Press Ltd (1973)
Goode, J & Neave, S. The Dominican Friary. Information boards
in Beverley friary (2002)

Jennings, B. Yorkshire Monasteries: Cloister, Land and People. Smithy Settle (1999)

MacMahon, KA. 'Bishop, Scholar Martyr 1469 – 1535'

MacMahon, KA. Beverley. Dalesman Publishing Company Ltd: Clapham, Yorkshire(1973)

Neave, D & S. '£100 Saves Minster from Demolition.' Friends of Beverley Minster Annual Report 1997/8

Palliser, D. '1548 and all that.' Friends of Beverley Minster Annual Report 1997/8

Salkeld, M. The Wartons of Beverley. BA dissertation, Degree in Regional and Local History University of Hull (1992).

CHAPTER 9. 1600 – 1700 CLIMB OUT OF THE DEPRESSION

Primary Printed Sources

Civil War Tracts (Beverley Library)

Inventory of possessions of Michael Warton of Beverley Parks, died 1688, by his servant Robert Cook (archives University of Hull).

Secondary Sources

VCH Beverley in the 17th century by GCF Forster

BM The Minster in the 17th and 18th centuries by WJ Sheils

Dennett, J (Ed) Beverley Borough records 1575 – 1821. Archaeological Society. Record series Vol. 84 (1933)

Hall, E (Ed). Michael Warton of Beverley: An Inventory of his Possessions. Centre for Regional and Local History, University of Hull in Association with Humberside Leisure Services (1986)

Hope, E (arr. by) A Puritan Parish Clerk – commentary on current events made in the register of St Mary's Church by Nicholas Pearson, Parish Clerk 1636 - 1653

Hopkins, P. 'The Wartons of Beverley Parks.' Friends of Beverley Minster Annual Report 2000/01

Hopkins, P. The Diary of John Jackson: Sometime Macebearer in 17th century Beverley (faction). Hutton Press Ltd (1991)

Markham, J. The Living Past. Highgate of Beverley (2001)

Neave, D & Woodward, D. 'Memorials to a Yorkshire Family.' Country Life Vol. 166 No. 4292

CHAPTER 10. 1700 – 1800. THE GENTEEL SLOPES

Primary Printed Sources

Diaries of John Courtney (University of Hull archives)

Georgii II. Regis – An Act for more effectually Cleanfing, Deepening, Widening, and Preferving a Creek called Beverley Beck, running into the RiverHull 1741

Secondary Sources

VCH Beverley, 1700 – 1835 by David Neave

BM The Minster in the 17th and 18th centuries by WJ Sheils

RCHM P. 35 Swine Moor Wells

English, B. The Great Landowners of East Yorkshire 1530 – 1910. Harvester Wheatsheaf (1990)

MacMahon, K. Roads and Turnpike Trusts in Eastern Yorkshire. East Yorkshire Local History Society (1964)

Moody, B. Ann Routh of Beverley. Friends of Beverley Minster Annual Report 1999/2000

National Trust Leaflet. 'An Introduction to Ormesby Hall, Cleveland'

Neave, D & S, The Diary of a Yorkshire Gentleman. John Courtney of Beverley, 1759 – 1768. Smith Settle Ltd. (2001)

Norfolk, R. Militia Yeomanry and Volunteer Forces of the East Riding. East Yorkshire Local History Society (1965)

Pinfold, F & Higginson, G. The Inn Places of Beverley. Hutton Press Ltd (1988)

Society of Friends. A Brief History of a Quaker Meeting

Stirling, A. The Hothams, being the chronicles of the Hothams of Scorborough and South Dalton from their hitherto unpublished papers, in two volumes. Herbert Jenkins Ltd (1918)

Woodward, D. Descriptions of East Yorkshire: Leland to Defoe. East Yorkshire Local History Society (1985) – extracts from journals of John Leland, Edmund Gibson, Ceila Fiennes, Daniel Defoe

CHAPTER 11. 1800 - 1900 THE INDUSTRIAL INCLINE

Printed Primary Sources

Peddie, R. The Dungeon Harp, being a number of pieces written during a cruel imprisonment of three years in the dungeons of Beverley (poetry and verse with a local setting).

Report of the Borough Surveyor as to the Walker Back 1893

Secondary Sources

VCH Modern Beverley by Lucy M Brown

BM Minster in 19th and 20th centuries by David Neave

RCHM Post-Medieval Buildings by Ivan Hall

Brown, P. Minster Life – Some Historical Themes of Beverley

Brown, P. Old Beverley. East Yorkshire Local History Society in association with Humberside Leisure Services (1983)

Crowther, J (Ed). Beverley in mid-Victorian Times. Hutton Press Ltd (1990)

Lawson, J. Primary Education in East Yorkshire 1560 – 1902. East Yorkshire Local History Society (1959)

Markham, J. The Old Tiger Inn Beverley. The story of a Georgian Coaching Inn. Highgate Publications (Beverley) Ltd 1988

Markham, J. 19th century Parliamentary Elections in East Yorkshire. East Yorkshire Local History Society (1982)

Markham, J. 'A Time for Greatness' (an article on Revd Coltman). Friends of Beverley Minster Annual Report (1994/5)

Moody, V. Doorways into Beverley's Past. Highgate
  Publications, Beverley, Ltd (1991)
Neave, S. 'St Mary's Manor' (a paper)
Oliver, G. Beverley.The history and antiquities of the town and
  Minster of Beverley, in the County of York from the most
  early period with historical and descriptive sketches of the
  abbeys of Watton and Meaux. B: M Turner (1829)
Poulson, G. Beverlac or the antiquities and history of the town of
  Beverley in the County of York and the collegiate church of
  St John. Beverley: George Scaum. 2 vols. (1829)
Speck, W. 'Clio the Computer' University of Leeds Review Vol.
  29 (1986/7)
Ward, J. East Yorkshire Landed Estates in the 19th century. East
  Yorkshire Local History Society (1967)

CHAPTER 12. 1900 – 2003 CONSTANT CHANGES IN THE LANDSCAPE

Printed Primary Sources

Beverley Guardian 1914/ 1990
'History and Growth of Richard Hodgson and Sons Ltd.'
  Company leaflet

Secondary Sources

VCH Modern Beverley by Lucy M Brown
BM Post-Reformation Monuments by David Neave and Ian
Sumner
Aldabella, P & Barnard, R. Hull and East Yorkshire Breweries.
  East Yorkshire Local History Society (1997)
Attwood The Wilsons of Tranby Croft. Hutton Press (1995)
Clifton-Taylor, A. Six More English Towns. Beverley. British
  Broadcasting Corporation (1981)
Markham, J. Colourful Characters. Highgate Publications (1992)
  (Admiral Walker, John Edward Champney and William
  Spencer)

Markham, J (Ed). Burton of Beverley: Pictures of Beverley and District by Thomas Bonfrey Burton. Photographs by Patricia Dean. East Yorkshire Local History Society No. 48

Markham, J. Beverley: a photographic history of your town. Black Horse Books for WH Smith Ltd (2001)

Neave, D & S. East Riding Chapels and Meeting Houses. East Yorkshire Local History Society (1990)

Robinson, P. Then the War Came. Beverley and District During the Second World War. Hutton Press Ltd (1989)

Toll Gavel Methodist Church. Toll Gavel Church Centenary 1891-1991

Wise, V. Frederick Elwell RA (1870 – 1958)

INDEX

bull baiting, 268, 269
Bulryng, 109
burgage plots, 41, **43**
Burlington, Earl of, 196, 197
Burney, Revd James, 160, 164, 170
Burton, Jeremy, 172
Burton, Thomas, 89
Butcher Row, 37, 268, 327, 359

Camidge, John, 305, 324
Campbell, Colin, 197
Carmarthen, Marquis of, 231
Carnival and Shopping Week, 315
Carr, John, 217, 222
Cartwryght, Simon, 105
Catfoss Lane, 228
Catterson, George, 292
Champney Rd, 322
Champney, John, 315-317
Chapter Act Book, 73
Chapter House, 151
Charles Deans of Hull Ltd, 313
Charles I, king, 158, 160, 162, 164, 170
Charter of Elizabeth I, 153
Charter of Henry I, 32, 42
Cherry Burton, 16
Cherry Tree Lane, 323
Cholmley, Sir Hugh, 166
Civic Amenities Act, 338
Civic Society, 338
Clark, George, 276
Clarke, Revd John, 191, 215
Clarke, Thomas, 170
Cobbett, William, 288
Cochrane, Hamilton and Cooper, 304, 311
Cockerills, 122
cockpits, 232
Coifi, 11
Collinson, Nellie, 248, 342
Coltman, Revd Joseph, 240, 256, 262

Dawson, Elizabeth, 172
Deans and Son, 342
Defoe, Daniel, 210, 256
Deira, 8
Dibdin, Charles, 235
Dings, 40
dispensary, 266
Dog and Duck Lane, 109
Dog and Duck, 248
Domesday, 28, 29
Dominicans, 54, 55
drapers, 125
Driffield, 56
Drypool Group, 343
Duffill, John, 282
Dymoke, John, 176, 179

Ealdred, Archbishop of York, 26
Eanfled, queen 12
East Riding Constabulary, 347
East Riding County Choir, 360
East Riding County Council, 305
East Riding House of Correction, 251, 252, 253, 255
East Riding Lunatic Asylum, 300
East Riding of Yorkshire Council, 349
East Yorkshire Borough of Beverley Council, 345
East Yorkshire Cart and Wagon Company, 313
East Yorkshire College, 334
East Yorkshire Militia Regiment, 230, 231, 331, 332, 359
Eastgate, 39, 112, 197, 199, 225, 291, 315, 340, 344
Educaton Act of 1870, 299
Education Act, 1902, 332, 334
Education Act of 1944, 333
Edward I, king, 49, 67, 68, 69, 72
Edward II, king, 69, 77, 83, 94, 95
Edward III, king, 69, 87, 107
Edward IV, king, 100
Edward the Confessor, king, 23, 24, 25, 29, 47
Edward VI, king, 149, 151
Edwards, Sir Henry, 272, 273, 291

Great Charter, 103
Green Dragon, 247
Green, John, 246, 356
Greenfield, W, archbishop, 79, 80
Green's Public Library, 246
Greenwell, Rev Canon, 6
Grey, Edward, 170, 179
Grigges, William, 151
grithmen, 62
Grovehill Rd, 71, 332
Grovehill, 37, 38, 177, 208, 211, 292, 303, 313
Guild of Minstrels, 132
Guild of St Mary, 93
Guildhall, 138, 216, 222, 249, 250, 266, 267, 275, 278, 286, 341, 345, 349

Haldene, William, 104
Hales, Sir Robert, 86, 101
Halitreholme, Robert, 132, 139
Hall Garth, 24, 48, 142
Hallam, John, 144
Hansby, Ralph, 168
hanshus, 33
Hargreaves, Revd Reginald, 360
Harold Godwinson, king, 25
Harold Hardrada, king, 25
Harpham, 12
harrying of the North, 27
Hawe, William, 296, 297
Hawksmoor, Nicholas, 201, 256
Hayton, John, 123, 124
Hengate, 19, 70, 277, 299
Henry I, king, 31, 32
Henry II, king, 31, 35
Henry III, king, 49, 54, 58, 67
Henry IV, king, 108
Henry V, king, 116
Henry VI, king, 116, 117, 118
Henry VII, king 128
Henry VIII, king, 14, 139, 140, 148, 149

Quakers, 171, 284 see also 'Society of Friends'
Queensgate, 71, 299, 328, 331, 332

racecourse, 216, 218, 233, 279, 318
Railway Street, 288
railway, 286
Rambla Café, 330
Ranby, Robert, 313
Ravensor, Richard de, 102, 107
Reform Act 1832, 272
Reform Act 1867, 272
Regal Cinema, 328
Register Square, 229, 286, 302
Registrar's Office, 229
Richard I, king, 31, 35, 49
Richard II, king, 69, 96, 97, 105, 108
Richard III, king, 128
Roger, Revd Ezekiel, 160
Rokeby, Lady Loan, 140
Rokeby, Sir Richard, 131
Rolleston, Robert, 117
Rolleston, Roger, 117
Roman Catholics, 261
Rome, John, 122
Roos, John of Routh, 123
Routh, Ann, 225, 347, 358
Rudd, William, 122
Rye House Plot, 179

Safeways, 346
sanctuary, 21, 27, 60, 114, 146
Sanderson, Christopher, 143
Sands, Alice, 122
Sandwith, Thomas, 256
Saturday Market, 39, 70, 262, 354
Scarr, Henry and Joseph, 304
Scheemaker. Peter, 195
Scott, George Gilbert, 259, 305
Scott, Oldrid, 259

waits chains, 270
waits, 100
Walker, Admiral, 308, 322
Walker, Caroline, 347
Walker, James, 308
Walker, Sir James, 273
Walkergate House, 223, 295
Walkergate Infant School, 363
Walkergate, 37, 70, 91, 211, 215, 261
Walter de Gray, archbishop, 58
Walter of Grimsby, 56
Waltham Lane, 348
Waltham, canon, 116
Warton, Charles Hospital, 347
Warton, Charles, 177
Warton, Lawrence, 155
Warton, Mary, 182, 217
Warton, Michael I, 155
Warton, Michael II, Captain, 161 (d. 1644)
Warton, Sir Michael III, 161, 163, 168, 169, 176 (d. 1655)
Warton, Michael IV, 175, 178, 180, 181 (d. 1688)
Warton, Sir Michael V, 181, 192, 201 (d. 1725)
Warton, Sir Michael, hospital, 224
Warton, Sir Ralph, 179, 194
Warton, Sir Warton Pennyman, 215, 217
Wartons of Beverley Parks, 155, 189, 195
Water Act, 301
Water Bill, 300
Waterloo, battle of, 249
Watton Priory, 16, 35, 67, 90, 133, 145, 146
Waugh, Edwin, 310
Weatherill, Christopher, 172
Wednesday Market, 70, 109, 141, 261, 288, 359
Well Lane, 229, 246, 247, 265, 316
Wesley, John, 204
Wesleyan Chapel, 308, 357
Wesleyan Day School, 315
West Saxons, 19
Westwood Hall, 295
Westwood Hither Mill, 281

.